Blaming the Victim

Blaming the Victim

How Global Journalism Fails Those in Poverty

Jairo Lugo-Ocando

PlutoPress
www.plutobooks.com

First published 2015 by Pluto Press
345 Archway Road, London N6 5AA

www.plutobooks.com

Copyright © Jairo Lugo-Ocando 2015

The right of Jairo Lugo-Ocando to be identified as the author of this work
has been asserted by him in accordance with the Copyright, Designs and
Patents Act 1988.

British Library Cataloguing in Publication Data
A catalogue record for this book is available from the British Library

ISBN   978 0 7453 3442 4   Hardback
ISBN   978 0 7453 3441 7   Paperback
ISBN   978 1 7837 1226 7   PDF eBook
ISBN   978 1 7837 1228 1   Kindle eBook
ISBN   978 1 7837 1227 4   EPUB eBook

Library of Congress Cataloging in Publication Data applied for

10   9   8   7   6   5   4   3   2   1

Typeset by Stanford DTP Services, Northampton, England
Text design by Melanie Patrick
Simultaneously printed digitally by CPI Antony Rowe, Chippenham, UK
and Edwards Bros in the United States of America

Contents

List of Tables

Acknowledgements

This book would have not been written without the generous support from the Carnegie Trust for the Universities of Scotland which provided me with a series of small grants during a period of time that led directly to the key ideas expressed in this book. In a time in which research funding in the arts and social science is being ruthlessly cut by governments that have given few signs of caring for those in a state of poverty, organisations such as the Carnegie Trust despite limited resources are making all the difference in the world.

As with any type of project such as this one, it is never really the work of one single person. Behind me, several people and institutions made this book possible. Nevertheless, let me start by taking sole credit for its flaws and declare myself responsible for any criticism that derives from its reading. Having said that, I want firstly to thank Pluto Press and particularly its Managing Director, Anne Beech, for having accepted my proposal and the support, feedback and encouragement they gave me throughout the preparation of this book.

I want to acknowledge the contribution of my co-authors in three of the chapters, Patrick Malaolu, Steven Harkins and Scott Eldridge II, whose help was indispensable. I was very privileged to be writing the book while supervising their doctoral theses and thankful for their willingness to set aside time to help me develop these ideas.

I also want to thank my present and former students from the MA in Global Journalism and the MA in International Political Communication at the University of Sheffield in the United Kingdom for the level of discussion and engagement when I presented to them many of these ideas in my lectures and seminars.

I am equally grateful to the Centro de Investigación de la Communicación at the Universidad Católica Andres Bello (UCAB) in Venezuela for the time I was allowed to spend there and work on many of these ideas, in particular to Marcelino Bisbal, Andrés Cañizalez and Caroline Bosc-Bierne de Oteyza. I am also indebted to Antonio Castillo and Miguel de Aguilera at the University of Malaga in Spain for inviting me to deliver lectures on these topics over the past few years. I also want to thank Anya Schiffrin at the School of International and Public Affairs at Columbia University in New York for allowing me to share with her students some of the ideas expressed here and for the discussion that fallowed.

The book was born from a series of discussions with many colleagues and friends about my previous life as a practising journalist. However, I would want particularly to mention Emma Briant, Martin Conboy, Muhammad Idrees Ahmad, An Duc Nguyen, Tony Sampson and John Steel. I owe to all of them a great deal for their ideas, suggestions and comments over the past two years.

Thanks to my partner Corinne Fowler, who was not only a second pair of eyes but also became a challenging testing ground for some of the ideas here expressed. My three sons Edgar, Victor and Rafael deserve however more than a thanks. They deserve all my ultimate recognition for showing infinite patience with me and my time-consuming obsession to finish this book. Their kisses and hugs in the morning, after a sleepless night, were the most important motivation of all in my life.

Finally, I want to dedicate this book to the memory of my late young brother, Adalberto Daniel Lugo Morales, who shared my quest for a better world. I hope one day his daughters, Sofia and Valeria, now perhaps too young, can read this book and appreciate how inspiring he was for all of us and what a difference he made in our lives.

Introduction

Back in the early twentieth century, one of America's finest journalists and authors, Upton Sinclair, wrote *The Brass Check*, one of the first comprehensive studies about journalism practices and media ownership. In *The Brass Check*, Sinclair warned that the United States had 'a class-owned press, representing class interests, protecting class-interests with entire unscrupulousness, and having no conception of the meaning of public welfare' (1919: 318). Others such as Hamilton Holt saw journalists as 'tools or vassals of the rich men behind the scenes' (1909: 4). In both cases, it was perhaps a harsh assessment of the overall state of the press at the time but these judgements do reflect some truth that even today resonates in the tone and approaches that still dominate news narratives with regards to poverty. News media today still offer simplistic explanations about why people live in a state of poverty, explanations that reflect dominant discourses that are shaped by class ideology.

Indeed, the two-times Pulitzer Prize winner, Nicholas Kristof, in his 2 November 2011 column in the *New York Times*, suggests that there is a solution to problems such as climate change, poverty and civil wars: 'birth control'. For Kristof, the impact of overpopulation is clear:

> One is that youth bulges in rapidly growing countries like Afghanistan and Yemen makes them more prone to conflict and terrorism. Booming populations also contribute to global poverty and make it impossible to protect virgin forests or fend off climate change. Some studies have suggested that a simple way to reduce carbon emissions in the year 2100 is to curb population growth today. (Kristof 2011a)

Sadly, these simplistic views are still widely held by many in newsrooms around the world, despite the fact that the overwhelming depletion of nature occurs at the hands of the richest individuals, who not only consume the most but also produce and supply the weapons that fuel the wars that have devastated places such as Afghanistan and Yemen.

Regrettably, we have heard similar arguments, albeit from different standpoints, for almost two hundred years. The singularity of Kristof's article is that, in many ways, it reflects the prevalent views among the most powerful media in the world today. Eric Ross calls it the 'Malthus Factor', an ideological paradigm which tends to blame the poor for environmental degradation (1998: 73). In the case of the so-called 'global media', we could also refer to these views as an Orwellian doublespeak that not only embraces a false paradigm as a discourse of truth, but that also evades reality by transferring responsibilities to the victims. In so doing, the international media seem to obviate, deliberately, the underlying circumstances that foster poverty, while displacing responsibilities to parallel political spheres where the possibility of any real action can be blocked.

Some scholarly literature has concentrated on national media representations of poverty, linking it, for example, with welfare (Franklin 1999: 6). This is perfectly understandable as poverty is mainly a national issue (Townsend 1993), despite its international dimension. In more recent times, academic work has focused on the way in which emotions connect spectators with those who suffer (Boltanski 1999; Chouliaraki 2006, 2013; Höijer 2004). These same works have looked at how those links create a common space between spectators in the West and those who suffer, which is also referred to as 'regimes of pity'. For these authors, this common space enables the mobilisation of the public, who pressure politicians to articulate some sort of response to these types of humanitarian crises (Robinson 2002; Shaw 1996; Zelizer 2001). They argue, nevertheless, that this can also lead to 'compassion fatigue' (Höijer 2004; Moeller 1999) and therefore to the exhaustion in the public's political will to engage with such events. Few scholarly works, however, have looked at the processes of news gathering, production and dissemination in relation to poverty and social exclusion from a global perspective. This global perspective is needed, as these structural elements are not constrained within national levels of political action: they are a direct by-product of historical international structures, which have been exacerbated by the process that we call 'globalisation'. As Pierre Rosanvallon (2012) points out, media globalisation has brought the world closer, while simultaneously deepening the gap between social classes. For him, the divided classes in our time are the equivalent of the separated nations of the nineteenth century and world inequality is no longer different from social inequality.

None of these works have been able to explain fully why journalists concentrate on the manifestation of poverty rather than poverty as a by-product of inequality, despite the fact that in order to fulfil its normative claim of social change, the reporting of poverty should go beyond describing the manifestations of exclusion. In facts, journalistic practice normatively demands an approach that should expose the structural elements from which poverty derives, such as the uneven distribution of resources and the limitations in accessing the means of production of wealth.

Indeed, poverty as a consequence of inequality has become a news story with a particularly international dimension that requires a distinctive explanatory framework. Reporting on poverty from an international perspective is important, as the 'experiences of the developed countries should be more widely publicised' so as to allow more informed choices (Chang 2002: 140). This book intends to advance precisely this view – one that is more transnationally focused and historically based. In so doing, it will also discuss different interpretations of poverty by deconstructing representations in the context of global media. It examines the way journalists and news editors working in mainstream media outlets understand the causes of poverty and how they view the different manifestations of this phenomenon in the news agenda.

The book presents a critical assessment of poverty in the newsroom from both the point of view of news-gathering/production/dissemination and through the analysis of the relationship between journalists and their sources. It investigates when and how poverty becomes newsworthy and how it is articulated in media narratives and subsequently represented throughout specific news discourses. It analyses the framing of poverty as a news story from an international perspective, while arguing that far from being considered a homogenous practice, journalists' framing of poverty should instead be seen as an example of the complex dynamics within the ecology of the newsroom.

Complex Definition

Poverty is a recurrent theme in the media, although not as widely reported upon as one might think. Nevertheless, as it is argued in the following chapters, it is mostly presented by journalists by means of its different underlying manifestations, such as overpopulation, famine, exclusion and conflict. Poverty in the news is therefore a true mirror image, as reality is regularly represented as an inverse truth in which poverty is a consequence of these tragedies rather than the other way around.

Another important problem has to do with the core views of news-makers and news-shapers in relation to poverty. Although the news coverage of some of these issues has changed over the years (Gráda 2009: 1), it is still anchored in certain values that dominate the worldview of poverty in the newsroom. In this worldview, poverty is rarely presented as a rational phenomenon that follows the logic of inequality. There are very few occasions when the public is told that the reason why so many have so little is because so few have accumulated so much. When exceptional journalists tell this side of the story, many accuse them of bias and partisan propaganda. In these cases, as we will explore later, objectivity is used by some as a deterrent for ideological analysis in the name of safeguarding journalism's neutrality. Because of this, most news stories concentrate on the palliative efforts of 'heroes' and the goodwill of donors. As the Indian journalist Palagummi Sainath reminds us:

> Too often covering the poor, for the media, gets reduced to romanticising the role of saintly individuals working among them. Often these heroes are from the same class and urban backgrounds as the journalists covering them. A latter-day version of the noble missionary working among the heathen savages. (1996: 295)

In reality, most journalists and news editors operate within specific ideological categories that define not only the way poverty is constructed in the newsroom but also the narratives that frame it as a news item (Devereux 1998: 21). The fact remains that global coverage of poverty is articulated within the frame of greater ideological discourses, but in such a way that these frameworks do not become explicit enough to challenge the status quo of wealth distribution. Nevertheless, news of poverty manages to present itself as political, mostly by deferring to the notion of objectivity, that is, presenting the political facts but without the much-needed accompanying structural analysis.

This is not to say that all coverage of poverty always takes into account political context. On the contrary, representations of the poor often tend to be based on views with little or no context (Meinhof and Richardson 1994), as they often follow the same type of articulation of other issues – that is, being manufactured and bearing little relation to actual events (Harcup and O'Neill 2001: 277). Indeed, poverty tends to appear on television screens and front pages only when there is a 'crisis'; structural day-to-day issues are largely invisible unless they present a justification for military intervention, or legitimise the colonial past of present intervention in the face of donations and foreign aid. This situation prevails despite the fact that these crises are by no means new, but merely visible manifestations of structural and more fundamental issues. Hence, poverty is mostly articulated in the news as an isolated issue which seldom challenges prevalent worldviews and ideologies.

Therefore, one of the key themes of this book is to explore how journalists themselves understand the notion of poverty. For news editors and reporters, the fact that the concept of poverty has been instrumentalised in ways which mean something very specific in the context of specific ideological narratives should be a matter of concern. This is because deferring to those promoting these worldviews has the unintentional consequence of framing news on poverty in ways which do not challenge the status quo by not exposing, for example, inequality or social injustice. The question then is what do we really mean when we use these terms in our debates and discussions about the media? This is important not only in terms of how journalists influence public policy but also in relation to the consequences for political action of reproducing prevalent discourses about poverty.

Poverty in itself is by no means a universal concept (Lister 2004: 4), at least not one that can easily be summarised in the news. Even when specialists refer to categories such as 'absolute poverty' (as widely discussed in the prolific debates between Amartya Sen and Peter Townsend), the 'universality' of the concept has been difficult to pinpoint. This is not to say that it is not a tangible phenomenon. Poverty is everywhere we look and, despite some very abstract discussions that are actually not that useful for political action, poverty is nevertheless a category that encapsulates the most pressing and real tragedy of our times.

Poverty, as originally suggested by Adam Smith, is about a lack of respect from others:

> ... it is chiefly from this regard to the sentiments of mankind, that we pursue riches and avoid poverty ... The reason poverty causes pain is not just because it can leave people feeling hungry, cold and sick, but because it is associated with unfavourable regard. (Smith 1776)

Poverty, therefore, is relative not only to what the poor lack, but also to what is available to the rest of society. As such, news stories about poverty should also be about inequality, which until relatively recently was often absent in those mainstream stories. This is one of the key arguments of this book.

It is also important to define what is meant in this book by the term 'global news media'. These are the news media outlets that are based in those countries with sufficient wealth and power to influence the most powerful elites and to mobilise people inside those countries; this group of nations is often called the West, but also includes countries such as Australia and Japan. There should be no doubt that in this book the term 'the West' is also a euphemism for wealthy and 'global' an indirect reference for 'powerful' and 'influential'. This is because the media systems that we talk about here are all part of the post-Second World War arrangement often referred to as the 'international community'. This 'community' is composed of the group of nations that after the Second World War went on to dominate the United Nations system and its institutions such as the Security Council, the World Trade Organisation (WTO) and Bretton Woods (which includes the World Bank and the International Monetary Fund, IMF) and major military forces such as the North Atlantic Treaty Organization (NATO).

In this context, we recognise the problematic nature of such generalisations; within this group of media outlets, there are important exceptions. However, what we have done in this book is to use these generalisations in order to make our analysis more accessible. Overall, what we want to highlight with this exercise is how the coverage of poverty by the global news media relies heavily on the conceptual frameworks developed over the years by undemocratic and unrepresentative organisations and institutions.

In one respect, the global news media nearly reflect reality: poverty in the international news coverage is as much about 'the others', as it is about power. Indeed, those who are excluded from the patterns of consumerism and wealth enjoyed in the West, and who have little or no opportunity to shape the editorial policy of those media outlets, exist in the news narratives only in relation to those who have access to the media and the resources to shape their agenda. Hence, the following chapters also examine the position of those in power in relation to the phenomenon of poverty.

Overall, this book is about the invisible society that surrounds us; the slums in the cities, the destitute farmers, the beggars in the streets and the places and people, who, metaphorically speaking, only show up on our screens when destiny and tragedy make them visible and useful in perpetuating and reproducing power structures. Therefore, it is a book about how we, the privileged ones, view our destitute fellows through the lenses of a small group of reporters, journalists and media owners. The media are not the only party culpable of this distortion; it is no secret that we in the West are more than willing to listen to those who act as a Praetorian Guard for the ideas, preconceptions and worldviews that allow us to continue to live in the comfort of our homes without having to face up to the moral dilemmas posed by our chosen lifestyles.

It would be naïve not to expect that in an unequal world, news reporting would also be anything but unequal, despite the fact that there has been widespread awareness of the problems of media representation of the developing world, well expressed in the 1980s UNESCO report, *Many Voices, One World*. Nevertheless, since its publication, very little has been done – in the context of traditional mainstream media – to improve the way people around the world perceive and understand poverty. The promised dialogues between the North and South have rarely materialised and many media representations remain as problematic as ever.

What this book suggests is that the news coverage of poverty needs to evolve and that in order for this to happen, journalists ought to take a step back and review their own role in enabling the prevalent discourses. Part of this reassessment will mean re-engaging with the imagination of the wider public and re-establishing real commitments towards structural transformations and challenging existing injustices. As Chandran Nair, founder of the Hong Kong-based think tank Global Institute For Tomorrow (GIFT) said recently, 'The extreme form of capitalism which has permeated the world, particularly in the last 30–40 years, is in deep trouble and we are [all] in denial' (BBC 23 September 2011).

Finding a Meaning

The inspiration for this book was born of frustration – with both reading the news media and with having to confront my own past as a journalist and news editor. Indeed, this book is in part a reflection of my own failures at reporting poverty and the type of experiences I and many of my colleagues share in this field. Therefore, I make no excuse for what was by any standards an appalling level of news coverage of poverty on my part. This book is not a patronising attempt to tell journalists what many of them already know. Instead, I wish it to become a reflective account that could help move things forward.

I understand all too well the unbearable pressures under which most journalists work. But journalism is what it is: a practice modelled by the pressing circumstances and demanding dynamics that surround events and facts that are covered on a daily basis. As very imperfect historians, journalists go about seeking truth with worn-out tools in a challenging and changing environment that is transforming the nature of what they do and who they are. However, rephrasing John Maynard Keynes, it is equally true that if we are intellectually honest people we should therefore change our minds when facts tell us to do so.

Journalistic practice and the environment in which journalists operate have changed in the past decades in ways which make this area almost unrecognisable; its unprecedented transformation is ubiquitous (Waisbord 2013: 174), but nevertheless still aspires to uphold some of its more cherished values. This dichotomy of context and practices, together with the aspiration to maintain the ethical framework that has defined journalism as a profession, challenges particularly the way news media attempt to cover poverty as a global phenomenon.

In a way, we could be forgiven for feeling a certain nostalgia for the former Soviet Union. It is not that we should somehow forget the brutal excesses of that regime or the ruthless and inhumane character of the totalitarian dictatorships behind the Iron Curtain. Having said that, the end of the socialist experiment meant that many in the West stopped talking about poverty in a serious way; many journalists and editors who used to place inequality at the centre of the news agenda started to disregard it in favour of the New World Order. Indeed, inequality was a central argument in the propaganda efforts during the Cold War; hence it was widely reflected in the debates and narratives of the news media. However, after the 1980s, inequality became almost invisible in the news agenda with few exceptions.

Furthermore, the collapse of the Soviet Union, which also meant the end of assistance to many places in Africa, Asia and Latin America, occurred almost in parallel to the debt crises in the developing world and the subsequent implementation of the IMF and World Bank Structural Adjustment Programmes (SAPs). This meant that these Washington Consensus-inspired type of policies were implemented in fragile societies in the developing world when they were at their most vulnerable and had no political alternative to use as a bargaining chip. Until then, the West had implemented a series of assistance programmes for developing countries that fostered industrialisation and even encouraged land reform in some countries, such as John F. Kennedy's Alliance for Progress aid programme in the 1960s; these were created as a propagandistic counterbalance to Soviet initiatives such as the purchasing of Cuban sugar at a premium price and similar subsidies to other countries. If that era could hardly be categorised as a 'golden age' for the world's poor, at least the Cold War put them at the centre stage of the propaganda drama between capitalism and socialism, which meant that inequality was present as a recurrent theme in the news narratives.

The end of that era introduced a predominant paradigm in which many argued for the end of utopias, best summarised in Francis Fukuyama's 1989 essay 'The End of History?'. Soon after, many journalists fell for the illusion that merely by means of economic growth, market deregulation and by modifying certain aspects of our current system of production, we would achieve the eradication of poverty. By then development had become, as Gilbert Rist (1997) argues, a 'global faith' and 'economic growth' the ritual that should be performed if we aimed for salvation.

Many of us working in the newsrooms across the developing world at that time enabled these types of policies to be implemented by insufficiently scrutinising these ideas and experiments in social engineering. To many of us, privatisation and open markets seemed at that time a logical and rational solution to the chronic lack of public services, waste and state inefficiency. For example, many in the developing world will still remember how one had to wait almost ten years for a phone landline or face chronic shortages of water or electricity cuts at the mercy of state-owned companies. Many of my own generation still remember how many resources were poured into state-owned airlines, hotels and manufacturing industries, while hospitals and schools were running on huge deficits and scarce resources.

However, in the end, the medicine was worse than the illness. We know now that the neoliberal promises of a better future never materialised in the Third World. In hindsight, it is easy to see how naïve many of us were to expect that these policies would actually work. But knowing this now is of little comfort for those in a state of poverty who have had to carry the heaviest burden of these policies and who have never received a proper apology from those of us who should have known better. If anything, this book is my own personal apology to them.

Poverty cannot, of course, be blamed solely on the spread of neoliberal ideology into policy-making during the 1980s and 1990s. World poverty existed before structural adjustment programmes were ever devised, before the arrival of what we now call 'modernity'. However, indiscriminate liberalisation, deregulation and privatisation, adopted as dogmatic ideologies in the past few decades, have certainly made things worse.

The inequality gap is today far wider than it has been: 1.5 billion people in the world are medically obese, while another 1 billion go to bed starving every day (EFE 2011). Furthermore, most experts will nowadays recognise that despite improvement in countries such as China, many other countries have experienced a deterioration in living standards.

Despite this, if one were to believe the reporting in the news media before 2008, things were only getting better. The general discourse and its associated narratives in the news overwhelmingly embraced the free market model in which consumerism, maximum productivity and economic growth were leading the world towards an era of prosperity never seen before. It was a series of discourses in which limiting state intervention and pursuing absolute efficiency were at the core of any solution for poverty. These discourses are of course connected by the same goal: maximising profits by allowing the concentration of ownership of industry and services, while discouraging governments from taxing the very rich.

From the 1990s onward, any attempt to address inequality was frequently attacked by the media, under the pretext of incentivising investment. In Britain, Gordon Brown's attempts to increase taxes on inheritance, first as chancellor and then as prime minister, were met with fierce opposition by the mainstream media. Later, in the United States, President Barack Obama's plans for an equality tax that would make a hedge-fund manager pay the same tax rate as a plumber or a teacher was labelled 'class warfare' by Republicans, and the president was called a 'communist' by several segments of the media.

The situation became so obscene that on 15 August 2011, the financial investor Warren Buffett, one of the three richest men in the world, expressed his disgust at the fact that he paid less taxes than many of his most junior employees, by publishing an op-ed piece in the *New York Times* with the title 'Stop Coddling the Super-Rich'. He called for an increase in taxes on those reporting more than US$1 million of taxable income a year in the US. President Obama reacted in his 2012 State of the Union address by announcing the introduction of legislation that would make people earning over US$1 million pay the same tax rate as the rest of the population.

The majority of Washington's mainstream journalists were caught out by this sudden change in the news agenda. As with the character of Brooks Hatlen in the film *The Shawshank Redemption* (1994), they were institutionalised in their views about poverty and inequality. After all, for the past three decades, the news media have dedicated time and resources to creating a pedestal for the super-rich, while avoiding critical narratives on inequality or the need for taxation; precisely the type of initial steps needed to start addressing poverty. When the undisputed king of the speculative financial world denounced this situation, things had to be really bad.

As discussed further in the book, there is no master plan or conspiracy that perpetuates the framing of news on poverty, but a series of objective conditions that have historically shaped journalism in Europe, North America and Australia. This type of journalism, with its associated editorial practices, prevalent news cultures and dependence on corporate and government interests, is responsible for providing an ill-informed view on poverty. From this substandard starting-point, it seems that a lot needs to be done in order to promote a news agenda in which wealth redistribution and not just economic growth are taken into consideration as solutions to poverty in the news agenda.

We can only hope that the 2008 financial crisis signalled a turning-point and that journalists wake up from the catatonic state that has characterised the reporting of poverty in the past few decades. Whereas it would be naïve to expect media organisations to change their approaches to poverty, as they are ultimately representatives of hegemonic values, journalists are a different matter altogether and with them there is room for hope. As Henry David Thoreau once pointed out, 'Corporations do not have a conscience, but individuals can have one' (1849) and maybe these individuals are able to influence corporate policy, we should add.

Indeed, over the years it has become clear to many journalists that poverty is neither systemic nor natural. Instead, modern poverty is entirely a man-made phenomenon that is perfectly avoidable, as we have the ability and the resources to terminate it once and for all. It is true that only a small, but powerful, minority of humanity lacks the political will to push for a solution for inequality, but that is precisely where journalism can play a leading role. It will not be by any means an easy path and this book is just one small step in that direction.

The Book

Each chapter of this book focuses on a specific aspect of poverty reporting, although the overall discussion of the book is closely interlinked. Overall, the book explores how poverty is articulated in news narratives and presented to the wider public by offering understanding and critical analysis of the issue of poverty in the context of the news agenda, media representation and news production.

The key concepts are discussed in all the chapters and they are exemplified with cases from around the world. The message is, however, very simple: news reporting of poverty needs to switch from covering the manifestation of poverty to focusing on inequality. In so doing, as it is argued here, journalism faces many challenges. Perhaps the most daunting is precisely the state of denial about what, by any standards, is an unsustainable news agenda.

To help with two specific chapters of this book, I have enrolled three of my current and former PhD candidates: Scott Eldridge, Steven Harkins and Patrick Malaolu. Their participation in this book has allowed us to produce a very comprehensive insight into how news reporting of poverty is framed and articulated. I would like to thank them for their insightful contribution and support during the preparation of this book. I am also very honoured by their contribution as I am sure they will become top academics in their respective fields.

Chapter 1 deals with 'the subjectivity of poverty' as a news issue. The chapter provides a general overview of how the mainstream media deal with poverty as a global news item. By making reference to specific examples in the news, the section explores some of the most common representations of poverty in the media and the ideological categories that frame news stories on the subject. Particular emphasis will be placed upon global media news outlets such as Associated Press (AP), Thomson Reuters, the BBC, CNN and other European and Australian global news media outlets.

Chapter 2 attempts to provide a brief history of ideas on poverty in the newsroom by asking where these ideas come from and where journalists dealing with poverty and related issues acquire their views and general perceptions. In so doing, this chapter traces the most influential discourses on poverty back to the nineteenth century and explores how these ideas shaped the concept of poverty in the modern newsroom. It analyses the evolution of the news agenda and media representations of global poverty in the past hundred years by exploring historical shifts and continuities. It also looks at the different factors that have influenced journalists and news editors in the construction of the imaginary on global poverty.[1]

Chapter 3 discusses why many journalists working with key news media outlets around the world tend to overlook the root causes of poverty in their reporting. Indeed, when reporting poverty or related issues such as unemployment, exclusion, or even famine, journalists tend to leave aside the causes for such situations (Franklin 1999: 22). In covering poverty abroad, the media tend to focus on foreign aid as a quick solution, rather than exploring the underlying reasons for why people are poor. The chapter discusses the construction of news narratives on the causes of global poverty in the context of change and continuity, from the Washington Consensus to the UN's Millennium Development Goals.

Chapter 4 examines the news coverage of Africa and how this continent is represented by the media as the epitome of poverty. Reduced to a 'scar' of humanity, the complexities of the continent are often visually simplified into images of starving women or children, while sidelining post-colonial contexts that play a critical role in explaining current events. This chapter analyses how Africa as a news issue is constructed and articulated in the news agendas of the global media. It considers media events related to poverty in Africa, particularly famines, conflicts and natural disasters, and assesses the influence of these in the construction and framing of media representations on global poverty.

Chapter 5 looks at the visual culture of global poverty and how it is represented in images, by making reference to issues such as gender and race hyper-visibility in the news agenda. It looks at the problems that derive from visual representations and misrepresentations of certain segments of the population. This section explores the visual construction of poverty in the news agenda, while discussing the global media's creation of heroes, villains and victims in their narratives. It analyses how the news media has shaped notions of poverty in the context of popular culture and explains why it is important to deconstruct these assumptions.

Chapter 6 addresses the use of poverty by spin doctors and public relation managers to advance specific news agendas. As discussed here, multilateral organisations, governments, NGOs, think tanks and corporations invest heavily in media campaigns to influence the public's perception of poverty. These campaigns are instrumental in the articulation of news agendas and framing narratives and representations of the poor in orchestrated campaigns that define many news stories. This chapter explores and explains how these campaigns are designed and implemented, who is behind them and how they affect the media's coverage of poverty. In so doing, the chapter looks at the broader concept of 'media campaigns' and explores the role of PR and lobbying in the articulation of poverty in the media narrative.

Chapter 7 looks at the emergence of alternative voices and their role in re-shaping news about poverty. It examines networks such as Al Jazeera, Telesur and alternative news media outlets such as Democracy Now!, Radio Pacifica and Inter-Press Services. In doing so, it discusses how these media outlets have managed to provide a different type of reportage which ultimately has added complexity to the ways the mainstream newsroom deals with poverty. This chapter assesses the impact of the 'new' media in the articulation of poverty as news and how the Internet has transformed the way in which alternative voices on poverty manage to reach wider audiences; to do so, it analyses examples which have had a direct impact on the media's coverage and representation of poverty.

The concluding chapter discusses the sustainability of the current news agenda, while asking if it is possible for the mainstream global media to maintain a news agenda where poverty is an aesthetic and exotic news item. The chapter analyses the future of poverty in the news agenda and argues that it is intrinsically linked to the concept of sustainable development and environmental action. It will look at what some authors have called the need to democratise the media. In doing so, it suggests that this has become a pivotal task for those wanting to change the news agenda and provide a voice for the excluded (Shieldsa 2001: 217).

Finally, I must say that this book is my own contribution towards an overdue debate in the news media. It is a necessary and urgent one, but one that has been postponed for too long. The debate is not only about how poverty is reported. The debate in this book also refers to what journalism is about. When I was doing my own degree in journalism many years ago my then Professor of Public Opinion, Ana Irene Mendez, asked us in class what journalism was about. I jumped up and said with all certainty, 'It is about telling the truth.' She looked at me and said, 'Well no, that is what it claims to be about, but what it really intends to do is to deliver justice.' It took me almost twenty years and many mistakes to realise what she meant by that. I hope that by reading this book, readers will be able to understand her point rather more rapidly than I did.

1

The Subjectivity of Poverty

Poverty is arguably the most important single issue in the global news agenda, but at the same time one of the most neglected ones. According to the United Nations' report *Rethinking Poverty. Report on the World Social Situation 2010*, 'global levels of poverty have changed very little over the past two decades' (2009: 31), while most experts doubt that more than a handful of countries will achieve the targets set in the Millennium Development Goals (Elliot 2011: 43). Despite this, most of the mainstream news media in the West either ignore the subject altogether or seem wedded to the positivist view regarding world poverty levels.

Indeed, scholarly research has pointed out that the average amount of reporting on poverty is negligible when compared to other issues (Golding and Middelton 1982; Devereux 1998; Kitzberger and Pérez 2009). Most observations of the media's coverage of poverty suggest that it tends to be a marginal issue in the daily news (McKendrick et al. 2008; Kendall 2005), while similar studies highlight that the media in general do not do a very good job when reporting poverty (Chouliaraki 2006; Golding and Middelton 1982; Clawson and Trice 2000), as they allocate minimal resources, space and attention to the issue on the one hand, while distorting many facts on the other.

With relatively scant coverage, news about global poverty is effectively an oddity, which tends to come to the fore mostly in cases of humanitarian crises in distant and remote places. News media in the West, such as news wire services and broadcast networks, tend to focus mainly on crises such as famines and wars, while failing to discuss in depth the structural causes of poverty or to provide alternative views of the so-called developing world (Boyd-Barrett and Rantanen 1998: 14; Diaz Rangel 1966: 23). In these predominant systems of representation, poverty is mostly presented as a collateral issue rather than the main topic, while images of poverty are often distorted by the media (Clawson and Trice 2000: 54). These representations tend to create a sense of hopelessness, and the voices of the poor are rarely heard.

The prevalent narratives also appear to suggest that there are profound disagreements on what to do about poverty. Based on a variety of news sources, they tend to suggest very contradictory policies that range from increasing foreign aid to cutting it all together; this is neither new nor surprising, as similar situations have arisen in the recent past. Expert opinions are often represented as diverse and contradictory with regards to issues such as, for example, acid rain, the link between cancer and tobacco and, more recently, climate change, despite broad agreement among the scientific community (Oreskes and Conway 2010: 16). To be sure, the media and journalists have always been susceptible to lobby groups and public relations (PR) efforts from people with vested interests opposing any policy that could potentially affect those interests (Miller and Dinan 2007); this situation has worsened over the years in the face of increasing cuts in the newsrooms (Davis 2008) and the need to rely increasingly on press releases and PR material (Lewis et al. 2008b: 2).

The current media ownership structure and the model that it uses to produce news in the context of the market-driven economy has been flagged as a major reason for bias and misrepresentation of reality (Allan 1999a; Schlesinger 1978; Herman and McChesney 1997), leading to the conclusion that news stories do reflect a reality, but one that is socially constructed (Soley 1992: 12) by the terms of those who own or are capable of influencing the news media.

Therefore, at a time when the media not only transform reality but also create it (Martin Barbero 1993: 28), it is not surprising that poverty, as a by-product of inequality, is presented ·in the way it is; as a contested term defined by the news values prevalent in journalism cultures. As these cultures have been expressed by practices, dynamics and histories linked to the emergence of capitalism, we must assume therefore that poverty is understood in terms of the mode of production within a particular historical context.

Inequality itself, as the *raison d'être* for poverty, was effectively missing from the news agenda until the 2008 financial crisis; this despite the fact that the UN and other international organisations have highlighted very clearly for years the urgent need for wealth redistribution on both national and international levels. More pernicious, however, has been the fact that important sections of the media still disregard the issue of inequality altogether. In these cases, the prevalent narrative continues to be that as long as there is growth at the top it would be possible to pull people out of poverty, thanks to the 'trickle down' effect.

Indeed, inequality has been the elephant in the room among the most prominent global news media outlets for decades, being only temporarily highlighted during the US electoral campaign of 2012 which saw President Barack Obama having to come out in defence of greater equality (not without being called a 'socialist' by the extreme right) and several billionaires, such as Warren Buffett and Bill Gates, paradoxically calling for higher taxes on the rich.

However, more recently, experts and the media themselves have become more aware of inequality as the key issue. In their seminal work, Richard Wilkinson and Kate Pickett (2009) shed light on the problem of inequality by arguing that it brings misery not only to the poor and excluded but also to the rest of society. More and more voices have taken the position of addressing inequality as a priority in policy making (Lansley 2012; Stiglitz 2012) and more recently the central question has shifted from how to achieve growth in order to reduce poverty – as important and problematic as this question is – to how to reduce levels of inequality in order to eradicate poverty altogether.

The evidence suggests that economic growth as a way of reducing social exclusion has reached its limit in many nations (Wilkinson and Pickett 2009: 11) and that inequality is the primary cause of poverty. Despite this almost consensual view among experts on the current situation with regard to poverty and what to do about it, a great part of the news media seems to tell a very different story.

Isolated dark-skinned faces of women and children in remote corners of Africa appear to dominate narratives that tell us, sporadically, very little about the root causes or the nature of the problem. An overall sense of despair and resignation is pervasive, as if nothing can be done except for a laconic relief effort to aid the suffering while at the same time the idea is put forward that foreign aid should be cut altogether, in order to push poor countries into confronting the hard choices they are somehow avoiding.

Meanwhile, the 'growth' narrative is still the dominant feature in these media debates, as if there were no other choices for policy makers. Moreover, the palliatives that have been used in the past to alleviate poverty as a result of market failures, such as foreign aid and the welfare state, are now not only under attack by those who think that they are inefficient, but are also being blamed for creating a trap that keeps people in poverty (i.e. Moyo 2009).

This chapter provides a general overview of how the mainstream media deal with poverty as a global news item and how it enters into the news agenda within the wider frameworks of ideology and political discourses. By making reference to specific examples in the news, the next section explores some of the most common representations of poverty in the news media and the ideological categories that frame news stories on the subject.

The Elephant in the Room

Let us start by calling a spade a spade: poverty is a political problem and therefore the nature of this problem is the result of the particular political context within which it has developed (Alcock 1993: 13). As poverty is associated with intra-national levels of exclusion and inequality, not every government takes the same approach to poverty. The United States, for example, conceives poverty in different ways to that of many European countries and even to its neighbours, Canada and Mexico. While most European countries place the poverty line at a percentage of the average income of the general population, the United States still treats it in terms of absolute income.

Indeed, many members of the European Union set a relative standard by basically saying that any family group earning 60 per cent or less than the national average should be considered poor. Instead, the current poverty measure in the US, established in the 1960s, measures poverty by an income standard that does not include other aspects of economic status, such as material hardship (for example, living in substandard housing) or debt, nor does it consider financial assets (including savings or property). The official poverty measure in the US is a specific dollar amount that varies by family size but is the same across the country. According to the official guidelines, the poverty level in 2009 was over US$22,000 a year for a family of four and slightly over US$18,000 for a family of three. A similar criterion is followed by the World Bank when it measures poverty by an absolute standard of whoever lives on less than US$ 2 a day around the globe.

Therefore, we can argue that despite having its own rationale, the way in which a given country conceptualises, defines and then measures poverty is, at the end of the day, an arbitrary decision. As some authors have correctly pointed out, there is no single concept of poverty that stands outside history and culture (Lister 2004). It is, in other words, a social construction; different groups and countries perceive and articulate the notion of poverty in different ways.   没有耳 · 相同 - 复国

The problem with this is that since the conceptualisation of poverty involves moral imperatives, it has practical effects and implications for the distribution of resources both within and between societies. Hence, as a contested political concept in the media, poverty entails an implicit explanation, 'which in turn underpins policy prescriptions' (Lister 2004: 3). By defining poverty in a certain way, the state, international organisations and the media set the ground rules about how resources will be allocated and how they will be gathered, that is, taxation, nationalisation, privatisation, and so on).   规定

It is in this context that global news media articulate their own conceptualisation of poverty; a process that means legitimising a certain ideological strand in the society in which they operate and which defines the way in which resources and means of production ought to be allocated. In accepting the definition and measurement of poverty in a certain manner, the news media are in effect ratifying a specific type of policy. This relativism in the way poverty is measured makes the reporting of poverty on a global scale very problematic. Moreover, normal conventions that apply in other areas of news reporting and which set universally accepted standards, such as international law, do not work for every country or region when it comes to conceptualising, defining and measuring poverty.

Journalists tend, at least in theory, to stick to widely accepted conventions. These conventions relate to the attempt or aspiration to perform the 'strategic ritual' of objectivity (Tuchman 1972: 661), moving within well-accepted frameworks when reporting news. For example, it is expected that journalists reporting conflict should adhere to the wider consensus when defining the issues they report. They should describe and explain the events happening on the ground to their audiences in the broader terms of international law (Friel and Falk 2007: 6). In cases such as this, they are expected to make at least some basic distinctions between 'soldiers' and 'civilians' and between 'occupation' and 'liberation', while referring to the conflict in terms of the referential framework provided by the United Nations system and related bodies.

However, these conventions are not as straightforward – or as easy to adhere to – when it comes to reporting poverty. To start with, and despite the prolific use of the term in different contexts, a universal concept of poverty proves to be elusive and problematic at best, because our understanding about it derives from our own 'political' and 'moral' values (Alcock 1993: 6). Therefore, given the diversity of interests and values in the context of the global media, any attempt to define poverty will be mediated through a set of very distinctive and competing notions already present in news agendas.

To complicate matters even further, the definition of poverty by international bodies – which is often used as a benchmark by journalists – varies greatly even within the UN system itself. For instance, the multilateral banks and the International Monetary Fund (IMF) have over the years developed an approach to poverty that is very different to that of the World Health Organization or UNICEF (Babb 2009: 165), while other institutions such as NGOs and think tanks will develop concepts and policies on poverty that sometimes contradict each other even when working together on the ground.

Because of this, journalists and news editors have little to relate to in terms of conceptual consensus and standards other than their own ideologies, personal experiences and the authority they confer upon their own news sources, which in many cases are the same people from the institutions named above. As a result, consensus is reached only in critical situations such as famine, genocide, natural disasters and other media events, and only in a way that does not allow for a critical and comprehensive examination of these events' root causes. Even then, the media's role in making the relief efforts accountable to those who donate to them has been very poorly covered by the news media (Gill 1986: 94), while other problems are often simplified and caricatured beyond recognition.

An example of this is the news coverage of famines and their causes, although they no longer tend to capture the headlines as they did in the past (Gráda 2009: 1). Does the term 'famine' imply hundreds, thousands or millions of starving people? Does it occur because of natural causes such as droughts? Are famines cyclical or sporadic? More importantly, what are the conventions of reporting famines in the news?

Niger's food crisis in 2005 is an emblematic case of the above. This crisis was localised in the regions of northern Maradi, Tahoua, Tillabéri and Zinder, and arguably was caused by severe weather conditions and high food prices in a society that faces many levels of poverty. At some point, media reports referred to it as a 'famine', which soon became a political issue. Niger's president, Mamadou Tandja, dismissed reports that his country was experiencing a famine. He went on to say that opposition parties and the UN aid agencies had exploited the situation for political and economic reasons. For its part, the World Food Programme denied that the scale of the problem had been exaggerated; its spokesman, Greg Barrow, emphasised that they did not refer to the crisis as a 'famine' but talked about 'pockets of severe malnutrition' (BBC 2005a). Very few governments acknowledge that their people are suffering in a famine and if they do, they often blame natural causes.

Indeed, one of the problems with the term 'famine' is that it is both contested and politically charged in different contexts. Although famines such as the Irish ones of the eighteenth and nineteenth centuries or the Bengal famine of 1943 have often been attributed to natural causes such as disease and drought, there is wide consensus that they have often occurred in places that have no food shortages (Sen 1999: 170). They can also be politically sensitive, as they grant *carte blanche* for intervention and military coups, as occurred in the 1974 Ethiopian famine and the subsequent overthrow of Haile Selassie.

It is well known that many countries suffering from mass starvation were food exporters at the time of those famines (Gráda 2009: 194). In an article in the *London Daily Post and General Advertiser* from 1 May 1740 (Issue 1722), there is a dispatch from Ireland (dated 22 April 1740) in which it is reported that despite moderate prices of corn and oatmeal, people had forcibly boarded a ship with 50 tons of oatmeal cargo bound for Scotland. We may infer that this must have been some sort of a riot, as after the event the authorities had to 'recover the ship from these people and return it with its cargo to its rightful owners'. After the riots, the authorities had to ban exports from Ireland and distribute several tons of meal and grain among the poor. One of the most interesting parts of this news report was that it blamed the influx of people from the 'North of the Country', whose actions in taking over the ship 'threaten us with famine'; that 'us', of course, being the people living mainland Britain.

Other famines, such as the famine in Ukraine (1933), the Great Chinese Famine (1958) and more recently the North Korean famine of the early 1990s have been completely or partially labelled as human-made. However, they remain problematic in terms of conceptualising them as such. In all these cases, the news media reports articulated prevalent views from their own side of the ideological spectrum that defined 'famines' in such a selective and arbitrary way that any disaster only became so when they or their sources decided to recognise it as such (Benthall 1995: 11). On the other hand, the governments facing those famines would rarely admit at the time that their own people were starving and, when they did so, they and the government-controlled media would place the blame on natural causes.

Even when hundreds of thousands of people are starving, the term 'famine' still seems to be contested and politically loaded, both in the political discourses and the media narratives. This is because for a journalist or news media outlet, to label a food crisis as a 'famine' is to take a political stance and that, as we will see in a future chapter, has important consequences for the news coverage of poverty in general, and for the ability of journalists to claim impartiality and objectivity in particular.

For now, let us accept that famines are arguably the most extreme manifestation of poverty in the context of media discourses and narratives. They symbolise the ultimate stage of crisis and are a dire reminder of how vulnerable is the human race in the face of adversity. Its notional image is powerful precisely because it is able to create some agreement or consensus even if it is difficult to underpin its exact meaning. In the context of global news stories on poverty, this is a great achievement, as it is one of the few circumstances in which poverty is seen as a tragedy.

Famines, however, are just one aspect of the ways in which poverty is represented. In many ways, famines are the most obvious aspect because, for all their ambiguity, famines symbolise extreme depravation. However, poverty appears explicitly and implicitly in many formats across global news media stories. Given the fact that these manifestations of poverty are built upon a series of historical legacies, geopolitical approaches, corporate interests and political baggage, the identification and articulation of poverty in global news will often depend on a set of micro-interests intrinsically linked across the globe, which are ultimately of concern only to the elites who hold power.

In other words, despite the assumption of being a 'global' player that articulates world news for a world audience, the western media's coverage of poverty is instead strongly influenced and defined by the domestic politics articulated and managed by small elites. There is an important amount of empirical research that shows how domestic politics defines and affects foreign policy (Miliner 1997). Media agendas that follow foreign affairs will therefore also be affected by these same elements and will articulate these affairs in similar terms. News of poverty in this context will therefore be defined by the global media outlets that are covering it and their relations with the dominant elites in the countries in which they are based.

The fact that these domestic matters are closely related to the interests of the key actors who set the global agenda on poverty creates a situation in which global media definitions of poverty occur in the context of the 'quasi-consensual ideology of the major Western countries; one which does not recognise itself as such, but that sees itself in terms of "natural" common sense' (van Ginneken 1999: 32). Referring, for example, to the news agencies, Boyd-Barrett argues that these contribute to the homogenisation of global culture in form and in source, while greatly multiplying the texts available within standardised discourses (1997: 143).

These standardised discourses form the bases of the quasi-ideology, tends to legitimise injustice by making disparities acceptable, almost as if they are part of the natural order. In a systematic and sometimes unconscious way, these media outlets also support the lifestyles of the powerful elites who are their main clients as consumers and advertisers. This is especially true in the more economically unequal and affluent countries, where most media outlets base their headquarters. In these countries, the injustice that frames news reporting is supported by a set of beliefs based on individuality and the notion that the rich are the most capable and hardworking people (Rosanvallon 2012: 35); these beliefs derive historically from the view that elitism is efficient, exclusion is necessary, prejudice is natural, greed is good and despair is inevitable (Dorling 2010: 2).

Consequently, poverty is often conceptualised in the newsroom through these beliefs and articulated in the context of this ideological framework. News rarely refers to the world 'out there', but instead reports a synthetic, value-laden account which carries within it the dominant assumptions and ideas of the society within which is produced (McNair 1994: 30). Subsequently, poverty is conceptualised as an anomaly, which needs to be 'normalised' by articulating it in ways that do not question or threaten the system of inequalities that creates poverty in the first place.

In covering poverty, the global news media also face another intractable dilemma: having to assume impartiality and objectivity while covering these events and, at the same time, having to display eloquently the idea of compassion. Ibrahim Shaw suggests that the solution to this dilemma is a type of journalism – which he calls 'human rights journalism' – that prioritises the idea of attachment over detachment, empathy over sympathy and advocacy over neutrality as journalists become moral witnesses (Shaw 2011: 55). The problem is, however, far more complex as individual journalists operate within media systems that embrace the notion of objectivity in order to appear as legitimate and neutral voices on the international stage.

Know Them for Their Deeds

Nevertheless, let us remind ourselves that the category of 'global media' or 'international media' is a problematic notion that runs parallel to and is interlinked with that of the 'international community'. Therefore, the media that 'really count' have historically been that which are able to influence public opinion and affect leaders' ability to remain in power in countries that had a veto in the UN Security Council or that possessed the political muscle, the economic resources and/or the nuclear-deterrent capability to bypass or ignore the UN system altogether.

In this context, the way the global media articulates news about – or related to – poverty is very similar to the ways they cover other topics. By framing social and political issues in specific ways, news organisations declare the underlying causes and likely consequences of a problem while they establish the criteria for evaluating potential remedies (Nelson et. al. 1997: 658). The current framing of poverty in the news is based on powerful assumptions that became widely predominant after 1945. These assumptions were set by the two dominant ideologies of the time, which paradoxically shared the worldview of progress and economic growth. As Arturo Escobar points out:

> Poverty became an organising concept after WWII and the object of a new problematisation, which brought into existence new discourses and practices that shaped the reality to which they referred. That the essential trait of the Third World was poverty and the solution was economic growth and development became self-evident, necessary and universal truths. (1995: 24)

This is exactly the notion that most of the global media have embraced since 1945. Global media outlets – in the face of news agencies, key media outlets in the West and international broadcast networks – became fixated on a certain idea of poverty and a certain solution to it. There is a contingent relationship between the fact that global news agencies and broadcasters are predominantly owned and controlled by western corporations and the fact that they present an ethnocentric bias with regards to the world's poorer regions and nations (Stevenson 1999: 134).

Because of this, and despite some degree of diversity and important exceptions in its coverage, the global news media overwhelmingly cluster around a specific notion of poverty in order to construct it as a reality. The media focus on a pre-conceptualised notion and, more importantly, stick to a prevalent moral interpretation of what it is to be poor and where poverty is situated; both in terms of physical and ideological spaces. Poverty is subsequently conceptualised, defined and measured in the newsroom in ways that reflect the same news values that perpetuate and propagate the core ideas that justify and legitimise the causes of poverty.

This process of 'domestication' is performed by journalists whereby poverty as a news item becomes familiar to their audiences in ways which do not challenge prevalent structures of power and wealth. Therefore, the victims become 'ours' but not our responsibility, allowing inequality to remain invisible in the overall narrative, which remains emotionally attached to the notion of charity and fundamentally ethnocentric in the way it explains the phenomenon.

One of the main reasons for this type of 'instrumentalisation' of the notion of poverty in the global newsroom is the way in which journalists select their sources. In theory, news sources are selected on the basis of expertise, but in reality this only partially applies as they are chosen for what they represent in terms of power and status. Journalists select news sources that allow them to claim objectivity, as this 'appears to be a function of their power and status within the profession' (Soley 1992: 16). In so doing, the use of sources and their quotes confers legitimacy upon journalists as impartial observers who are only presenting what others say. In the case of those covering poverty, the use of news sources presents the only way to reconcile the eloquence of compassion with the lack of subjective responsibility.

Scholarly research on news coverage of the homeless in Canada, for example, suggests that the use of authoritative sources is a key strategy through which journalists achieve legitimacy: they gravitate to expert sources because they are seen as a more neutral authoritative option. In these studies, when the journalists were asked about the use of sources in their reporting on homelessness, they focused on their use of various kinds of expert sources. However, few mentioned the homeless themselves as potential news sources (Schneider 2013: 53). The voices of those actually living in poverty are rarely heard.

One of the key reasons for this is that selection of sources depends mostly on perceived credibility (Reich 2011: 19) and the homeless and those in poverty in general are perceived as unreliable, whereas those in positions of power or who display authority are axiomatically credible in the eyes of journalists, who see them as offering a more general and contextualised account of events. For journalists covering poverty, these expert sources are credible because they have 'technical authority'. This authority derives in part from the fact that many of these sources have been educated in the West and/or work for western institutions. It also means that they embrace views about poverty that are closer to that of the majority of the mainstream news people in the West. These views are characterised by what William Easterly calls the 'technocratic illusion', that is, the belief that poverty is purely a technical problem amenable to technical solutions (2013: 6). In so doing, these sources tend to offer a picture of poverty that tends to reflect the views of poverty as merely a technical problem, even in those cases when the expert sources are sympathetic to those in poverty.

Therefore, the construction of poverty as a concept in news stories is an exercise in symbolic power, as many journalists and editors use the sources to reinforce rather than to explore specific pre-conceptions. By so doing, the exercise of reporting poverty makes the clear, although sometimes indirect, distinction between 'them' and 'us', while presenting poverty as a phenomenon that happens to others in distant places (geographically, politically and morally), and in which there appears to be no direct link between the wealth of the very few and the exclusion of the many.

This situation has been aggravated by cuts in the newsrooms of major media outlets, which makes it very difficult to place reporters on the ground in these places, unless a major crisis is occurring. As the location of the news crew is key in defining what is covered by the news media (Dominick 1977: 96), the global media are prevented from interviewing local voices and the poor themselves, and journalists become increasingly dependent on official sources based in Washington, New York and other western capitals, or on the mediation and facilitation of charities and NGOs (Dogra 2012: 73). In other words, cutbacks in the newsrooms make them depend more on news agencies and public relations, which have come to fill in for the deficit of newsgathering (Davis 2008: 101). Cutbacks have also translated into an increase in the use of 'news shapers' (Soley 1992: 31), that is, people who provide opinions about events – such as 'experts' and 'commentators' – and a decrease in the use of those actors who are really involved in the story. Many newsrooms have become dependent on 'invitations' from multilateral organisations and NGOs to fly their journalists to the remote places in which poverty 'happens'. For all the altruism that one could assume from these organisations, this relationship presents the same types of moral dilemma as are found amongst those who are 'embedded' with the military during conflict and war.

Overall, journalists covering poverty rely on the available sources and these tend to be mostly those that provide official accounts. To illustrate this, an analysis of 98 news articles and editorials in the British newspapers the *Daily Telegraph* and the *Guardian* (between July 2010 and March 2011) regarding Sudan provides a clear indication of the way this reality is constructed. Nearly 66 per cent of all quotes used in these articles were provided by western officials and aid workers. Overall, less than 10 per cent of the news sources interviewed by journalists were of Sudanese origin and these included many working for international NGOs.

Early studies regarding the construction of news showed that most news sources are white, male and from elite institutions (Gans 1979: 125), something that has changed very little over the years. There are very few occasions when the poor themselves are given a voice in news reports. Studies carried out in places such as Britain indicate that those who experience or are at risk of experiencing poverty represent less than 12 per cent of the news sources used by journalists (McKendrick et. al. 2008: 24). Other studies in Canada suggest that experts dominate as sources, while the homeless are not completely denied a voice, but are consigned to the 'devalued voice of experience' (Schneider 2011: 71).

Of course, poverty in the global media is not only constructed through the use of specific news sources. The prevalent narratives are also articulated by the framing of the stories and the use of audio-visual images. In a study of five key American news magazines, Clawson and Trice concluded that African Americans were disproportionately portrayed as poor. African Americans were especially over-represented in negative stories on poverty and in those instances those in a state of poverty were presented with stereotypical traits, while, in addition, the 'deserving' poor were under-represented. The researchers suggest that the images of poor people in these magazines do not capture the reality of poverty; instead, they provide a stereotypical and inaccurate picture of poverty which results in negative beliefs and antipathy towards the poor (Clawson and Trice 2000: 63). These findings are consistent with other scholars' work (Golding and Middleton 1982; Devereux 1998; Franklin 1999).

Poor Features

One of the key features of the narratives describing the poor is that of 'passivity', often present in terms of the 'devalued voice of experience'. As well as being 'the other', the poor are commonly represented in the media as self-marginalised and self-excluded. A poverty-stricken person is merely surviving, expecting to be rescued by a saviour, or waiting for death to put an end to their misery. The passivity of the poor is represented at all levels, as we will discuss later in more detail. However, there are some important differences in the attitudes towards passivity and consequently distinctive discourses take place when referring to it. These attitudes can be seen in a *New York Times* article by the journalist Lydia Polgreen, in which poverty is presented as being of the Nigerians' own making. Polgreen cites Kayode Fayemi, then a candidate for governor in the state of Ekiti in south-west Nigeria; the article goes on to highlight that

> Nigeria is the fifth-largest supplier of oil to the United States. It is the economic, social and political fulcrum on which West Africa balances. Fayemi, the gubernatorial candidate in Ekiti, says he hopes to transform the political culture. He spent much of the 1990s in exile opposing military rule and now brings his resume studded with graduate degrees and international accomplishments to the local political scene. He also has a network of high-level contacts that includes, among many others, the liberal American financier George Soros, whom he befriended while serving on the board of Soros's Open Society Justice Initiative. 'We have allowed our politics to be so debased by money and violence that of course nothing but misery can come of it,' Fayemi said. 'It is the politics of the belly, and it is destroying us.' (Polgreen 2006)

It is important to examine the double standards that take place in this type of representation of passivity. Indeed, while passivity tends to have negative connotations when referring to the poor, it is presented as a virtue when referring to the wealthy.

One of the most interesting examples of this is provided by the comparative analysis of news coverage during the weeks after the earthquake in Haiti in 2010 and the one which hit Japan in 2011. The descriptions and images showed both a slow recovery and extreme passivity from the Haitians themselves. A photograph taken by Ramon Espinoza for

Associated Press is more than eloquent: a group of people is looking at a team of rescuers standing in front of a pile of rubble. The caption reads, 'People watch French rescuers use equipment to determine if a person is still trapped alive under the rubble of the St. Gerard University in Port-au-Prince.' The passivity is expressed in the faces of the earthquake survivors, who are waiting to be rescued by the representatives of the West, who are well-equipped, white French aid workers in helmets and uniforms, with their superior resources, knowledge and technology. This type of visual coverage appears frequently, despite the fact that most rescues after earthquakes are carried out by locals with little or no equipment.

Images and descriptions that suggest passivity dominate the media's narratives when covering the aftermath of events such as famines, earthquakes and other natural or human-made disasters that are characterised by poverty and destitution. However, passivity in rich societies facing events such as these is interpreted very differently. In a report from the US network ABC, on 15 March 2011, under the headline 'Japanese, Waiting in Line for Hours, Follow Social Order After Quake', we are told:

> Four days after a 9.0 magnitude earthquake and resulting tsunami, 'They are doing OK,' said Ron Provost, president of Showa Boston Institute for Language and Culture, a campus of the University of Tokyo. 'These are tough, strong, strong people. I think they are coping as well as could be expected or even better, if you imagine us being in that situation,' he said. 'That strength and resilience are rooted in a culture that has historically relied on social organization.'

Indeed, the same passivity that is often so negatively portrayed in poor countries in similar situations is labelled as 'resilience' and presented as a virtue in the case of developed nations when facing similar circumstances. There is no mention of the fact that Japan is one of the richest economies in the world and that in contrast to places such as Haiti, the institutional resources to confront these types of situations are in abundant supply. Instead, the Japanese resilience is explained in the following terms: 'Some of that community-minded resilience may come from its geography and dense population. Japan is only slightly smaller than the state of California and has a population of 127 million people.'

The fact that people in Japan have some certainty that help will arrive and that the state has resources to deal with the emergency, contrasts with the fact that Haitians are well aware of their own state's limitations, and that many Haitians were already living at subsistence level before the earthquake struck. To ask for serenity from those who know there is nothing for them at the end of the tunnel and then judge them for rising with fury and anger against adversity is hypocritical, to say the least. As Escobar suggests, how can we ask for more austerity from people who do not know anything but material austerity as a fundamental fact of their daily existence (1995: 213)? Yet that is precisely what a great part of the global media has done in the past when reporting the suffering of others.

Passivity is not the only feature that defines poverty in the news reports. References to 'chaos' are also widely used in news reports on the poor in different situations. Again, as in the case of passivity, 'chaos' has a double function: it legitimises intervention and justifies reporting by implying the presence of conflict. In a *Washington Post* article from 18 January 2010, under the headline 'Security fears mount in lawless post-earthquake Haiti', Manuel Roig-Franzia, Mary Beth Sheridan and Michael E. Ruane wrote:

> There was almost no Haitian law enforcement presence on the streets of Port-au-Prince on Sunday. For years, blue-helmeted U.N. peacekeeping forces have patrolled the city in armoured personnel carriers and trucks. But the U.N. force is deeply unpopular, and its ability to respond to the crisis has been hampered by leadership problems. The force's acting commissioner died during the earthquake, and his replacement did not arrive for several days.

The paragraph confirms the sense of chaos that seems to justify intervention or displace responsibility. The overall editorial approach that highlights chaos often ignores the reality of unequal resources. While the authorities in the developing world facing these events are often absent from the media reports or presented as chaotic and corrupt, in the industrialised nations they are very present in the news media, showing all their resources. As Simon Cottle points out:

> In the aftermath of catastrophic disasters politicians and other elites invariably go on 'media parade', symbolically positioning themselves among the carnage and devastation, conducting walkabouts and meeting survivors and commending emergency service and relief workers on their professionalism and heroic efforts – all in front of the cameras. (2009: 54).

The message in the industrialised world is clear and emphatic: the state and the elites are in control. However, when analysing CNN's 2012 news coverage of the possibility of famine in Sudan, we find that only 9 per cent of the reports made any reference to local or national authorities in the handling of the crisis. The suggestion in these types of narratives is unequivocal: poor people cannot articulate proper responses to the dilemmas/challenges they face and therefore intervention is necessary. Like Shakespeare's Macbeth, the suggestion in the reporting of tragedy is also very explicit; these people cannot govern themselves.

Conceptualising Poverty

At this point, it is possible to argue that the way in which newsrooms conceptualise poverty is closely linked to the process of 'othering'. The fact that journalists working in global news media outlets still 'other' those in the state of poverty in their narratives is perhaps illustrative of the fact that journalism has not yet managed to respond fully to the challenges raised by the transnational patterns of communication that characterise a de-territorialised world (Guedes and Harindranath, in Allan 2005: 278). Poverty is therefore conceptualised and reported in the newsroom as an issue that happens to 'others' in spaces/places far from home, even when it takes place in the same country.

In a few cases, global news media outlets reflect poverty as a domestic issue; that is, a problem for 'us' or better said, 'our problem'. Narratives of aid and help are constructed around 'will and need' for intervention, in which the 'must do something about it' is commonly regarded as an act of 'moral will' rather than as a socio-economic and geopolitical set of interests. Indeed, terms such as the 'community of donors' underscore the image of passivity among the poor 'other', while reinforcing the status and image of the 'us', whose power and wealth provides the luxury of feeling sorry and deciding whether to intervene or not, but about which very little is said in terms of responsibility for wealth concentration and inequality.

As Escobar suggests, the body of the malnourished – the starving 'African' portrayed on so many covers of western magazines, or the lethargic South American child to be 'adopted' for $16 a month portrayed in the advertisements in the same magazines – is the most striking symbol of the power of the First World over the Third (1995: 103). A whole economy of discourse and unequal power relations is encoded in this body of news about poverty, in which this phenomenon is conceptualised as a label that provides agency to some and denies it to others.

Moreover, labels are essential to the production of discourses of poverty in the media; the poor live in 'villages', in 'slums', in 'shanty towns'. They are defined by these labels so they can be excluded from our own living space. But as Susan George reminds us, labels are not neutral; they embody concrete relationships of power and influence in the categories which we use to think and act. More importantly, they confer access to resources (1986: 53), as they set in motion the discourses for action and policy. This is why one can argue that in labelling poor individuals, groups and whole societies, the global media also deprive them of power and rights. Africa, for example, becomes, in the news stories, a hopeless continent. Latin America is described in the journalistic narratives as an unfulfilled promise while parts of Asia are represented as a woman and her child who have embarked on an eternal begging journey from which there is no point of return. The corollary of course is the West's right to intervene and the 'other's' duty to comply with the values, institutions, rules and settings of that intervention, which is euphemistically called 'globalisation'.

These types of specific ideological categories that define not only the way poverty is constructed in the newsroom but also the narratives that frame poverty as a news item (Devereux 1998: 21) are not, however, universal. The process of news gathering and the selection and the dissemination of poverty as a news item tend to be also strongly influenced by the mindset and symbolic frameworks that operate in the different newsrooms. These frameworks have been historically recycled, as we will see in the next chapter, and they persist in the description of poverty and, most importantly, in defining 'who is' and 'what it is to be' poor. Although these representations are not always a general pattern to be found in all newsrooms, they are nevertheless a common experience for those of us who have covered poverty.

In this common space, all these competing and complementary approaches to poverty in the different newsrooms seem to respond to a process of 'othering' the poor, a process which takes place in a systematic and persistent manner and presents historically crucial continuities. In this process, reporters, journalists and editors tend to defer to those who lead in the organisation, or who have become references in the process of agenda setting within the profession, when shaping their understanding and subsequent articulation of news stories about the poor.

One could almost paraphrase Bernard Cohen (1963: 20) and argue that top international journalists in key media outlets do not tell others what to write, but they surely tell them what to write about. Moreover, since these journalists and news organisations hold power or control access to power in terms of promotion and recognition in the profession, their own views tend to become the referents for the way the news on poverty will be framed, something that has been well described by several authors (Allan 1999a; Altschull 1995; Curran 2000; McNair 1998).

This being the case, we can safely assume that journalists' backgrounds and their experience of poverty are key elements in defining the way they conceptualise, cover and report it, but only in relation to the dynamics of the news culture in which they operate. This assumption is backed by an ample body of scholarly literature regarding the conceptualisation of issues in current affairs with regards to the process of manufacturing news (Cohen and Young 1973; Schlesinger 1978; Gans 1979; Herman and Chomsky 1988; McNair 1998; Harrison 2006). These works highlight the role of the journalists' background in constructing news and there is no reason to suppose that it is different in the process of conceptualising poverty in the news. If this is the case, then it is possible to understand why, despite their best efforts to show some empathy and engagement with poverty, many news reports ended up in the vicious circle of 'pity and dismiss'.

Let us start by pointing out the obvious: Most journalists and editors working for the global news media outlets lack first-hand experience of poverty. For example, a study carried out by the Sutton Trust in Britain showed that roughly half of the hundred leading journalists in the country attended one of the country's top two universities, Oxford and Cambridge (2006: 4), neither of which offers a journalism degree.

Many of these people are journalists working in the so-called 'global media', which would not be problematic in itself were it not for the fact that more than 55 per cent of Oxford and Cambridge students come from private schools. In fact, 54 per cent of Britain's leading journalists were educated in private schools, which account for just 7 per cent of the school population as a whole. This is also the case in some of the most influential news outlets. For example, journalists graduating from Oxford and Cambridge predominate among the most senior positions on the British newspaper the *Guardian* (Elliott, C. 2011), where most new senior positions are filled by white, middle-aged males. There are few editors of ethnic background and women have only just started to access the top positions in this type of media organisation.

The latest recruits to the news media in Britain are even more likely to come from privileged backgrounds than those from previous generations, as a result of the bias towards those with family or personal connections within the industry amid a largely informal but highly competitive recruitment process and the stronger skills and attributes exhibited at an earlier age by those from private schools. New graduates from upper-class backgrounds are also able to afford unpaid training schemes, which may land them one of the few entry-level journalism jobs in times of recession.

These numbers are very similar in the United States, Australia and other western European countries with regards to the origin and background of journalists, who tend to come disproportionately from privileged families. Studies show that the average journalist in the US is a white male Protestant in his forties, usually from the East Coast (Weaver 2005: 44), while in Britain only 18 per cent of the top journalists are women and less than 5 per cent are non-white. The situation in places such as Germany and Sweden is no better (Graf 2011), while Aboriginal indigenous Australians are almost invisible in the mainstream newsrooms in that country (Meadows 2001). The newsrooms of the global media outlets seem to bear no resemblance to the real world and are particularly unrepresentative of their own societies.

The conclusion is obvious: few media professionals have direct knowledge of poverty, even in those cases in which they have shown themselves to be very sympathetic. Their views and perceptions on poverty are constructed by hierarchical education systems and a family ethos which situates them at the opposite end of society; consequently, the formulation of ideas about poverty follows similar rituals to the construction of any other aspect of social reality, which is mostly designed to reinforce existing power structures.

The (Social) Reality of Poverty

As Brian McNair points out, it is almost a commonplace to say that news and journalism are social constructions, but nevertheless in truth this idea remains central to our understanding of journalism (1994: 30). This can be applied to the articulation of the concept of poverty in the news. It is made up of referents that we use in our daily life to filter the world around us and to understand it in our own terms. Indeed, 'there are portions of the real world, objective facts in the world that are only facts by human agreement' (Searle 1995: 1).

Therefore, those factors which make poverty an 'objective' news reality are precisely those things that exist because we believe they exist; intangible elements such as money, property, governments, education. These are the things that the poor lack and that the global media try to call for when covering poverty. However, these objects are not neutral; instead they carry a very heavy ideological baggage, which defines them in very subjective terms.

As a result, the construction of poverty as a social reality happens in the context of specific ideological frameworks in which this phenomenon is conceptualised and defined by arbitrary measurements. Because an ideology is taken on by a group because of specific theoretical elements that are conducive to its interests (Berger and Luckmann 1966: 141), these frameworks act as blinkers through which the world is seen solely in the forward direction of 'progress', fuelled by economic growth in general and consumption in particular.

For the global media operating within these ideological frameworks, closely interlinked to the corporate world, poverty is defined as a temporary but at the same time natural reality – one that should be expected to exist for an indefinite period of time. There is no room for critical examinations of poverty as a by-product of a system that is by definition unjust and structurally incapable of addressing the issue. In most news stories, people 'are' poor, as if that was an inherent condition rather than a temporary state. In such a context in which people are constantly dehumanised and responsibilities are individualised, the coverage of poverty brings about a type of pseudo-responsibility that calls for intervention either by means of military power or through compassionate but highly politicised foreign aid and international assistance. But in very few of those global stories are members of the public made to question their own role in creating that poverty in the first place.

2

The Poverty of Ideas in the Newsroom

Jairo Lugo-Ocando and Steven Harkins[1]

Despite journalistic normative claims that news accounts on poverty are driven by a quest for social justice, the way poverty is articulated today by the global news media is instead a convergent by-product of more down-to-earth organisational dynamics and interests that happen within the newsrooms. First, we can point to the media's editorial and news policies, which are shaped by a multiplicity of interests and objectives; second, we have the ideological interventions and approaches of journalists and editors in the process of news gathering and dissemination; and, third, the framing provided by news sources and news shapers in the construction of explanatory narratives for the events and issues about which they are consulted and interviewed.

In all three cases, the historical construction of knowledge and the continuities in news cultures play a pivotal role in the configuration, understanding, perceptions and general articulations of discourses regarding poverty. Indeed, journalists have always belonged both to a specific culture and to a specific professional subculture; they live in a common-sense world in which the meanings of things, facts and relations are shaped differently by the process of socialisation (van Ginneken 1998: 65). These are processes that imprint their cultural and historical baggage in the construction of social reality.

Almost equally important is the fact that the ideas about poverty of journalists, as a professional body, as well as those of their news sources, news referents and those implicitly defining the ethos of the media outlets for which they work, are determined one way or another by class conscience. This is not to say that the notions of poverty in the newsrooms are by any means static or completely homogenous. On the contrary, they are constantly mutating and adapting to fit the prevalent discourses of each era. These historical dynamics lead to a wide range of interpretations and diversity of views in which the old and the new converge to construct the journalistic idea of what poverty is. In the newsroom, the notion of poverty is overall the result of a professional subculture that tends to recycle ideas and practices but that nevertheless manages to evolve and adapt to new circumstances. As Martin Conboy reminds us, for as much as we would want to celebrate its triumphs, the history of journalism is, at the end of the day, characterised as much by ruptures as continuities (2004: 2).

Therefore, to understand why global journalism represents poverty in the way it does, it is necessary to look at the history of the ideas of poverty in the newsrooms and to raise fundamental questions about the formations and origins of the ideas of poverty in the global newsroom. Indeed, if we want to understand the prevalent journalistic discourses about poverty we should then ask questions such as: Where do these ideas come from? Where do journalists get their views and general perceptions about poverty? How do these views translate into the articulation of poverty in the news and subsequently affect the practices of gathering and constructing news on poverty?

This chapter aims to address these questions while tracing historically the origins of the most influential journalistic discourses on poverty and exploring how these ideas have shaped the concept of poverty in the modern newsroom. It analyses the evolution of the news agenda and media representations of global poverty in the past by exploring shifts, continuities and trends. In so doing, it looks at how practices and approaches in the modern newsroom have been shaped over the years by the wider set of cultural referents, while exploring how these have affected both media practices and journalistic approaches towards poverty.

There are many different factors that have influenced journalists' and news editors' imagining of poverty, from the literary and journalistic works of Charles Dickens to the political writings of Karl Marx and Friedrich Engels to many forms of media cultural representations – from films such as Charlie Chaplin's *Modern Times* and D.W. Griffith's *The Birth of a Nation*, to more current influential references for journalists such as Oscar Lewis's *Five Families*, Jeffrey Sachs' best-seller *The End of Poverty* and staged media events such as Band Aid, the protests against the World Trade Organization (WTO) meeting in Seattle in 1999 and against the G8 Gleneagles summit of 2005. Moreover, journalists are after all individuals subjected to particular experiences that would have shaped their own individual views of poverty.

However, it is equally true that journalism as a professional body shares a common discourse that is widely reflected in the output that is generated in the form of news reports. Indeed, the pay-off for journalistic profession-alisation over the past two hundred years cannot only be seen as a social one, but also needs to be considered as corporate (Maras 2013: 25). In other words, we need to consider journalism as an 'epistemic community' that cultivates distinct forms of knowledge within its own professional logic (Waisbord 2013: 130). In the case of British and US journalistic practices, this common discourse can be traced back to the political debates of the Victorian era and the accompanying literature of that period, which created important ideological referents that remain present today in the forms of journalistic professional values and assumptions regarding poverty.

These referents from which men and women in the newsrooms derive their understanding and interpretations about poverty as a social phenomenon are historically consistent with who they are as a professional body, where they come from as a social group and to whom they ultimately respond to in terms of the political economy that underpins their profession. These referents are the basis of the modern conceptuali-sation of poverty in the newsroom which have become popular and then fallen from favour over the years only to later re-emerge and be recycled in different forms. The key question is therefore, why do these ideas continue to persist over time in the minds of journalists?

The aim in this chapter is to use this question as an excuse to examine and debate the way in which journalism as a professional body in the West constructs social reality in relation to poverty. This chapter does not pretend to be a full account of the history of all journalistic ideas about poverty in the newsroom. Instead, it is a modest attempt to try to understand why some of these ideas remain almost immutable or have changed so little over time. In so doing, it wants to analyse the three factors mentioned above that shape the construction of poverty as a news item in the articulation of news stories.

From Then to Now

Current journalistic approaches to poverty have been developed from prevalent notions of the past and tend to reproduce the more general views on poverty that have developed over the years. These continuities in the articulation of poverty in journalistic discourses are deeply rooted in the Industrial Revolution. It was then that the balance between urban and rural populations began to shift, and poverty started to become a reality in the public eye and to be discussed in the public sphere as a political issue.

Indeed, the Industrial Revolution was a definitive period in terms of conceptualising poverty in the newsroom. During that time, especially because of the so-called 'moral imagination' of the late Victorians (Himmelfarb 1992) but also because of workers' radical movements (Hollis 1930), ideas about society and poverty would profoundly change. It was during this period that social Darwinism took formal shape by linking with Malthusian conceptions of populations and demography. Social Darwinism was certainly one of the most multi-functional, all-purpose ideologies of the late nineteenth and early twentieth centuries (McCarthy 2009: 75) and it played a pivotal role in shaping the idea of poverty in the second half of the nineteenth century.

We can, of course, find many connections with previous ideas of poverty. From the time of the Elizabethan Poor Law, we find classifications of the poor, mainly distinguishing between neighbours and strangers (Katz 1989: 11), while providing the foundations for settlement rights and obligations towards the other. Indeed, poverty as a news item was already well-represented in British newspapers as early as 1800. The 1–3 January 1800 edition of *Lloyd's Evening Post* (Issue 6608) displays several letters on its front page informing the reader about the charitable activities of some members of society. One is from the Bishop of Hereford, in which he uses the paper to call for the attention of the 'Nobility, the Gentry and my Reverend Brethren Clergy of this Diocese' to offer help for the poor. Nevertheless, he makes it clear that there is no imposition or obligation to help them. He merely reminds readers that 'God loves the giver.' In many ways, we find in this type of narrative the origins of the discourses that today see foreign aid as an act of will rather that a statutory obligation. It is in these pieces that we can observe some of the early manifestations of 'compassion-with-no-obligation' discourse in the media.

The second letter, by William Cavendish-Bentinck, 3rd Duke of Portland, to the lieutenants of the different counties is even more interesting. The letter basically calls on them to enforce a King's Act that specifically dictates the amount of wheat that bread should contain. It reminds the public about the increasing cost of wheat and grain and how this could affect the 'industrious' poor, while suggesting that special measures are necessary if charity contributions are to be effectively distributed. The piece is made even more relevant by the fact that he calls upon magistrates to guarantee that the poor have access to food. Again, this is a news item that has a great deal of resonance with today's news narratives about food shortages and escalating prices worldwide and how they affect the poor.

However, it was only in the mid-nineteenth century that newspapers all over Europe and the United States started to publish stories about poverty from around the world as a regular feature. In many cases, these reports came from newspapers in other countries, while in others they were based on reports from correspondents in distant places. Examining some of these pieces in the archives, we find many similarities with today's news accounts. During that epoch, the concept of poverty was already evolving in the newsroom, following and reflecting the wider debates in society. It incorporated the ideas of exclusion as a 'necessity' and elitism as a 'reality'. Overall, it provided the justificatory seeds to see poverty not as a manifestation of deep-rooted problems, but as a problem in itself.

This was because the narratives of Europe as the evolutionary pinnacle of human society were well-established, as is evident from the works of Jakob Böhme (1575–1624) and Georg Hegel (1770–1831). However, by examining newspaper collections in England, one may suggest that two of the most influential discourses in the newsrooms of the first half of the nineteenth century were those shaped by the ideas of Adam Smith (1723–90) and Thomas Robert Malthus (1766–1834). It is in this epoch's newspaper pages that we are able to observe, in its crudest form, the questioning of charity as an unnecessary prolongation of poor people's suffering and overall the consolidation of the ideas of the 'deserving' and 'undeserving' poor as a mainstream reality. Indeed, Malthusian tradition was quick to identify overpopulation as the key root of poverty. Soon after, Malthus's adherents went on to promote birth control, although Malthus himself, as a Christian, proposed celibacy (Jones 2004: 210). These ideas had a powerful political influence on the 1834 Poor Law Amendment Act, which made life far more difficult for poor people in Britain, while Malthus argued against poor relief for the able bodied (Avery 1997: 62).

It was during the nineteenth century that some of the core values and definitions of poverty became embedded in journalists' jargon and discourse. In his 'Letter I', English journalist Henry Mayhew (1812–87), defined poor 'all those persons whose incomes are insufficient for the satisfaction of their wants' (cited in Thompson and Yeo 1973: 121). Mayhew's view, ahead of his time, was that poverty was the product of the economic system (ibid.: 88). However, like many of his contemporaries, he also drew a distinction between the 'honest' and 'dishonest' poor, echoing the old Elizabethan notion of 'deserving' and 'undeserving' poor.

These ideas were partly a reflection of the political context of the time, which demanded the constant legitimisation of empire, slavery and colonial rule. Hierarchical order, necessary exclusion and racial superiority were acceptable ideas that justified the existence of the British Empire. During this time, dominant representations conceptualised race as a product of culture under the application of a dichotomy that distinguished between white 'civilised' Europeans and non-white, non-European 'savages' (Peters 2013: 10–11). In 1848, Europe experienced a series of revolutions led by 'working-class radicals and middle class liberals in Paris, Milan, Venice, Naples, Palermo, Vienna, Prague, Budapest, Krakow and Berlin' (Rapport 2009: ix). Unlike Karl Marx, who famously interpreted these types of revolutions as class struggles, Robert Knox (1791–1862) interpreted them as a 'race war' (Peters 2013: 10). Knox's unorthodox shift of focus from cultural to biological explanations of race appealed to the emerging scientific discourses that defined the Victorian era.

Another important aspect to consider is the scientific revolution which was taking place during that era. Indeed, the late nineteenth century saw rapid advances in the fields of mathematics, medicine and physical science that 'altered the way people might understand life or locate themselves in the universe' (Lightman 1997: 179). This spirit of scientific enquiry was to have a profound effect upon journalism and the journalistic culture, which shifted away from a 'traditional ethic of avid partisanship' towards a 'professional code of objectivity' (Allan 2010: 25). As Kaplan suggests:

> Under objectivity, journalists adopt the pose of scientist and vow to eliminate their own beliefs and values as guides in ascertaining what was said and done. Supposedly avoiding all subjective judgments and analysis, the journalist strives to become a rigorously impartial, expert collector of information. More than just ending formal political alliances and external control, the objective press must eliminate any organizing philosophies or social commitments from influencing the news. (Kaplan, in ibid.: 26)

These ideas shaping the notions of poverty, and especially of hunger, lasted well into the 1940s (Vernon 2007: 272), which explains why they still matter in this analysis. After the publication of Charles Darwin's *Origin of*

Species in 1859, these ideas would go through a very important mutation, giving rise to notions of race, mainly because they seemed to add scientific evidence to all the existing prejudices and assumptions about the 'others'. The interpretation given to Darwin's work serves to consolidate a language and discourse that had been in formation for the past two hundred years in a way in which they would provide a post-Enlightenment distinction between 'civility' and 'barbarism' or what we consider 'rationality' from 'faith' (Fitzgerald 2008: 6).

Unlike Robert Knox, who believed that different 'races' were different species of men (polygenism), Darwin was 'convinced that humans were a single species', a line of thought that was interpreted as 'monogenism' (Steinbach 2012: 244). One of the important concepts that sprang from monogenist approaches to 'race' was the idea of 'an ideal type, often associated with whiteness, from which all other races have degenerated as a result of their particular environment' (Peters 2013: 16). This line of thinking constructs the poor as a threat to civilisation because they are at risk of degenerating into savagery. Following Malthusian thinking, charity and poor relief will increase the risk of degeneration as they simply subsidise procreation beyond the poor people's means of subsistence. This is an idea that has been recycled and can be found in contemporary press accounts of poverty, and certainly we find them among many news reports that focus on a violent 'underclass', which has developed because the welfare system is deemed to be 'too generous'. Journalists and commentators used these ideas to construct an explanatory framework for the 2011 London riots, which were blamed on the existence of a widespread 'underclass' (Biressi and Nunn 2013: 44–7).

Associated with 'social Darwinism', these ideas became prevalent in the late nineteenth century as an ideological construction. They mostly referred to notions such as that of the 'survival of the fittest', while justifying actions and practices that excluded those unable to support themselves. Among these practices was the implementation of laissez-faire economic policies, the pseudo-science of eugenics (to improve race) and the justification of colonial rule. Later, in the twentieth century, these ideas would evolve into the type of ideologies that justified Nazi expansionism and the genocides of the 1930s and 1940s.

These were, of course, not the only ideas being disseminated at the time. Five years before Mayhew's first letter on the conditions of the poor in London, Friedrich Engels (1820–95) had already published, in German, *The Condition of the Working Class in England* (1844), in which he linked the Industrial Revolution with pauperisation. In a detailed account, he showed how mortality rates actually increased in cities such as Manchester and Liverpool after the introduction of the mills. These ideas would certainly have challenged Victorian assumptions of progress, which were rapidly spreading among journalists and writers. But Engels' – and also Karl Marx's – ideas were kept at bay in the newsrooms despite being far better substantiated by 'facts' than those of the Malthusians and social Darwinists. In his articles about the debates that had taken place in the Diet of Rhenish, Marx himself would underline that the press at that time deliberately ignored structural interpretations of poverty because of class interests (Marx and Engels 1841: 121). Indeed, looking at historical archives of the five main newspapers at the time in London, Friedrich Engels's name or works are not mentioned or referred to until 1886, and thereafter only a few times, mostly in highly contested political reports. Engels's book was not published in English until 1887 in the United States and it would take four more years to appear in Britain, this despite strong links between English and German intellectuals at that time.

However, less radical journalism did make its way onto the front pages and was able to disseminate important ideas that led, for example, to the reform of housing. Many of the so-called pamphleteers and sensationalists of the 1870s and 1880s saw themselves as social explorers who penetrated the deep and dark territories of poverty (Golding and Middleton 1982: 23). Among such explorers was George Sims, whose work on the living conditions of the poor in England appeared in the *Pictorial World* in 1883, and Andrew Mearns, whose work on the 'outcast' for the *Pall Mall Gazette* was in many ways a prelude to reporting social exclusion. The news coverage of poverty by these pamphleteers proved to be very popular in terms of circulation and for some years it drove many more into carrying out ever more systematised reporting about poverty.

Nevertheless, the ideas inspired by Malthusianism and social Darwinism finally became the prevalent explanatory frameworks for news narratives. Accordingly, journalists at the time assumed that individuals were responsible for their own poverty, attributing their condition to the lack of fitness to survive. This idea became more prevalent during a time in which the ideology of objectivity was also taking shape as a core value in journalism practice (Schudson 2001: 149). No longer did journalists have to explain explicitly where poverty came from, but just develop the stories based on facts and allow prevailing assumptions to say the rest. As James

Carey pointed out, by elevating objectivity and facticity into cardinal principles, the press abandoned explanation as a primary goal (1986: 29).

This shift also coincided with a carefully orchestrated exercise in disseminating the ideology of empire and white European supremacy. Indeed, nineteenth-century industrialisation saw the spread of theories which were translated into newspaper stories, attempting to justify the inequalities in the income and wealth of the new age, which were becoming more prevalent in British society and across the empire. As David Spurr suggests, the concept of nature became pivotal for the colonial discourse. This is because 'natural law' grants domination over the earth and over less advanced people. Therefore, the land belongs to the power which understands its value and is willing to turn it to account. By 'naturalising' the process of domination, this discourse justifies domination and conquest of nature and primitive people (Spurr 1993: 156).

From this 'naturalisation' came the need to propagate an evolutionary theory that could support and legitimise the notion of the few very able, who would preside at the top, and the many. whose role was to follow those chosen few. In contrast, the same argument runs, there was a

> ... residuum of inferior but similar interbreeding human who were much greater in number. Often these people, the residuum, came to rely on various poor laws for their survival and were labelled 'paupers'. Between these two extremes was the mass of humanity in the newly industrialising countries, people labelled as capable of hard working but incapable of thinking. (Dorling 2010: 103)

In this scheme of things, one of the most important distinctions between the 'deserving' and 'undeserving' poor became closely interconnected with the notion of the survival of the fittest. It was Herbert Spencer (1820–1903), in his book *Principles of Biology* (1864), who coined the phrase 'survival of the fittest'. Moreover, throughout his life he believed (as did many of his contemporaries) that hereditary talents were passed from individuals to their families. This of course is an extreme oversimplification of Spencer's intellectual contribution, as some of his biographers would attest (Duncan 1908; Francis 2007). Nevertheless, the simplified version of his ideas about race became the basis of mainstream journalism's reporting about poverty for the subsequent years. Using Jean-Baptiste Lamarck's (1744–1829) theory of the inheritance of acquired characteristics, Spencer argued that the principles of biological evolution could be applied in order to understand society. He became, among the Victorian era's newspapers and their journalists, a 'celebrity' by modern standards and a permanent news source for the most important news media at the time.

To be fair to Spencer, many of those writing for British newspapers at the time selected many of his ideas in a way that served to reinforce their own discourses and worldviews. However, Spencer did actively lobby newspapers to use close friends and acolytes as columnists or writers, who would reflect similar views to his own and would reinforce the ideas that he was selling to the world. Like the think tanks of today, Spencer and company made sure that their own ideas were disseminated and constantly validated. He was not only a prolific writer, but also an effective networker, who corresponded with the most influential people of the time, even when he disagreed with their views.

Another, later, but very important influence in reinforcing these discourses on poverty was Francis Galton (1822–1911). Although he explicitly rejected the idea of the inheritance of acquired characteristics, he was nevertheless an early proponent of the heredity of attributes by means of selection. Through the use of statistics, Galton provided the necessary 'rigour' to make race a scientifically strong argument in the public debate about poverty. Once statistics were incorporated into the discussion, newspapers' reports had to embrace them as rational facts that were beyond scrutiny. Galton himself, a half-cousin of Charles Darwin, was a proponent of the term 'eugenics' in 1883, in his book *Inquiries Into Human Faculty and its Development*. His ideas were later embraced by Karl Pearson (1857–1936), who would have a definitive influence on modern science and statistics. Their ideas translated into claims that races have different levels of intelligence, which led to the formulation of the first mental intelligence tests. In their current forms (that is, IQ, GMAT, GRE 11-Plus, Psychometric Tests, and so on), these tests, with their pretension of measuring intelligence levels, have been responsible in part for barring many from education and from the top jobs around the world as the tests continuously validate the notion of inferiority (Zuberi 2001: 56).

However, as is often the case with ideological constructions in history, it is never clear that these constructions had any influence on the development of ideas or if they simply synthesised existing preconceptions and already well-established practices. Indeed, the main draft of what would later become Spencer's *A System of Synthetic Philosophy* was presented in 1858, one year before Charles Darwin published his own masterpiece. Furthermore, Spencer's ideas were well known to newspaper editors even before then. Indeed, in a column titled 'Rationale of a Poor Law' published in the *Bradford Observer* on 21 July 1842 (Issue 442), we find a very critical discussion about land rights and the need to reform land ownership in order to eradicate poverty:

> In another column will be found the third of an able series of letters from the pen of Herbert Spencer, on the proper sphere of government, in which a settled provision for the poor is greatly deprecated, and it is contended that it is better to give men their rights, than to give them charity. When God sends hither into this world man, endowed with fitting corporeal and intellectual powers to make cultivation of the earth serve his wants, is it proper by any conventional arrangement, utterly to exclude a given number of men from any participation of the common inheritance? Property is the offspring of social laws, and antecedently to society could scarcely exist. Government is called into being to give protection to property, and this indeed is its main function. Man has a right to subsistence here – the title deeds to which were dated long prior to either property or government – has a right to claim that his industry not his idleness, shall serve him for a living. If owing to the complicity of the machine which we call society, honest industry ceases to be available to secure the supply of daily wants, the state, or the body politic, is bound, under such circumstances, to furnish and equivalent for the original right of inheritance, which for its own advantage has been abolished. A poor law we look upon, not as a state charity, but as a partial and imperfect substitute for man's native right to enjoy fruits of that earth which God hath given him. No man is sent into this world under the obligation to starve; and conventional arrangements which created the danger must, of necessity, provide the remedy. – Nonconformist.

This letter illustrates the complex and sophisticated level of the discussions on poverty taking place in the media of that time. In his initial interventions, Spencer argued for land reform and votes for women, although later in life he opposed these same ideas, becoming more and more conservative over the years. Therefore, his views on race were presented in the context of what seemed to be an overall progressive positivist discourse that drew on the Enlightenment tradition. Consequently, Spencer's views were incorporated in the mainstream newspaper narratives as a justification of empire and industrial progress.

By the late nineteenth century, the main British commercial newspapers were discussing poverty in terms of social Darwinism; even when they were advocating support and charity:

> In the wake of Darwin's *Origin of Species* (1859), and through the intermediation of Herbert Spencer and his American disciples, social Darwinism became the dominant ideology in a period that saw the establishment of a racial cast system in the South, the completion of Indian removal in the West, the shift from continental expansion to international imperialism in the war with Spain, and the rise of organised opposition to immigration from Southern and Eastern Europe in the Northeast, and from Asia, especially China, in the West. (McCarthy 2009: 69)

By the time these ideas started to become popular on both sides of the Atlantic, most mainstream newspapers had been transformed into complex commercial enterprises, especially in the light of the emergence of the 'penny press' (Nerone 1987: 377), a more commercial and less politically driven form of newspaper. As newspapers became more and more profit driven, they became more interlinked with the industry and commerce that provided the much-needed advertising revenue to prosper and thrive.

The commercial press changed the way newspapers operated, creating the economic model which would dominate the industry for the next century. The majority of British and US newspapers started to pay more attention to their surrounding communities and to report rather than editorialise. By the end of the nineteenth century, they changed the nature of their news coverage, as they could no longer rely on just subscriptions and daily sales to make a profit (Campbell 2003: 12). In this context, the editorial markets necessitated the distribution of news in a far more public form (Allan 1998: 298), which brought about profound changes in journalistic and editorial practices. The roles of the objective reporter and the fact-checking sub-editor began to take shape in the modern sense and with them the definition of what constituted 'news'. By this time, information gathering and distribution had become a business on its own, and news merely another way of attracting audiences which are turned into commodities.

A Whole New World

The twentieth century also saw the consolidation of transnational media in the face of the expansion of the international news agencies. These agencies represented geopolitics in its purest sense. Indeed, the main structural feature of the emerging news organisations in Europe until well into the twentieth century was an oligopolistic division of the market (Boyd-Barrett 1980: 157). News agencies such as Havas in France, Wolff in Germany and Reuters in Britain, demarcated their news coverage and audiences along the lines of their own empires. Although they all started more or less in the nineteenth century as information services providing commodity and stock market prices, their information soon began to be acquired by newspapers and other clients. By the end of that century, these news agencies were providing news stories from abroad, which complemented the dispatches sent by the newspapers' own correspondents.

The news agencies began hiring those they considered to be the best news editors and journalists, who brought with them the skills and ideological baggage of the era. It was in this way that views and preconceptions about poverty, incubated in the Victorian newsrooms, were passed on to what would become the most influential media in the world. The end of the nineteenth century saw the dissemination of ideas about poverty, wealth and property throughout the world. News agencies, which were paradoxically global operators of a national character (Boyd-Barrett 1980: 31), became propagators of an ideology in which the poor were seen as an inevitable result of human nature.

Indeed, political events that exposed the structures that caused poverty were widely framed in the news of that time in ways that would portray the poor as passive actors and any attempt to rebel against the status quo as the prelude to chaos. Reuters's, Havas's and Wolff's dispatches of the 1871 Paris uprising and the establishment of the Commune were, as expected, biased against the insurgents. As in many cases today, reporting on the conflict mainly consisted of propaganda. Reuters's reports of 'Insurgents firing into an unarmed crowd' (*Bradford Observer*, 24 March 1871: 3; Issue 2572) were spiced up by using comparisons with Robespierre's regime of terror in France. Articles about beggars being persecuted by the Commune authorities and other similar pieces were disseminated by the main news agencies at the time. In not one case did the insurgents' motives appear in their reports or in the newspapers that bought the articles from these news agencies.

The consolidation of these news agencies as oligopolies in the distribution and dissemination of world news coincided with the emergence of eugenics as an accepted science at the time. As mentioned before, social Darwinism already dominated conceptions of and views on poverty in the newsrooms. These ideas received a scientific veneer, mutating into the eugenics movement, a pseudo-science that would become one of the most influential frameworks used to explain poverty. These ideas would cross the Atlantic and find a home in the vibrant and growing media industry in the United States before travelling around the world to countries such as Australia. They came to define in the early twentieth century the conceptualisation and understanding of poverty within the newsrooms of the West and its colonies.

However, it was also in this same period that one of the crucial dilemmas regarding poverty started to pose important questions. Indeed, if poverty abroad was easily explained as a natural consequence of uncivilised societies undergoing modernisation by their colonial rulers, it was not so easy to account for the growth of the '*lumpenproletariat*' that the Industrial Revolution was creating on Britain's doorstep or the famines in British-controlled territories. An illustrative example of how journalists would explain poverty abroad is a dispatch by the Tehran-based correspondent for a London newspaper:

> Tehran is not so striking as the native town of Agra, and without any of its embellishments – all mud and a few dabs of paint at the King's palaces. Cholera is rife all over Persia. The country is impoverished by misgovernment, whose sole aim is to extort money from all and every one by fair or foul means to gratify its own poor ideas of show. The failure of the silk cultivation of the Gilan and Mazanderan provinces owing to disease amongst the worms has put a finishing touch to the misery and poverty which is palpable throughout the 300 miles I have travelled. I am within the mark when I say that five villages out of six were deserted and in ruins. In spite of this, the King insists on getting his revenues. (*The Examiner*, 1 January 1870; Issue 3231)

Apart from the more formal language, the similarities with current accounts of poverty are striking, especially when reporting on places such as Africa, where government officials' corruption is often viewed as the sole cause for poverty. Notice also the subtle criticism against taxation, when this correspondent writes that 'the King insists on getting his revenues.' This criticism against King Naser al-Din Shah Qajar, who was paradoxically a pro-European monarch, was nevertheless problematic, as judgement was being passed despite the fact that Persia was facing intense droughts and was on the verge of the worst famine in its history, one which would leave an estimated death toll of over 2 million people (Okazaki 1986: 183). Furthermore, in the same article the correspondent mentioned that 'cholera is rife and some Europeans have died', which would become a common feature of reports about poverty abroad in the global media of our times.

It was not so easy, however, to explain the same phenomenon happening on British or European soil. In these cases, very complex, often contradictory, narratives were deployed which did not usually offer a clear explanation. In an article in the *Northern Echo* from Darlington, England, 7 January 1870 (Issue 6) reporting on a councillors' meeting, the newspaper describes how fever and cholera could strike in that city. It warns that the lack of hygiene and clothing not being disinfected are probable causes for the spread of these diseases. At no point do these reports mention poverty but instead call for intervention by the authorities to clean up the houses of those at risk.

Well before this, in 1854, John Snow had already proved his theory that cholera was linked to a contaminated water supply and, with regards to that specific case, to a single water pump in Soho, London. Despite this evidence, journalists in England found it difficult to explain how major epidemics such as influenza, typhus, typhoid and cholera were still occurring at a time of supposed prosperity and progress; they basically ignored the obvious relation between health and public investment in better infrastructure for the poor. For these journalists, it was always going to be easier to deal with the manifestations of poverty abroad, than with the causes of poverty at home.

This was perhaps the first time that modern journalism had to deal with the fact that economic growth does not necessarily bring prosperity. This contradiction was well-documented and highlighted by anarchists and socialists of the time and thoroughly explored by party political newspapers, which in most cases had limited circulation. However, it was rarely discussed in mainstream newspapers which, incapable of dealing with this contradiction and fearful of the public's reaction if exposed to these ideas, suppressed and ignored them as much as they could. Fear of political agitation and the links being built between the now commercially driven press and their sponsors set the basis of what some scholars today identify as the press's commercial filters, that is, ownership and dependence on advertising revenues (Herman and Chomsky 1994: 2). At the turn of the century, this model of media ownership and the journalistic practices that derived from it firmly established the basis upon which poverty is still reported today.

A New Order

From the beginning of the new century up to the 1930s, Europe witnessed extraordinary changes that altered the way it perceived itself; arguably one of the most important was the collapse of what remained of the Ottoman Empire. This single event reinforced the idea of Europe, especially of the British Empire, as a superior civilisation (perhaps, one could argue, similar to the way in which the Soviet Union's collapse reinforced the neo-Hegelian notion of western superiority, and the 'end of history' as articulated by Francis Fukuyama in 1992).

The emergence of the United States as a world power during the first two decades of the twentieth century was also attributed to race, which was then used to justify social Darwinist ideas in other countries. This happened at a time when the geopolitical scheme of things was changing, especially with regards to information provision: the United States was on the road to becoming a world power and had set up its own news agencies, such as Associated Press (AP) and United Press International (UPI). During this time and even through the Great War, ideas of racial superiority, exclusion and inequality became the default explanatory framework in the newsroom for understanding poverty. Although the First World War caused major disruptions to world commerce, especially in relation to the British Empire, nevertheless ideas about poverty experienced very little change and journalistic and editorial approaches remained almost untouched until the 1929 financial crash and the Great Depression that followed. It was in this period that news organisations such as the BBC became an integral part of the hegemonic mechanism of state control, playing a detrimental part in the workers' struggle for their rights.

Indeed, despite the BBC's claims of impartiality and objectivity with regards to the 1926 miners' strike (Wilby 2006), many media historians agree that the corporation sided with the Tory government. The then-director general Lord Reith wrote anti-union speeches for Tory Prime Minister Stanley Baldwin and broadcast them to the nation, while refusing to allow the labour leaders to put their side until the strike was over. The rest of the global media would adopt similar approaches to working-class struggles around the world.

The Great Depression of 1929 had a lasting impact on mass culture (Barnard 1995) and consequently on journalistic values, cultures and practices as well. We know little about how that crisis impacted the coverage of poverty as most accounts have focused on the way in which financial crises were covered (Schiffrin 2010; Starkman 2014; Suttles 2011), and few scholars have yet explored the way in which that era's journalists' and editors' views changed in the light of these events (Liebovich 1994). However, we do know of personal accounts of many journalists (Lerner et al. 2012; Terkel 1997) who lost their jobs and saw significant losses to their own privileges. These journalists lived in a time when poverty was happening near to home and therefore impossible to ignore. How their experiences were later reflected in their own work remains under-researched by media historians and limits our understanding of news and poverty. One can assume, from the few accounts to which we have access, that the 1930s must have been a traumatic period as the Great Depression hit home. Indeed, because poverty became such a common feature for so many (including journalists and news editors), and because so many were exposed to the risk of being poor, audiences in general became far more receptive to liberal views.

It was in this context of crash and recovery that ideas of state intervention and wealth redistribution, embodied by Franklin Delano Roosevelt's New Deal, became a dominant paradigm in the public imagination. Furthermore, Roosevelt's federal relief agency linked journalism with the creation of public policy by hiring journalists, most notably Martha Gellhorn (1908–98), to provide reports on the conditions of the poor (Gellhorn 2012: 10). This happened despite the fact that Roosevelt lacked support from the main newspapers and news agencies, which mounted vicious attacks even when he was highly popular (Winfield 1990: 6). Roosevelt's administration faced commercially controlled media and other interest groups who fiercely opposed the implications in terms of the taxation and wealth redistribution that the New Deal represented.

In Britain, on the other hand, by the end of the Second World War and especially the electoral triumph of the Labour Party under Clement Attlee (1883–1967), new approaches in the news coverage of poverty emerged. This was not necessarily because the media owners had modified their views,[2] but because the political agenda had changed dramatically.

Journalists began to describe an environment in which Keynesianism had been embraced by most of the political class and in which there was a broad consensus for welfare reforms. These views refuted the neo-classical idea that free markets would automatically provide full employment, as long as workers were flexible in their wage demands. John Maynard Keynes (1883–1946) instead argued that aggregate demand determined the overall level of economic activity, and that inadequate aggregate demand could lead to prolonged periods of high unemployment. By arguing this, Keynes called for strong state intervention to alleviate poverty. These interventions included fiscal and monetary measures to mitigate the adverse effects of economic recessions, which overall focused on stimulating economic growth.

Another systemic change emerged from the ruins of the war. In the face of the mass extermination camps and in the light of increasing demands from the working classes after the war, newspapers could no longer justify, at least openly, Malthusian narratives about the 'deserving' and 'undeserving' poor. Indeed, the Second World War turned everything upside down and for a time, everyone seemed to be equal, at least under international law (Rist 1997: 69).

However, this did not necessarily bring about an entirely new discourse about poverty in the news media. Moreover, contrary to the common understanding, belief in eugenics in the newsrooms did not come to an abrupt end after the horrors of the Nazi concentration camps were revealed. Between 1945 and 1955, many articles in key newspapers in Australia, Britain and the US that were reporting on poverty offered openly racial and eugenicist views as explanatory frameworks. What did change was the way world poverty was conceptualised in terms of development and modernity, rather than just in terms of individual responsibility and race. As the United States emerged as the new power in the West, the need was not to justify empire or colonial rule in the traditional sense, but capitalism and its markets in the new world order. More important, there was the need to provide a counterbalance to the socialist model of the Soviets and their allies. As Arturo Escobar writes, after 1945, the task of governments was to make poverty useful by fixing it to the apparatus of production that planning sought to deploy. A completely utilitarian and functional conception of poverty emerged, linked inextricably to the processes of labour and production (1995: 89). This new conceptualisation became very popular in US and western European newsrooms and would dominate discourse regimes until the early 1980s.

The end of the Second World War meant that 'growth' became the main strategy for the alleviation of poverty by newly established multilateral organisations such as the World Bank and the International Monetary Fund (IMF) (Babb 2009: 165), especially under the presidency of Robert McNamara. This consensus permeated the newsrooms of news agencies and other key global media, as journalists and editors deferred to their sources in the Bretton Woods institutions. Economic growth became the paradigm to reduce poverty and is still a view widely held across the globe, even in places such as Communist China, where President Hu Jintao said, marking the Chinese Communist Party ninetieth anniversary, that the economy must keep growing in order to address poverty and ensure stability (Coonan 2011).

In light of the Marshall Plan's success in Europe, economic growth became the 'silver bullet' in policies and discourses with regards to development and poverty during the post-war period. In part because the capitalist system is based on constant growth and in part because of the prerogatives of the Cold War discourses, economic growth also became the leitmotiv of journalism narratives when exploring solutions to poverty. For many, Keynesian economic theory and the creation of the welfare state and economic growth had saved the West from the jaws of communism.

However, not all would embrace these ideas. To some, economic collectivism was a dangerous threat. In the late 1930s, a group of intellectuals met under the banner of the 'Colloque Walter Lippmann' in order to reinvigorate classic liberal economics by favouring 'the market economy over state intervention' (Mirowski and Phlewe 2009: 13). One of these intellectuals, Friedrich von Hayek, who later published *The Road to Serfdom* (1944), where he argued against state intervention in economic matters; the book was 'written in some haste' following the publication of the Beveridge Report, which led to the establishment of the British welfare state (Cockett 1995:79). More important, in 1947, Hayek set up the Mont Pelerin Society in order to create an intellectual opposition towards the developing Keynesian economic consensus. However, the society's ideas remained largely ignored until the 'troubled years of the 1970s' (Harvey 2005:22).

The energy crisis after the Yom Kippur War of 1973, in the context of the general world economic downturn of the 1970s and the apparent exhaustion of the Keynesian model, brought to power two of that era's most controversial leaders: Margaret Thatcher (1925–2013) in Britain and Ronald W. Reagan (1911–2004) in the US. Both leaders introduced a new conservative 'order' based on neoliberal ideas, with monetarist and free-market policies at its core. These ideas would be disseminated by the media, especially key US and British global media outlets, which sold the notion that the market was the best way of dealing with poverty. To achieve this, their followers used think tanks and well-funded lobby operations, which played a pivotal part in disseminating these ideas. They were set to promote and spread these ideas at a time when Keynesian economics was considered to be outdated.

It was these institutions that set the new tone for journalists and editors when reporting poverty. While think tanks such as the Institute for Defence and Security Studies (RUSI) and the Fabian Society in Britain and the Brookings Institution, the American Enterprise Institute for Public Policy Research (1943) and the RAND Corporation in the US had existed for years, the 1970s and 1980s saw the formation of neo-conservative think tanks such as the Heritage Foundation (1973) and the Cato Institute (1977), which became far more active in steering the news agenda towards the right (Abelson 2002: 32). The US-based Heritage Foundation was an offshoot of Hayek's Mont Pelerin Society, as was Britain's Institute of Economic Affairs (IEA) (1955) (Harvey 2005: 22). Part of this news agenda was an increased call for the dismantling of the welfare state, linking this to the notion of the undeserving poor (Golding and Middleton 1982: 77). Margaret Thatcher 'relied on the IEA for detailed economic analysis of the welfare state' from the moment she became leader of the Conservative Party (Cockett 1995: 147). Some of these think tanks targeted foreign aid, by arguing that aid went from the poor of rich countries to the rich of poor countries (another way of categorising the undeserving poor on an international level). Babb (2009) argues, for example, that the Heritage Foundation influenced a whole new era in the World Bank's policies towards the poor during the Reagan administration and articulated a set of discourses that reflected its own views on poverty abroad. As the multilateral organisations were the referent for journalists, when their experts changed their discourses, so did the journalists and news editors.

Indeed, multilateral banks and government officials were not the only target of these think tanks. Journalists and editors were also wooed and important resources were poured into propaganda efforts to set a new framework for economic news in general and on poverty in particular. Public records in the US reveal that, during the Reagan administration, right-wing think tanks were supported by both public and private contributions; needless to say, many of these resources went into lobbying the media, in a well-orchestrated effort that sold a set of ideas over the course of nearly two decades. Right-wing foundations emphasised that the poor had no incentive to work, they called for more choice for the middle and upper classes and argued that the market could deal with almost anything, including poverty, as long as the state did not intervene (mostly synthesised in Milton and Rose Friedman's *Freedom to Choose*, published in 1980).

In Britain, the IEA spawned more think tanks (Mirowski and Plehwe 2009: 431). The Centre for Policy Studies (1974) was created in order to 'convert the Tory party' to economic liberalism (Cockett 1995: 237). The Adam Smith Institute (ASI) (1978) followed four years later and attempted to promote economic liberalism through the media. These think tanks created the core policies of Margaret Thatcher's Conservative government (Cockett 1995: 322). One of the key arguments put forward by these think tanks was a sustained critique of the welfare state, which translated into a media campaign of 'social derision of the poor so punitive in its impact' that it was to 'threaten the very props of the modern welfare state' (Golding and Middleton 1982: 5).

A similar set of discourses surrounded political debates in the United States. Welfare spending debates were heavily influenced by Charles Murray's 1982 book *Losing Ground*. Murray's work had been funded by the Manhattan Institute which was yet another offshoot of the Institute of Economic Affairs. Murray's book was welcomed by the *New York Review of Books* as 'the most persuasive statement' of a 'new variation on Social Darwinism' (Jencks 1985: 1). In 1989, the *Sunday Times* brought Murray from the US to Britain, where he argued that Britain's welfare programme was funding the growth of an 'underclass' (Murray 2001: 1). In 1994, Murray followed up on the 'underclass' theme with *The Bell Curve*, co-authored with Richard J. Herrnstein, in which race was a central concern. By doing so, they brought into the public realm the more traditional and cruder aspects of Malthusianism and social Darwinism.

Indeed, using IQ tests as 'scientific' proof, the authors of *The Bell Curve* argued that black people were less intelligent than white people and that welfare cuts were necessary in order to stop those members of society with the lowest IQs from procreating (Herrnstein and Murray 1994: 548). The authors argued that by allowing people with lower IQs access to welfare, the US was creating a divisive society whereby the 'mansions on the hills above' are threatened by the 'menace from the slums below' (ibid.: 518).

Just as Francis Galton had done many years before, Murray used statistics to give his work a veneer of scientific objectivity which helped to sell his ideas to the media on both sides of the Atlantic. These arguments resurrected several tropes from the Victorian era, including social Darwinism, racial science, eugenics, degeneration and the dichotomy of civilisation versus barbarism. They were enthusiastically taken up by the press and the idea that welfare was the catalyst for creating a caste of inferior people – this time labelled as the 'underclass' – came to dominate domestic news coverage once again.

In the international arena, these ideas would take the form of a consensus shared by leading corporations, institutions, politicians and opinion formers in the most powerful centre in the world. The Washington Consensus was, therefore, not an academic theory 'but a policy programme shaped by intellectual and political forces' (Babb 2009: 176). As Peter Townsend observed (1993), exchanges in the late twentieth century about the nature, extent and causes of poverty were largely dominated by individualistic and structuralist perspectives – on the one side, by those who place poverty as a consequence of individual choices, and on the other, by those who see the capitalist system as the problem.

This dichotomy in perceptions of poverty is best illustrated by the neoliberal approach in the United States which continues to insist on identifying individual characteristics and subcultural phenomena as the prime sources of interest. In this worldview, those in poverty should embrace free-market values and should not be distracted from this by state patronage in the form of welfare. It is also illustrated at the other extreme by those who in one way or another theorise a structural perspective, drawing on dependency theories of development, and theories of stratification, neo-colonialism and state policies designed primarily to deal with the casualties of the market (Townsend 1993: 96).

Most content analysis on discourses of economics suggests that the individualist perspective has, since the 1980s, received far more news coverage and interest in the global media than the structuralist one. Individualistic approaches have dominated not only the news agenda but also the discourses of those who produce news about the poor. However, it is difficult to understand why these discourses are still recycled so uncritically by so many journalists. For that, we must look instead not so much at their status as a professional body and their historical relation to power but to the elements that shaped the journalistic imagination.

The Objectivity of Poverty

Objectivity continues to retain a central, if disputed, place in discussions of journalism as a profession that works across national frontiers, despite very distinctive historical-national origins (Maras 2013: 5). Even with a far more sophisticated discussion of what objectivity really means, the practice nevertheless often translates into the normative claim that journalists' work is somehow detached from their own feelings and that it is scientifically objective. Historically speaking and in relation to news coverage, it meant that journalists' compassion should not cloud their impartiality when reporting poverty.

Henry Mayhew (1812–87), in his 'Letter I' in the *Morning Chronicle* on 19 October 1849, explained how he intended to carry out his work of examining and reporting the conditions of those in poverty living in London:

> However alive I may be to the wrongs of the poor, I shall not be misled by a morbid sympathy to see them [the poor] only as suffering the selfishness of others. Their want of prudence, want of temperance, want of energy, want of cleanliness, want of knowledge, and want of morality, will each honestly set forth. This done, I shall proceed to treat of the poor receiving parish relief, outside and inside the union; after which, the habits, haunts, and tricks of the beggars of London will be duly set forth; and finally, those of the thieves and prostitutes. (Cited in Thompson and Yeo 1973: 121)

Implicit in these words are the claims of 'detachment' that characterised the Victorians. However, these claims had more to do with ideological positivist aspirations than with the imperatives of reality. It is this notion that has since then characterised the reporting of poverty, in which journalists are required to be morally detached and objective, and yet to immerse themselves in local life (Mitchell 1988: ix). This has become ever since one of the biggest obstacles to improving the coverage of poverty, which instead tends to be reported as a decontextualised phenomenon in which manifestations rather than causes are at the centre of the stories.

Journalists, therefore, seem obsessed with the object but rarely concerned with the subject and are unable to deal with other realities except the ones provided and framed by those in power. In their own normative claims, they are offering an objective story, although, as we know, 'no story can be told, no account of events given, without contextualisation around a set of assumptions, beliefs and values' (McNair 1998: 5). Hence, the supposedly objective reporting of poverty does not really happen in that pretended vacuum, but occurs always within a meta-narrative that is already assumed both by journalists and their audiences. Consequently, prevalent discourses not only remain unchallenged, but in most cases they see themselves reinforced by news stories about poverty that claim to be objective but that nevertheless fit into an already present worldview.

Looking at the historical development and consolidation of objectivity as a journalistic norm, one can see the importance of what has been lost through the years. In many ways, by embracing objectivity as a paramount value, journalists, to paraphrase Herbert Marcuse, have become 'one-dimensional' fact finders that selectively choose those events and voices that can somehow reinforce the socially constructed reality that has already been preconceived. What has been lost is the freedom for journalists to think critically about reality and produce news from their own imagination, which in some cases has proven to be far more accurate than reality in portraying the excruciating pain and suffering of the 'others' (Sontag 2003: 16). This is the real tragedy in the history of ideas about poverty in the newsroom.

3

What Lies Beneath?

When reporting on poverty or related issues such as social exclusion, unemployment, or famine, journalists around the world tend to present their articles mostly as hard news stories. Overall, news about poverty in the global media is more often than not reported following the traditional narrative style and structures often referred to as the '5WH' and the 'inverted pyramid', even when the article adopts the feature style. The first technique refers to the ability to answer the basic questions: Who is it about? What happened? Where did it take place? When did it take place? Why did it happen? How did it happen? The second technique requires that the most important aspects of the story appear at the beginning of the news article.

The adoption of this aesthetic by mainstream journalism has helped it to comply with the notion of objectivity, which is central to the prevalent news cultures that shape and define how journalists understand poverty and present it as a news item to the general public. While objectivity is still a contested notion, it 'continues to play a central role in media and journalism in linking concepts of truth, accuracy, impartiality and independence' (Maras 2013: 228). Therefore, objectivity still shapes the understanding and representation of poverty by the news media.

News about poverty is reported in generic terms and under time and space pressures just like most news items. Let us not forget that most news stories are actually produced by reporters who are generalists lacking a tremendous in-depth knowledge of the issues covered (Gans 1979: 138). This is also the case with global news on poverty, as what we often refer to as 'foreign correspondents' are reporters who are likely to be parachuted from one place to another without the expertise and in some cases not even the language of the place they are sent to, beyond some very general awareness of the people and issues they are covering.[1]

By taking this approach, the news media limit their ability to offer structural analysis of issues or provide contextual background to what is happening. The end result is that the explanations as to the causes of economic deprivation are often incomplete or superficial (Philo et. al. 1995: 21). Because of this, the majority of news reports concentrate on economic growth and foreign aid as quick solutions, rather than exploring the underlying reasons why certain countries suffer high unemployment, why so many people are poor and why some parts of the world endure crises such as famines with such frequency.

The effects of globalisation, the lack of sustainable industries, unfair trade agreements, and the historical legacy of colonial rule, among other root causes, are ignored or mentioned only briefly in many dispatches carried by the western news media. Instead, the public is fed with simplistic explanations that attribute poverty to 'overpopulation', 'corrupt leaders' and 'tribal or religious disputes' which fuel wars, while suggesting a lack of western 'values' and the absence of modern 'institutions' as a recurrent explanatory framework for those societies in which poverty is rife.

This chapter examines the construction of news narratives in relation to the causes of global poverty in the context of historical changes and continuities. In the previous chapter, we looked at the evolution of ideas about poverty in the newsroom. We saw that there are important links in the historical construction of these concepts, visions and perceptions that have shaped the way in which journalists and news editors interpret the stories. Over the past sixty years, these ideas have been largely determined by the notion of modernisation, which in itself had a huge influence on international intervention, foreign aid and development policy.

The idea of progress and modernisation, so prevalent in the global newsrooms, is one that proposes a model of societal transformation that embraces western service and manufacturing technology, liberal political structures, the West's values and its systems of mass communication (Shah 2011: 21). The post-Second World War idea of development was one of westernising the developing world in order to modernise it.

Indeed, the overall journalistic discourse about the developing world is heavily influenced by colonial and post-colonial ideas that have survived over the years in different forms, mimicking the colonial imaginary of the Third World (Spurr 1993: 91). After the Second World War, these discourses become wedded to the design and implementation of the Bretton Woods system, then in the 1980s attached to the neoliberal agreement often referred to as the 'Washington Consensus' and then, more recently, aligned with the palliative set of minimal aspirations known as the United Nations' Millennium Development Goals. In all these cases, mainstream media news coverage was generally uncritical of the core values and ideas of those institutions, policies and programmes and their respective ideological frameworks.

Take, for example, a report by Mark Tutton for CNN which was broadcast on 9 July 2011 under the headline '10 million at risk from East Africa drought'. The dispatch opens by attributing most of the drought's causes to natural conditions:

> East Africa is in the midst of its worst drought in more than 60 years, with as many as 10 million people at risk. The drought has led to crop failures and food shortages in parts of Ethiopia, Kenya, Djibouti and Somalia, and now a refugee crisis looms as people leave their homes to escape hunger. The UN says thousands of Somalis are leaving their country, ending up in parched and overcrowded refugee camps.

Citing Judith Schuler of the United Nations' World Food Program (WFP), the report goes on to say that the *La Niña* phenomenon and climate change have made things worse, as farmers had to plant their seeds late and deal with erratic rainfalls that washed them away. 'No one expects two consecutive failures of rainy seasons,' Schuler was quoted in the CNN report. Meanwhile, the delayed response in the delivery of foreign aid is blamed primarily on the ban imposed by the Al-Shabab group with links to Al-Qaeda.

This is the type of news report that often dominates the coverage of poverty on an international level, in which not a single source from the affected country itself is included and the whole story is articulated through the voices of Westerners. The reports also failed to acknowledge other important facts affecting food shortages in the country, such as fishing boats belonging to, or sailed by, European-owned companies under flags of convenience which have been engaged for years in illegal fishing off the coast of Somalia, depleting stocks that would normally feed people in that country. There is no mention either of the contexts in which poverty in Somalia grew to its current levels or any explanation as to why it is still such a recurrent feature among certain societies in the twenty-first century. Instead, the public is fobbed off with a laconic complaint from the representative of Save the Children: 'Unfortunately, this is a disaster that hasn't had much attention from the international community or donors.' The focus is clear – foreign intervention in some form is required.

Journalists use discursive strategies to represent social actors and their actions in the news in a certain way. For example, in the case of Somalia, the news reporting tends to emphasise the legitimacy of a western military presence (Way 2013b: 19). By extending this strategy, the news media are able to recontextualise piracy events in terms of security rather than poverty. These strategies are used systematically throughout stories of Somali piracy which articulate discourses that privilege the West and disadvantage Somalis (Way 2013a: 14).

Furthermore, alternative context, such as the need for state-building and critical analysis about the root causes of poverty, are often absent in news reports because many of the news sources used to produce the stories have a specific political agenda or want to appear politically neutral so as not to jeopardise possible contributions from donors, as in the case of NGOs or foreign aid workers. There are indeed a number of institutional reasons why NGOs tend in some occasions not to tell the full story and highlight the complexities and contradictions present in aid efforts (Franks 2013: 14).

Writing about his own experience while reporting famine in Ethiopia in the 1980s, journalist Peter Gill recalls how antagonistic positions and criticism of the donor countries led to delays and reduced help from the West (1986: 32). International NGOs and similar organisations constantly face the struggle of producing a coherent message for the news media amidst the tensions between fundraising and budgetary needs, and performing advocacy as a moral duty (Dogra 2012: 189).

Beyond this, there are also the issues of how news reports tend to ignore historical responsibilities and unfulfilled commitments from donor countries. For example, western countries' aid budgets intended to help poor countries achieve the United Nations Millennium Development Goals (MDGs) are to be cut drastically in the face of the financial crisis. Since 2008, most donor nations, with few exceptions, have confirmed they will be making sizeable reductions to previous financial commitments. In 2012, both the United States and Japan announced significant cuts to their foreign aid budgets. In addition to this, there has been an important reduction of available private resources because of diminishing donations from urban centres in the industrialised world.

Despite this, not a single report about the impending crisis in Somalia and Ethiopia from either the BBC or CNN in July 2012 made any mention of the effects of these cuts in undermining efforts to deal with the crisis. Nor was there any mention of the fact that while some western governments had decided to cut foreign aid, they nevertheless maintained their military expenditure at very high levels, while providing military aid to regimes with the most appalling human rights records. There was nothing in any of these news dispatches about the paradox of little additional money being made available for foreign aid but trillions of US dollars being wasted on military adventures and bailouts paid to bankers despite the colossal mismanagement and corruption shown during and after the 2008 financial crisis.

This should not come as a surprise and we would be naïve if we thought that the global media, which have generally acted as a Praetorian Guard for the interests of the rich and the powerful for so long, would behave differently. However, one would at least expect journalists to examine policy making and properly scrutinise key palliative policies (mostly relating to foreign aid) which at least had the potential of doing some real good for those suffering, even if expecting a critical account of inequality and social exclusion is perhaps too much.

Poverty as a Cause

Poverty is a manifestation of exclusion and injustice; *that* is the news story. People are poor because we have international systems of trade and historical-political legacies embedded in our societies that promote and reinforce inequality (Dorling 2010: 195). As a society, some of us are better off than others because a few 'take' more from humanity's common wealth than the rest. Some have done it unconsciously, others ungratefully.

In the past, we invaded other countries to secure their natural resources in order to acquire privilege and geopolitical advantage; from Francisco Pizarro to Donald Rumsfeld, the world has witnessed a series of architects of inequality who killed, enslaved, invaded and destroyed to become or remain rich and powerful. The immense wealth created by the blood, sweat and tears of black slaves, which fostered and maintained the Industrial Revolution, is still today in the possession of a few families that have passed on from generation to generation the possibility of accumulating capital beyond their needs (Westley 1998: 429). Furthermore, access to capital, to education and the whole system of wealth creation is designed to perpetuate these inequalities, both nationally and internationally. As Eduardo Galeano puts it succinctly in the opening of his book *The Open Veins of Latin America* (1971), the international division of labour consists in some countries specialising in being rich, while others specialise in being poor.

Despite this, the story mostly portrayed by the news media seems to be about corrupt officials, about 'poor individuals' who are unable to face adversity and about communities incapable of governing themselves. Paul Ricoeur highlights the fact that every action has its agents and its patients. Therefore, he points out, passivity is in fact an activity in which enduring and suffering are as much data of interaction as data of subjective understanding (1994: 157). Hence, we can argue, in these media representations, not acting is read as an open invitation for intervention.

Another important aspect is that news stories about poverty in the developing world are often placed in juxtaposition with 'discredited ideology that is recycled into hard facts' (van Ginneken, 1998: 42). There are many reasons for this, as global media outlets and the news editors and journalists who work for them operate within specific organisational structures and ideological frameworks that define the parameters in which they can move and articulate their discourses, often referred to as 'news cultures' (Allan 1999a: 3). This is because the media, although notionally free from government and corporate direct control and intervention, act nevertheless as an agent to legitimise the dominant ideology (Thussu 2000: 68).

This statement could be seen as a broad generalisation, and very few would support the idea that journalists and news editors deliberately pick facts and ignore others in order to be able to articulate news on poverty in a certain way. Instead, this is the by-product of a systemic process in which ideological rituals are performed in the construction and legitimisation of news. This process describes a series of practices that take place in the newsroom and that end up imposing organisational and professional worldviews which define, in this case, how poverty is articulated in news stories.

For media institutions such as the BBC and CNN, organisational cultures are pivotal in the way that news is constructed (Schlesinger 1978; Küng-Shankleman 2000; Ojer Goñi 2009). In a case such as that of the BBC, this means that external factors such as the ideology of those in power and the social climate in which news is produced are crucial in determining how this organisation approaches issues and delivers news content (Ojer Goñi 2009: 29). Something very similar might be said about CNN, with the addition that it must also pursue commercial considerations (Küng-Shankleman 2000: 13). Therefore, in international news organisations such as the main western broadcasting companies, the construction of news about poverty is defined by a whole set of elements which in many cases have nothing to do with dealing just with the facts.

Poverty, then, is examined through ideological, political and corporate frameworks that shape and define most of the other news issues that are reported on a daily basis. This is no different from the way the rest of the news is produced, which has been well described by Herman and Chomsky (1994) in their propaganda model. However, as poverty is an end result of the same structures and systems that allow these news organisations to exist and flourish, its coverage in particular is mediated by a series of discourses that are generally uncritical of the relationship between the wealth in affluent western countries and the poverty in others.

On 12 June 2011, the British newspaper, the *Observer*, considered a highly influential newspaper of the centre left, produced a very interesting example of this type of coverage. The paper dedicated two entire pages to the issue of foreign aid (pp. 8 and 9). One page was almost completely devoted to a piece written by Prime Minister David Cameron, with a very small note about what the Melinda and Bill Gates Foundation are doing for those in poverty. The second page had a commentary by Andrew Haldane, then an executive director of the Bank of England, basically defending the need for banking regulation and financial support for the financial market in the UK (nothing to do with the supposed theme of the page), as well as a short article about how the developing nations 'need more than money to escape poverty' [sic] which mainly quoted a report from the Overseas Development Institute (ODI) think tank. There is not a single voice from the people on the ground or any of the recipients of British help. To add insult to injury, for some bizarre reason the newspaper decided to advertise its food supplement on that same page, with a picture of a well-fed white man surrounded by hens – bringing to mind issues such as food waste in the West and subsidies for farmers in rich countries, which are core in explaining poverty in the developing world.

This is not an isolated case and the reason I am pointing to the *Observer* is because it is one of the news media outlets whose reputation leads us to expect a slightly different outlook when reporting on these issues. We constantly see news media reports about poverty in which there are no voices or very little reflection from those who are actually poor. In these cases, the voices of those in poverty are not only absent but also excluded from the microphones and the screens. In some instances – often well-intentioned feature articles or reports – human interest is allocated at the core in order to appeal to the public's interest (Cottle 1993: 79), especially with regards to television audiences. Yet these same pieces are often produced in ways that, even when the intention is to create empathy, present those in poverty as 'other'.

'Othering' Poverty

Journalists are able normatively to claim commitment to social justice while actually detaching themselves from the subjects they report on, thanks to their ability to 'other' those in poverty in their reports. Othering, as a cultural studies concept and as a journalistic practice, refers to the process in which people or groups of people are made to seem mildly or radically different. The representation of otherness is based on a duality described by Karl Marx as *Vertretung* and *Darstellung*. From a politico- economic point of view, *Vertretung* refers to someone representing others, embodying them and speaking for them. *Darstellung*, on the other hand, refers to the act of representing the other by shaping the image of who they are or how they are (Spivak 1988: 275).

This double function of representations occurs in the media's construction of those in poverty as 'the other', which allows journalists to decontextualise reports of poverty from its wider structural causes. In this way, journalists can avoid their work been seen as ideological, rather than scientifically objective. Consequently, those in poverty are presented as a homogenous group by voices that are external to their experiences (that is, experts, government officials and NGOs speaking about the suffering of third parties). According to Spivak, the subalterns – that is, those in poverty – are represented as ignorant of their own interests, having no history and unable to speak for themselves (ibid.: 287), and therefore silent on both local and international levels.

Furthermore, through 'othering', people are positioned as an out-group, 'while outsiders tend to perceive the others as a homogenous category' (Riggins 1997: 5). Implicit in this process is a hierarchy in which 'the other' is thought of and represented as being subordinate and/or inferior, even in those cases in which the narrative seems benign. This hierarchy operates as an organising metaphor (Franklin et. al., 2005: 185) in which the story's narrators present themselves as impartial but enlightened and as detached observers able to produce an account of reality from the perspective of a discourse of 'civility' (Fitzgerald 2008); in other words, an account in which the narrator assumes for themselves scientific and objective rationality against the irrationality and subjectivity of those being reported about.

'Othering' is a historical by-product of what Amanda Anderson calls 'the cultivation of detachment' (2001: 180), which emerged in the Victorian era in order to examine one's own life. By so doing, the Victorian narrator was able to confer upon themselves a cosmopolitan status which came along with the assumption of neutrality and balance in the judgement of others. This is one of the historical and philosophical bases for what we call today 'journalistic objectivity' (Maras 2012: 23).

'Othering' theory is a useful model for the critique of news coverage of poverty, despite some limitations. Indeed, 'it lacks the potential to overcome some important epistemological dilemmas that journalists' face (Fürsich 2002: 57). Nevertheless, by understanding the way in which journalists present those in poverty as a different group, we can come to comprehend why it is such a narrow approach. Indeed, most mainstream western journalism on poverty does not report people in a state of poverty as fellow world citizens who have the right to live on the same terms as we do and the right to share equally in our wealth, but as separate entities that, in the best cases, deserve our pity and in the worst, our contempt.

Because of this, the process of 'othering' of those in a state of poverty is one of the most important debates when examining the way in which the global news media cover poverty. In this process:

> People in poverty are thought about, talked about and treated as 'Other' and inferior to the rest of society. A dividing line is drawn between 'us' and 'them' and the dividing line is imbued with negative judgements that construct 'those in poverty' variously as a source of moral contamination, a threat, an undeserving economic burden, failures in the meritocratic race, an object of pity or even as an exotic species to be studied. (Lister, 2008)

More importantly, 'othering' is still widely the default position in newsrooms and remains well-embedded in journalists' worldview; especially when the media reports on people who are excluded both nationally and internationally (Bailey and Harindranath 2005; Besteman 1996; Petros et al. 2006). As a journalistic practice, the process can also be described as a 'culture of othering' (Allan 2010: 30), which is essential in the construction of social reality in terms of objectivity. Without 'othering', there is no distance between journalists and those in poverty and therefore, it would be impossible to produce decontextualised narratives.

This detachment is crucial in the articulation of a journalistic discourse that can claim an objective and unbiased understanding of the issue. Indeed, 'the very multi-vocality at the heart of the "narrativisation" of human rights issues renders problematic any claim to truth, and in so doing reveals that witnessing is socially situated, perspectival and thus politicised' (Sonwalkar and Allan 2007: 35). It is thanks to this 'narrativisation' of poverty that social exclusion becomes subject to 'us' and 'them' dichotomies, instead of being explained to the public in the context of equality.

To be truly representative of reality, news on poverty would require instead a perspective that assumes equal human rights and not just minimum subsistence standards of consumption. It should then call for action and mobilisation towards real change – that is, towards structural transformation and redistribution of the means of production and of accumulated wealth. This, however, becomes incompatible with a type of journalism which claims to be objective and that in practice is unwilling to take sides with those in poverty. Journalists who campaign against injustice and promote structural change for equality are more often than not regarded as biased and therefore unworthy of a profession that claims detachment and impartiality.

Detachment is also essential in creating a separation between the news audiences and poverty as a by-product of their lifestyle. In so doing, the global media outlets can construct poverty as a social problem which does not link back to the patterns of consumption and wealth accumulation in western societies. The argument goes something like this: those in poverty are 'there' and they are the 'other'; 'we' might see them and feel pity, 'compassion', even empathise with their pain, but only on a specific emotional level through a 'regime of meaning' (Chouliaraki 2006: 70); this 'regime of meaning' appears to shorten the geographical distance by connecting sufferer and spectator by emotion, but nevertheless keeps everyone apart in terms of identity by reminding us all just who are the 'we' and who are the 'others'. 'We' may even feel an obligation to contribute, to some degree, to the alleviation of 'their' pain and try to justify this as a legitimate response. This is done without these audiences having to acknowledge that poverty is a direct consequence of colonial history, current lifestyle and western patterns of consumption in general.

This is why media reports rarely incorporate the voices of those in poverty into the news. Even when the news coverage of poverty is carried out in terms of a regime pity, it still must confront the problematic and paradoxical relation that sustains with 'distance' (Boltanski 1999: 13). Indeed, the distance between the audience who consumes the news and those in poverty is not overcome by emotions, as some suggest, but just mediated. Therefore, people in the West can still feel sorry for the 'other', while nevertheless seeing the 'other' as part of a detached object that has nothing to do with their own reality.

Images from suffering poor people brought into our living rooms are presented in such a way as to not create an empathetic connection beyond the suffering. In this sense, news coverage often provides a notion of pseudo-empathy in which power is still very present: those watching the screens think that 'they' have the ability to 'help' the 'other' without any responsibility to share their wealth in equal terms. Because of this, the public does not see those in the developing world as equals who have the same rights we do, but as others for whom we can feel sorrow.

These views can be partly explained by the nature of journalism in the West. John Steel (2013) argues that modern journalism is basically defined by neoliberalism. In so doing, what he is suggesting is that journalistic practices are strongly influenced by a utilitarian rationale in which each story is used as an opportunity for both the individual who produces the story and those consuming it to maximise the use of the information in their own interests. In other words, while the journalists want to disseminate (sell) their work to the widest possible audience, those same audiences want to consume something that does not constantly challenge their lifestyle and can be amusing and to some degree enjoyable (that is, being able to see stories about poverty in Africa and then feeling good about donating to charity). Because of this, journalists must decontextualise their stories from ideology or structural reasoning as a way of guaranteeing news consumption.

In relation to this, Lilie Chouliaraki (2013), has pointed out that the communication of solidarity in the West faces a turning-point, in which the separation between the public logic of economic utilitarianism and the private logic of sentimental obligation towards vulnerable others is becoming blurred. This transformation in the aesthetics and ethics of solidarity in the West, she says, reflects a wider mutation in the communicative structure of humanitarianism. According to her, in the post-humanitarian scenario there is no longer the theatrical element in which the encounters between the spectator and the vulnerable other meet as an ethical and political event. Instead, she continues, the spectators and the victims of tragedy and suffering meet in a mirror structure where the encounter is reduced to an often narcissist self-reflection that involves people like 'us' feeling good about mediated performances of compassion.

Some have argued in favour of cosmopolitanism as a journalistic approach to overcome these challenges (Heikkilä and Kunelius 2008; Ward 2005). But the ideal of cosmopolitanism seems to have become just another chimerical illusion, as current mainstream journalism is incapable of meeting cosmopolitanism's demands (Hafez 2011: 484). It is also, I must add, an idea that allows western journalists and their audiences to think that they can feel the suffering of 'others' and that they can connect to them through images and texts and by means of acts of compassion that take place – such as pressing the red button to donate, writing letters to their political leaders, donating to the most acceptable NGO, or holding short-lived protests with little or no impact.

To be sure, if 'cosmopolitanism is possible' (Chouliaraki 2006: 13), it is only so in the terms set by the West and its intricate systems of production and consumption of reality. In those terms, cosmopolitanism still mediates reality by means of power and knowledge, because it retains the hierarchy of 'them' and 'us' in which western journalists and audiences have a self-perception of superior morality, knowledge and the correct allocation of resources.

Despite this, cosmopolitanism is still seen as an imperative in the context of global journalism. The central claim made is that the news media's globalisation requires a radical rethinking of the principles and standards of journalistic ethics, through the adoption of a 'cosmopolitan attitude' towards the news (Ward 2005: 3). According to this line of argument, this could overcome the limitations imposed by nationalism and patriotism.

However, the main problem with cosmopolitanism is precisely that it favours further detachment from subjective values such as patriotism, imposing greater obstacles to journalists' ability to engage, advocate and commit to the eradication of inequality. Instead, cosmopolitanism becomes a subtle way of practising 'othering' which is able to achieve some degree of legitimacy by artificially suppressing the notion of belonging in the journalistic narrative.

The other main problem with this proposition of a cosmopolitan ethics for journalists is that it implicitly assumes the universality and superiority of western values. The idea that, through cosmopolitanism, journalism can obtain a more accurate picture of the world is nothing more than a recycled version of the old notion of objectivity and detachment by other means. As such, it links with the idea of a greater worldview that pretends to be universal but that is nevertheless historically and politically connected to colonial and imperialistic institutions, views and ideas.

Cosmopolitanism has at its heart the prevalent Victorian preoccupation with the distinctly modern practice of detachment (Anderson 2001: 3). The historical ideal of critical distance, derived from the Enlightenment, is widely absorbed by modern journalism in the terms of 'sympathetic othering' or 'acceptable detachment', in which cosmopolitanism is a strategy that can allow empathy without losing its claim of having an 'objective' understanding of reality. Thanks to this process, people can still 'substitute doing something about an issue for knowledge about the problem' (Lazarsfeld and Merton 1948: 27).

Subsequently, the idea of cosmopolitanism with regards to journalistic practices can be considered as an attempt to reconcile objective detachment from those in poverty – the subject of the news coverage – with the imperative moral need to commit oneself to changing the structural conditions that drive so many into this state of exclusion. In relation to this, I side with Kai Hafez who has suggested instead that, in order for global journalism to be underpinned by a sort of global ethics, it needs to understand the complexities and multi-layered stories, while being able to connect with what often seem to be paradoxical and contradictory developments (2009: 331). This of course includes recognising one's own position in relation to and as part of these complexities.

Policy in Practice

What is the relevance of critically examining the way in which journalists present poverty to the world? Why is this so important? Most surveys confirm that people's knowledge of and attitudes towards current affairs are, to a great extent, shaped and defined by media exposure. Poverty is mediated through representations and the mass media are a crucial source of such representations. This worldview is not uni-directional as, first, the media are only one of the providers of texts, even though perhaps the most important, and second, because these texts are negotiated with the audiences: 'Making sense of the world we live in can be seen, in part, as a textual practice, where representations of many kinds and at many levels interact in the consciousness of individual subjects' (Meinhof and Richardson 1994: 1). Therefore, the role of language in defining what we think of poverty and how we feel about is tremendously powerful:

> It is through language and images that the discourses that frame how we perceive and act in the social world are articulated. Othering can thus be understood as a discursive practice, which shapes how the 'non-poor' think and talk about and act towards 'those in poverty' at both an interpersonal and an institutional level. (Lister 2004: 103)

This being the case, we should then accept that journalistic narratives will have an impact on individual choices regarding the understanding of poverty and on the constructions of social reality in relation to exclusion. The main problem with this is that these discourse regimes are tied to practices (Escobar 1995: 154). These regimes of representation – which can be analysed as places of encounter where identities are constructed and also where violence is originated, symbolised and managed (ibid.: 10) and are not a reflection of reality but constitutive of it (ibid.: 130) – allow journalists to articulate narratives that can define and/or influence policy.

Given the ideological framework upon which the global journalistic discourses are based, it is easy then to envisage what type of policies they promote and support. Therefore it is futile to try to encourage a 'global patriotism for humanity' (Ward 2010: 42) as this supranational patriotism is still ideologically anchored to the very Victorian notion of cosmopolitanism – a notion that looks to evangelise the West's institutions and values as universal.

To be sure, in order to overcome what journalistic objectivity perceives as nationalistic and patriotic worldviews, journalists tend to rely on sources and discourses generated on a supra-national level, which seem institutionally legitimate and neutral (that is, NGOs, the World Bank, the United Nations, and so on). However, as Mark Alleyne suggested, these same institutions are post-Second World War discursive constructions that present themselves as a democratic and independent community of equals when they are not (2003: 180).

Therefore, journalists use these institutions as news sources and award them a degree of neutrality and credibility that over time has proven to be questionable and problematic. Journalism that pretends to be cosmopolitan often forges connections between news discourses on poverty and policy formulation in terms of mutual reinforcement, where dissident voices and points of view outside these international institutions and organisations are often excluded or marginalised.

This, of course, goes against the notion of the media as watchdog, one that is critical in their scrutiny of policy, wherever it comes from. In the case of news on poverty provided by many journalists in the mainstream western news media outlets, there is a track record of a lack of scrutiny in relation to calling to account the conceptualisation and implementation of policies and the allocation of resources made by the international foreign aid system, transnational cooperation institutions and development organisations.

The global media's failure to overall examine critically the structural adjustment programmes (SAPs) implemented in developing countries in the 1980s and 1990s is a testament to the collusion between news people and international policy makers. In fact, news coverage of development programmes and initiatives is often driven by the agenda of those who set the policies. News reports were often presented in a fragmented manner with no context or background to the policies or the people implementing them. More important, these policies' ideological foundations were rarely questioned. For example, in the 1950s and 1960s, when population control policies and forced sterilisation were at their height, few news reports noted that these policies had derived from the then already discredited notion of eugenics (Connelly 2010) because journalists saw population control as a 'global' issue.[2]

This cosmopolitan view of population control deliberately obviated how natural resources had been – and continue to be – depleted globally by the few rich nation states in the North rather than by the many poor of the global South. Take, as an example, *How Many People Can Live on Planet Earth?* (2009), a programme broadcast originally in Britain by the BBC. In it, the well-known presenter David Attenborough discussed whether the world is heading for a population crisis, while reflecting on the profound effects of this rapid growth, both on humans and the environment. By the year that the programme was made (2009), Attenborough had joined the Optimum Population Trust, a population-control think tank, as a patron.

In the programme he warned that the projected growth in human population 'is likely to come from the developing world' [*sic*]; which set the tone of the rest of the documentary. The programme opens with a satellite circumnavigating the earth. While Attenborough's voice tells us how we are the dominant species, the screen shows a succession of images, from highways with cars, to what appears to be a western metropolis; then, suddenly when the voice-over says only one species 'can dominate the planet', the image that appears is that of a mother with her baby in a hospital bed just after giving birth. The mother's facial features are clearly those of a woman who appears to be from a Third World country.

To Attenborough's credit, he did denounce the fact that the lifestyle enjoyed by the few in the West has the most impact on the planet, while examining whether it is the duty of individuals to commit not only to smaller families, but to change the way they live for the sake of humanity and Planet Earth. He also makes it very clear that western patterns of consumption are not sustainable. However, while making these points, the images and examples used in the film prove at best to be problematic.

For example, when discussing government intervention, he mentions the 1979 Chinese 'one-child' policy and India's sterilisation programme. There is no mention of the involvement of western governments, multilateral organisations and even NGOs in the forcible sterilisation of hundreds of thousands of people, as was the case with the US State Department, the Rockefeller Foundation and Oxfam, all of which provided financial and/or technical assistance to Indira Gandhi's government to carry out sterilisation in India (Connelly 2010). Because of their sponsors, these types of interventions are regarded as development policies, and are subsequently reported uncritically, with little or no historical background and hardly any criticism from an ethical dimension of past failures in terms of policy.

Professor Jeffery Sachs's Millennium Villages Project presents another important discussion as it has received wide attention from the global media, especially those based in the United States. Nina Munk, in a *Vanity Fair* article, starts by describing Sachs as

> Visionary economist, saviour of Bolivia, Poland, and other struggling nations [presumably Mongolia], adviser to the U.N. and movie stars – won't settle for less than the global eradication of extreme poverty. And he hasn't got a second to waste. (Munk 2007)

The article goes on to highlight how, for many years, during the 1980s and 1990s, Sachs was known as 'Dr. Shock':

> The brilliant macro-economist from Harvard who prescribed radical fiscal and monetary discipline, so-called shock therapy, to countries

emerging from Communism. These days, he's better known glibly in the media as 'Bono's guru' and as the professor in MTV's masterful documentary 'The Diary of Angelina Jolie and Dr. Jeffrey Sachs in Africa'. In the movie, Jolie calls him 'one of the smartest people in the world'. (Ibid.)

The article says that Sachs's plan for Bolivia 'actually worked: strict fiscal and monetary discipline quickly lowered the country's annual inflation rate to about 15 per cent.' However, it hardly mentioned that his advice led to industrial collapse, widespread unemployment, pauperisation and a rise in mortality rates in Bolivia and other places such as Russia and Mongolia. Instead the piece argues:

> In hindsight, Sachs was probably naïve. Assuming that his reforms could be imposed on Russia as they had been on Bolivia and Poland, he was defeated by a massively bloated and stubborn economy. Russia was not resuscitated by Sachs's shock therapy; on the contrary, Russia was ravaged while Sachs and his ideas were ignored. The country's state assets were looted, and everything valuable wound up in the hands of a few clever men. (Ibid.)

The narrative places the blame on 'natural conditions' – in this case, a 'bloated and stubborn economy' – and politicians who were corrupt and did not do as they were told. In the most uncritical manner, the article details the 'experiment' of the villages project by pointing out that in 2006:

> Sachs named Ruhiira a 'Millennium Village', one of 79 villages in 10 African countries where his controversial theories on ending extreme poverty are being tested. He approaches alleviating poverty as if it were a rigorous scientific experiment, allocating exactly $110 per person each year for five years to implement a prescribed set of basic 'interventions': fertilizer and high-yield seeds, clean water, rudimentary health care, basic education, mosquito bed nets, and a communication link to the outside world. The results are tested and monitored, his goal being to prove that the same scientific model can be used on a grand scale to save the lives of hundreds of millions of people trapped by poverty. (Ibid.)

The report is basically a descriptive piece that aims at presenting the idea that giving foreign aid in this controlled way, by setting up sustainable villages, does work. In other words, it presents this type of project as a 'good' investment when it states:

> One of Sachs's biggest supporters is the financier and philanthropist George Soros, who recently donated $50 million to the Millennium Villages Project. (The project is a partnership among the U.N., Colombia, and Sachs's own nonprofit organization, Millennium Promise). According to Soros, whose foundation gives away between $350 million and $400 million a year, investing in Sachs offered an attractive 'risk-reward ratio'. 'Even though it's a large amount of money, $50 million, I thought there was really little downside,' Soros told me. 'As a humanitarian action, it was a good investment on its own. But if it succeeded, then of course you would get a reward that would be way out of proportion to the investment made'. (Ibid.)

Another important aspect is that managerial language is widely present in these types of narratives. As Escobar points out, management is the twin brother 'of gluttonous vision, particularly now when the world is theorized in terms of global systems' (1995: 193). These policies are therefore not really there to solve poverty, which is 'unsolvable', but to manage it so that everything remains the same.

To be fair to Professor Sachs, his is one of the few voices that have kept poverty in the spotlight in the global media. In the *Vanity Fair* article, he also insisted that 'extreme' poverty could be eradicated and he criticises 'excessive' military expenditure, compared to how little is provided for foreign aid. Nevertheless, he does not mention inequality nor question the fundamental ideological flow of the idea of development.

Of course, not all reports on Sachs's project are as favourable as this *Vanity Fair* article, but it is an example of how the key voices on poverty and development policies tend to articulate their ideas through the global media. Overall, the news coverage of poverty-alleviation policy presents many complexities worth exploring. It is loaded, for instance, with self-serving links that construct and reconfigure news and policy in a diversity of ways that none the less repeat and recycle similar ideas.

In order to develop further these recycled ideas about poverty, news coverage uses 'metaphors' (Lakoff 2004: xiii) and linguistic strategies such as labelling policies with words that pretend to say one thing when they actually mean another. For example, let us pause for a moment and think what the use of term 'alleviation' really means in this context; that is, policies that do not aim at solving the problem, but merely making the suffering less painful. In the same sense, the news coverage presents a parallel notion of addressing the suffering as the Good Samaritan (Moeller, 1999: 318) that concentrates on making the suffering bearable, but not really addressing the root causes of it. These discursive strategies avoid the need to address structural issues, while allowing for palliatives to become acceptable substitutes for the lack of real change. As Palagummi Sainath, one of the most eloquent journalists reporting on poverty, points out, 'development is the strategy of evasion' (1996: 331): people's needs are one thing, what policy makers deliver is entirely different.

Journalism about development reflects, in many ways, this same pattern of evasion. The issues are clear and present, but the stories seem to refer to a parallel universe. Let us not forget that most news media outlets from the West colluded with policy makers in the implementation of SAPs back in the 1980s and 1990s, enabling an ideologically driven neoliberal agenda that destroyed economies and shattered lives. Meanwhile, many journalists and their news editors failed the most vulnerable and excluded by uncritically reporting about the SAPs. That many journalists and news editors have changed their tone nowadays, as they now face similar policies in Europe, is no excuse for the past.

This failure to stand up for those affected by these policies is even more problematic in moral terms; news reporting of poverty has in fact an important effect on policy design and implementation, as it exercises an important degree of influence on both policy makers and the public from donor countries. This is the case for allocation of resources for foreign aid as suggested by Julia Cagé (2009) in her study about aid flows and information transparency. In her work, she argues that aid tends to be volatile, non-predictable and, in many cases, not delivered in a transparent way. This creates asymmetric information between the citizens and the recipient government about the amount of aid received by developing countries. By using a political-economy model, she shows that information is a key determinant of aid efficiency, while asymmetric information encourages rent extraction, reducing aid efficiency. In other words, the better informed the people from the donor and recipient countries are about aid programmes, the better these programmes will work. Other studies point in the same direction, suggesting that phenomena linked to agenda setting (such as the so-called 'CNN effect', or the ability to mobilise decision makers and the public through news coverage) take place with regards to foreign aid allocation (Van Belle 2004), while questioning the lack of transparency regarding the rationality in assigning these resources (Lugo-Ocando et al. 2013: 528).

This lack of transparency in the way resources are allocated – often driven by the donor nations' political agenda – contrasts abysmally with the post-colonial tone of many news reports that emphasise patronage over the resources allocated, under the implicit premise that the recipients are corrupt and incapable of managing these resources in an efficient and transparent manner. Take, for example, a radio chat show from the Australian ABC network on 31 May 2011, broadcast at a time when the government was announcing cuts in foreign aid despite a sound and stable economic performance:

> Australia's aid budget has more than doubled in the past five years and it's expected to double again in the next five years to reach $9 billion. But is Australia's aid money being spent effectively? And what is the objective – to alleviate poverty, increase our national security, or both?

By asking if the aid 'is being spent effectively', the radio programme was reinforcing that it is 'us' in the West who know best where and how 'our money' should be spent while supporting the 'efficiency criteria'.

This is, of course, not only a problem of coverage but also a problem of how foreign aid policy is designed and implemented in the first place. The manner in which resources for foreign aid are allocated is in itself a very complex and problematic process, starting with the fact that a great proportion of the resources is used to buy products and services from the donor countries (including military procurement, which takes a big slice of the pie); from the 'Oil For Food' programme in Iraq, through the loans made by the export-import banks, all the way to who provides the computers for media labs for schools and the grain to feed people during famines.

Linda Polman has produced a particularly devastating account of what she calls the 'aid industry' and how it operates. Journalism, she emphasises, bears a responsibility in all this, as news reports 'scarcely question aid organisations';

> They are content to let NGOs guide them around refugee camps, for example. If such camps were in the Netherlands or the UK and contracted out not to an NGO but to a care company or a catering firm, then journalists would want to know precisely why it was needed,

whether in fact it really was needed, how much money was being raked off and by whom, whether the aid workers had the proper diplomas for aid work, whether they are paying due attention to the rights of the residents, to neighbours and to the environment, what kind of aftercare the care companies intended to provide and whether or not local authorities were sharing the benefits. (Polman 2010: 162)

Polman calls these organisations 'business dressed as Madre Teresa' and points out that because they are NGOs, journalists let them get away with no questions asked.

To make matters worse, few reporters are trained to deal with issues relating to foreign aid accountability or have the will or time to do so. As a result, the foreign aid news coverage is generally abysmal when compared with the news coverage of other issues (Lugo-Ocando et al. 2013). Journalists often adopt a fall-back position and rely heavily upon institutional public relations sources representing the establishment and which provide a very institutional view.

Overall, the news agenda setting regarding anti-poverty policy is a complex process in which government officials, multilateral institutions, NGOs and a wide range of stakeholders intervene and shape the ways in which it is reported and represented. However, as we have mentioned before, most of these reports rarely include the voices of those living in poverty. From the classical political economists to today's neoliberals at the World Bank or the IMF, economists have monopolised the power of speech when it comes to development and poverty (Escobar 1995: 100). In the news stories, these economists seem to know better, 'even when the real specialists are those in poverty themselves'.

Policy in the Mirror

The issue of who determines development policy is fundamental in understanding the type of news agenda and overall coverage, not only because it matters in terms of identifying to whom these policies are accountable, but also because it tells us a lot about the intention of those designing and implementing these policies (agency) and therefore the media's role in justifying them. Furthermore, since the global news media covering poverty operate within a functionalist framework that 'assumes that order in international relations is a higher goal than justice and equality' (Alleyne 2003: 30), then maintaining order of a certain type becomes the default intention rather than questioning objectives, transparency and results.

The design and implementation of development policy is normally carried out at national and multilateral levels. Countries may assume that they have independence in formulating policy, but of course this is an illusion as interdependence on a global scale involves both influence and power. This creates a paradox in which success is often attributed to multilateralism and failure to national governments in developing countries in most news narratives.

However, multilateralism has reached its limits and the shortcomings of universal recipes for distinctive nations and societies are now clear. This became particularly apparent after the 2008 global financial crisis. For the global news media reporting poverty, these events had a transformational effect as the media could no longer count on common referents to articulate discourses. That being the case, reporting solutions for poverty went from the 1990s post-Cold War 'certainty' of deregulation and market-driven policy to the 2010s 'ambiguity' and 'uncertainty' of neo-Keynesian policy that operates now without an industrial-powered economy.

Indeed, for journalists around the world looking at the theme of poverty, there is no longer a fixed model to follow, as the supposedly rational assumption of private-managerial ideology fell apart under the enormous weight of the trillions of US dollars thrown at the bankers and their subsidiaries; brilliantly symbolised by Alan Greenspan, former chairman of the US Federal Reserve, admitting before the US Congress that his whole worldview had a fundamental 'flaw'.

Put more simply, one could suggest that journalism in the global news media went from covering news stories about poverty in a way that reinforced and legitimatised neoliberal assumptions of individual rationality and westernised models as the way forward for poor societies, to a scenario in which this same type of coverage happens in a situation in which this 'order of things' no longer makes sense or has the legitimacy it once had. The new emerging paradigms are instead riddled with contradictions, posing challenges for journalists' traditional worldviews.

The case of the news reporting of calls from Western leaders to address corruption in developing countries is symptomatic of these types of challenges. There have been several well-publicised scandals, such as that of the former World Bank's president, Paul Wolfowitz, who resigned in 2007 when an internal committee report found that he broke ethical rules in awarding a substantial pay rise to his girlfriend, or the decision of the then British Prime Minister Tony Blair to cancel, on national security grounds, an investigation on bribes paid to a Saudi prince to guarantee arms contracts for British defence companies.

Furthermore, at a time when the World Bank officially stated 'that its views on good governance and anti-corruption are important to its poverty alleviation mission' (2010) and just one year before the Wolfowitz scandal, the world learnt about a general amnesty programme-policy in which private firms which had defrauded the World Bank in the past would not be penalised as long as they admitted their wrongdoing. That is, the World Bank offered an amnesty to private companies, NGOs and individuals who had stolen or defrauded the bank, a criminal act in itself, if they fully disclosed past malpractice and promised 'to stick with the rules' in future:

> Under the new scheme, they could bid for work on future World Bank funded schemes if they meet strict criteria. World Bank boss Paul Wolfowitz said it would 'prevent and deter corruption'. The World Bank says it is trying to tackle corruption and weak governance, seeing it as a major obstacle to economic development in the world's least developed countries. It has barred 330 firms from working on projects it funds following fraud investigations by its Department of Institutional Integrity. (BBC 2006)

In other words, companies and NGOs which had been caught red-handed would receive a mere slap on the wrist and be allowed to continue business as usual. At no time did the BBC question the World Bank's central argument as to why it was allowing criminals, who had stolen money originally destined for those in poverty, to be let off the hook. Instead, it went on to present only the institution's version:

> The World Bank said the initiative would identify corrupt organisations and individuals and ensure its funds were spent properly. 'While there are individual firms that may hope to profit, the private sector as a whole stands to lose when corruption is pervasive and the rule of law is undermined,' Mr Wolfowitz said. 'The Voluntary Disclosure Program is a new tool that will help the Bank further its anti-corruption agenda in a practical and cost-effective way.' (Ibid.)

By not challenging this policy, the BBC failed to fulfil its duty to disclose the intentionality of the policy. Indeed, this policy was not only a reflection of the ideological principle of self-regulation, so embedded in neoliberal minds; it was also a clear example of the double standard that characterises the overall discourses on poverty and development with regards to the Third World.

In fact, it is often the case that those journalists who are often so keen to denounce corruption in a poor African state tend to be very slow to highlight western countries' own wrongdoings when it comes to foreign aid mismanagement. They embrace a narrative that enables discretion at home but vociferous denunciations abroad. These narratives constitute the basis of a discourse in which rhetoric and reality operate in distinctive ethical (or unethical) dimensions, but nevertheless *seem* universally legitimate.

We can observe these differences more precisely when it comes to investment intended to alleviate poverty. For example, 'alleviation' from multi-lateral banks can be better explained by the loose definition of terms such as 'small farmers' and 'small entrepreneurs' or by how 'human development' seems to encompass so many things that do not refer to those in poverty (Babb 2009: 167). By developing a language that refers to many things that seem to be about poverty but which are not, the organisations and institutions dealing with poverty are able to treat it as a commodity in the marketplace.

The Remains of the Day

Overall, the imbalance between those with resources and those without is extraordinary (Escobar 1995: 213). At the bottom of this is the stark reality that by 2005, 95 per cent of the population in developing countries – that is, almost 80 per cent of the world's population – were subsisting on less than US$10 a day (Ravallion et al. 2008). The situation has improved very little recently and in some places has become much worse. This is most compelling evidence not that foreign aid has failed, as Moyo (2009) suggests, but that the policy and approaches were inadequate in the first place – something which many global news media outlets have missed altogether. By treating poverty in developing countries as a separate issue – under labels such as 'development policy' or 'development assistance'

– the industrialised nations' global media have ghettoised the issue, 'othering' it by making distinctions between 'us' and 'them'.[3]

Development is in itself a problematic notion and the policies and strategies to improve poor people's lives need to be an integral part of a comprehensive set of economic and political policies deeply integrated into structural changes in the international system, at least if the aim is to provide dignified living standards to all the world's citizens. But to achieve this, individuals must contribute directly to human rights protections and promote rights-enhancing political integration between states (Cabrera 2010). In so doing, news reporting of poverty can play a crucial role in mobilising people towards this end. That is what should be at the core of the news coverage of poverty.

Moreover, as global citizenship is about equal human rights, the unequal way in which the world's resources and wealth are allocated should be the central objective of news reports about poverty and become the prevalent narrative when examining policy and actions towards those in poverty. The news agenda should expose the responsibility and ultimate culpability of our way of life in the West in relation to poverty in the rest of the world. We should no longer see ourselves as a House of Medici, acting as patrons aspiring to be saints, without considering the sacrifice that sainthood really entails, which is to leave aside our obsession with worldly luxuries and possessions and follow a very different life path – one that focuses on policy and actions that bring about total equality.

Meanwhile, the privilege that the western industrial states 'possess over the rest of world, the reality of politics, society and culture, especially in faraway countries, remains fragmented and often highly distorted in most media systems around the world' (Hafez 2011: 483). Under these circumstances, ghettoised journalism continues to support policies that, over the years, have failed spectacularly in highlighting inequality.

Inequality is indeed the real news story and should be the focus of policy scrutiny. The fundamental question in the mind of any journalist covering poverty should be: do the discourses and policies trying to eradicate poverty embrace the principle of redistribution in order to create a less unequal world? Even when the answer is no or does not seem relevant, it should be asked repeatedly, until the question itself starts making more sense than the traditional questions and answers that we get on a daily basis from the news coverage of poverty. Then, perhaps, we could have news coverage that is both thorough and ethically committed to a better society.

4

Africa, That Scar on Our Face

Jairo Lugo-Ocando and Patrick O. Malaolu[1]

In his speech to the annual Labour Party conference on 2 October 2001, the then British Prime Minister Tony Blair said to the audience: 'The state of Africa is a scar on the conscience of the world. But if the world as a community focused on it, we could heal it. And if we don't, it will become deeper and angrier.'

By reducing Africa to a scar, Blair was effectively following a long tradition of colonial rhetoric that has reduced that continent to a simplistic caricature in the western imagination. One hundred and twenty-eight years before and not very far from where Blair addressed that audience, the Scottish explorer David Livingstone used very similar words when referring to Africa, 'All I can add in my solitude, is, may heaven's rich blessing come down on every one, American, English or Turk, who will help to heal this open sore of the world' (Pakenham 1990).

The metaphors used by both Blair and Livingstone are problematic at very different levels and reflect a wider trend in which Africa is commonly represented in the media as 'hopeless' (for example, the *Economist* 2000). In this context, the continent's complexities tend to be visually simplified in images of starving women or children, while the sole mention of Africa, in many news stories, typically conjures up stereotypical images of lush jungles and wild animals, poverty and famine, corruption and tribal warfare, death and deadly diseases (Schraeder and Endless 1998: 29). Overall, these narratives foster media representations that depict Africa as an 'issue' characterised by the four Ds: disease, disaster, debt and death.

This chapter investigates these media representations in relation to the influence of culture, race, technology and ideology, but in the context of journalistic narratives and practices. In so doing, it interrogates the way in which the news agenda is set in relation to geopolitics and foreign policy. While sketching Africa's situation in alternative perspectives, we consider the impact of colonial legacies on the way Africa is constructed as news by the global media.

Representing the 'Dark Continent'

The modern construction of Africa in western imagery can be traced back to the 'scramble for Africa' (Pakenham 1990) that took place during the Victorian era, when the continent and poverty became intertwined in the narratives of journalists, explorers and travel writers. While reporting poverty in Britain in the late nineteenth century, journalist George Sims (1847–1922), for example, remarked that his task was 'equal to reporting from a dark continent' (cited by Golding and Middelton 1982: 23).

Media representations have been in fact the most influential source of information in the construction of Africa in the public imagination. These representations, by and large routinely based on stereotypes, tend to present Africa as an homogenous block (Harrison and Palmer 1986: x; Hunter-Gault 2002: 76). They tend to obscure Africa's progress in the areas of increasing democratisation and socio-economic advancement (Olujobi 2006) and instead present a grossly incomplete picture of the continent to the western world.

Moreover, if we had to choose one word that characterises news reporting from Africa it would be 'crises', epitomised by notions such as 'famine'. Crisis constitutes one of the few times when we hear about the continent on a regular basis in mainstream news reports. It is true that some news organisations have developed more comprehensive and positive programmes about Africa, such as CNN's *Inside Africa* (a weekly, half-hour, lifestyle programme), but the overwhelming tone in stories about Africa in the western news media continues to be crisis-related and conflict-driven.

It is because of this crisis-driven news agenda that 'intervention' in its different forms has been accepted so widely by the public as a legitimate way of dealing with poverty in Africa, becoming in the public's mind, as Rudyard Kipling once put it, 'the white man's burden'. Indeed, the concept of intervention is pivotal in understanding the way Africa is constructed in the public imagination by the news media, this because the concept contains a very subtle argument that 'they' (Africans) are 'passive' and 'hopeless' people (Botes 2011) waiting for 'us' (civilised western society) to bring modernity through intervention in the name of progress.

Equally important is to consider that crisis reporting happens in the context of the historical geopolitics of 'news flows' (Taylor 1997: 38) that take place between the 'news centres and the peripheries' (Harris 1985: 263; van Ginneken 1998: 128–32). Moreover, despite normative claims of detachment from government intervention, these news flows take place in an international geopolitical setting and are mostly determined by foreign policy prerogatives from the centres of power where the global media are based.

For example, the CARMA Report on Western Media Coverage of Humanitarian Disasters concludes that there is almost no link between the scale of a disaster and media interest in the story. In other words, death tolls have nothing to do with the amount of air time or space given to a story. However, the report continues, there is a clear correlation between the perceived economic impact of a disaster on western markets and the quantity of media coverage (CARMA International 2006: 6).

Here, journalism's propagandistic function in supporting foreign policy becomes clear. As journalists represent an ideological force (McNair 1998: 7) and are by all means chief sense-makers (Patterson 2013: 5), they are able to recycle a picture that makes the general public accept the inevitability of intervention by convincing them that western foreign policy operates in the best interests of Africa. In their narrative, crisis becomes an excuse for intervention, this being a euphemism for implementation of Western foreign policy. Journalists' narratives therefore have an agenda-setting function and in Africa's case, that function is to frame the inequality in power relations in a way that appears to justify intervention.

In the case of British journalism, for example, this idea of the need for intervention has mostly been articulated in the news narratives by means of humanitarian discourses, although since 9/11 increasingly in terms of security. In this sense, David Livingstone still represents, for many in the West, the 'acceptable' face of Empire and colonial rule (Conboy et al. 2014: 3). However, let us not forget that this humanitarian discourse is based upon a sense of racial and cultural superiority that gives a licence to intervene in order to help those who cannot help themselves. This hierarchical classification is key to the West's power to intervene, as this is dependent not only upon commitment to black inferiority, but also upon the affirmation of white civilisation's superiority (Spelman 1999: 202–15).

Although this idea of classifying people and cultures in hierarchies is an ideological mechanism that originated many years ago, it still resonates powerfully in the structuring of geopolitical discourses that constantly reproduce these hierarchies to normative effects. Consequently, we find on a daily basis numerous examples in which African conflicts are referred to as 'tribal', or their politics as 'tribalism'. By reducing African politics to representations of the savage stereotype, western news media are able to bring back colonial discourses that effectively justify and reinforce imperial hegemony (Anand 2007: 32). To explore this specific point, we will examine the case of Nigeria and the way that country is represented in the British media.

A study of 3,127 articles about post-independence Nigeria in *The Times*, the *Daily Telegraph*, the *Financial Times*, the *Guardian* and the *Independent* between 1997 and 2007 reveals how ideas and stereotypes of African countries are presented. These findings suggest that Nigeria is predominantly portrayed negatively by these news media outlets. Articles linking Nigeria to democracy, infrastructure and sport constitute only 41.1 per cent of coverage while a larger percentage, or 58.9 per cent of the articles studied, links Nigeria to corruption, fraud and crime (see Tables 4.1 and 4.2).

Similarly, there is a common denominator in the articles examined. Of the overall sample, 2,654 (representing 84.8 per cent) contain language or words suggesting condescension. They are written in a magisterial tone – derisive, dismissive or, at least, adopting the conspiratorial tone of 'After all, it is Africa: what do you expect?' What is almost always missing in the news construction of poverty and human suffering in Africa is 'empathy', which Chouliaraki calls the 'universal value of common humanity' (2006: 165), while Boltanski defines it as 'a strong gesture of humanity that recognises and formulates the common interest which links the one it touches to the other' (1999: 92).

In contraposition to this data, Chouliaraki cites how a Danish consul being interviewed on US television 'linguistified' his evaluation of the consequences of the September 11 attacks. She highlights how the diplomat shifted from a descriptive 'they', for the sufferers, to an all-inclusive 'we', which refers to humanity as a whole, suggesting a 'universal' being endowed with humanity like 'ours' (2006: 165). However, as one can often notice, that type of empathy is not necessarily a consideration in the construction of news about Africa, which is instead often treated as a distant cultural 'other' in western news.

Table 4.1 Post-independence Nigeria: Total news coverage, by category

Category	1997–99			2000–02			2003–07		
	No. of articles	No. of words	Words %	No. of articles	No. of words	Words %	No. of articles	No. of words	Words %
1 Democracy	235	147,218	31%	130	97,723	18%	163	152,677	12%
2 Infrastructure	73	65,725	14%	81	65,761	12%	243	211,470	17%
3 Sport	92	75,338	16%	134	89,264	16%	137	134,186	11%
4 Corruption	137	93,702	20%	181	124,866	22%	410	320,115	26%
5 Fraud	47	31,078	6%	110	59,713	11%	244	161,119	13%
6 Crime	99	63,068	13%	208	118,339	21%	403	257,711	21%
Total	683	476,129	100%	844	555,666	100%	1600	1,237,278	100%

Table 4.2 Post-independence Nigeria: Average news coverage, by category

Category	1997–99		2000–02		2003–07	
	No. of articles	No. of words	No. of articles	No. of words	No. of articles	No. of words
1 Democracy	47	294,436	26	195,446	32.6	305,354
2 Infrastructure	14.6	13,145	16.2	131,522	48.6	685,912
3 Sport	18.4	150,676	26.8	17,852.8	27.4	5,9757.6
4 Corruption	27.4	187,404	36.2	249,732	82	1,077,366
5 Fraud	9.4	6,216	22	119,426	48.8	50,382
6 Crime	19.8	126,136	41.6	238,712	80.6	878,236

African Sources

Another important factor in the negative depiction of Africa in the western news media is the role played by the selection of sources, which are 'the primary definers' of news agenda (Hall et al. 1978). Some sources are routinely over-accessed to the detriment of alternative but crucial viewpoints (Allan: 1999b: 71). Indeed, only 876 (or 28 per cent) of the sources quoted in the 3,127 articles coded on Nigeria are Nigerian, 2,102 (or 67 per cent) are European, foreign or non-African/Nigerian sources; 149 (or 5 per cent) are anonymous sources (Malaolu 2014).

In other words, Africans had little voice in their own stories – the 'knowledgeable' Western 'experts' speak for them, analyse their developmental problems for them and proffer the 'necessary solutions' (Easterly 2013; Malaolu 2014). It does not matter if these experts' knowledge of the African terrain is limited or if they have made only one high-security trip to an African capital city. Their value-laden opinion prevails and forms the basis for numerous intervention programmes. Consequently, there have been countless western interventions (including SAPs, poverty reduction policies, and so on) through multilateral agencies such as the World Bank, the IMF, the UNDP, and others. When these interventions fail, as they often do, the 'primary definers' of the news agenda heap the blame on corrupt African leaders, just as pre-colonial interventions were justified as necessary to counter the savagery and despotism of the native rulers (Anand 2007: 26).

An African leader who rubber-stamps western policies becomes a 'good' leader, notwithstanding his democratic credentials or the type of government that they deliver. In return, the leader is granted aid from the centre and praise from the global media. The reporting about leaders in South Africa, Zimbabwe, Kenya and Rwanda over the past three decades is a testament to how the western news media turn heroes into villains and vice versa according to the need to legitimise foreign policy in their own countries.

In this picture of good and bad governance, corruption is commonly cited by columnists, news sources and journalists as the cause of poverty. In their view, the media tend to emphasise the inability of Africans to govern themselves and obscure the fact that corruption is a two-way street. Take, for example, a Thomson Reuters agency news dispatch from 21 May 2006, under the headline, 'Bono Presses Africa to Tackle Corruption', where the singer is quoted as saying:

'I'll go further and say that the single biggest obstacle to business and the renewal of the economies in the South is corruption and the single biggest obstacle to getting start-up money for those businesses, if you want to look at aid as investment, is corruption,' he added. He said taxpayers in developed nations were also demanding more accountability from their own political leaders to ensure that money going to Africa was properly used. 'There is a window of opportunity but it could close if things like the corruption issue are not tackled or the peer review mechanisms are not felt to be real,' he told reporters travelling with him before addressing African finance ministers in the Nigerian capital of Abuja.

The report presents western taxpayers as demanding accountability, when in fact western corporations' tax evasion in African countries is a key problem facing these societies. Our argument is not that reports of corruption in Africa are entirely unfounded but that it is simplistic to identify corruption as the main reason for poverty in Africa, as many news reports suggest. This is also a critique of the way that global news media tend to exempt the West from any culpability, which is highly problematic, as such double standards have often led to the formulation and application of certain development antidotes. Bernard Porter put it succinctly in an article in the *London Review of Books* (26 March 2009): 'For every African leader taking bribes there is usually a western company dispensing them.'

For example, in 2010, Global Witness, a London-based NGO, published 'International Thief: How British Banks are Complicit in Nigerian Corruption'. The 37-page report, which comprehensively detailed the British financial institutions' involvement in the theft of funds meant to give succour to poor and desperate Nigerians, was practically ignored by the British press; instead, other reports such as those carried out by Chatham House detailing the criminality of Nigerians tend to receive more coverage (Press Association 2006).

Another example is the type of report produced by self-appointed global corruption watchdogs such as Transparency International (TI), which tend to focus on the African public sector. When using these organisations as a news source, reporters often fail to mention the links between the founder of TI, Peter Eigen and the International Monetary Fund (IMF) and to question how Eigen's organisation is funded.[2] Journalists also fail to acknowledge that the TI index of corruption is based on surveys carried out mostly among elites whose own views are shaped by what they read in the media and their own relationship with the local government and business community. However, as TI represents an 'authoritative' source – given its status as a western-recognised organisation staffed by Western-educated officials – its claims remain largely unchallenged.

Indeed, the particular selection of news sources for news coverage of Africa is not a random phenomenon but a consequence of the western news media's dependence on official sources and their complementary role in legitimising foreign policy. In her study of the *New York Times*'s news coverage of the Darfur crisis, Ammina Kothari points out that although the coverage is not entirely homogenous, it 'largely reflects support and justification for the enforcement of US foreign policies in Sudan' (2010: 221). Several other studies on the use of news sources confirm the role of the media in enhancing foreign policy and articulating legitimising discourses to support intervention (Alleyne 2003; Friel and Falk 2007; Herman and McChesney 1997; Herman and Chomsky 1988; van Ginneken 1998; Wasburn 2002; Way 2013a). Therefore it is impossible to understand why Africa is represented in the way it is without looking at the linkage between the news agenda and western foreign policy.

Role Models

The colonisation of Africa and the destruction of its indigenous civilisations mirror in many ways what the Spaniards had done in Latin America some centuries earlier, but on a larger industrial scale. By the nineteenth century, over 12 million enslaved Africans had been transported to the Americas, of which over 3 million died either en route or upon arrival. The scramble for Africa saw greed and destruction on an unprecedented scale. In a few decades, the Dark Continent became a testing ground for an ideology which had one single purpose: exploitation. Ten million square miles were stolen from Africa's people, then divided and finally gobbled up by the European powers (Pakenham 1990: xxiii). Natural and human resources were devoured by the new capitalist machine's infinite appetite that demanded ever more. If Africa was no heaven for its indigenous people before the white man set foot there, it certainly became hell afterwards; one that would witness its own 'African Holocaust' (Stannard 1994: 317). Colonial rule provided little or no economic growth in the colonised nations themselves; this was the case of British rule in India, where that country saw little or no economic growth for the last forty years of colonial rule (Sachs 2006: 147) and instead a dependence model was deliberately fostered in which cheap raw materials and minerals were exported from the colonies, then processed in the West's industrial centres only to be sold back to the new markets on the periphery (Furtado 1967: 19).

Therefore media narratives, often closely associated with foreign policy, had to explain poverty in Africa by other means if the legitimacy of colonial rule was to remain unchallenged. The news media of the late nineteenth and early twentieth centuries not only found plausible explanations for African poverty – a 'lack of civilisation' and the 'inferiority' of the African race – but also made sure that those ideas were widely disseminated across the globe. Fredrick Lugard's demeaning depiction of the African personae remains a vivid example of the discourse of 'lack of civilization and inferior races':

> In character and temperament, the typical African of this race-type is a happy, thriftless, excitable person. Lacking in self-control, discipline, and foresight. Naturally courageous, and naturally courteous and polite, full of personal vanity, with little sense of veracity, fond of music and loving weapons as an oriental loves jewellery. His thoughts are concentrated on the events and feelings of the moment, and he suffers little from the apprehension for the future or grief for the past. His mind is far nearer to the animal world than that of the European or Asiatic, and exhibits something of the animals' placidity and want of desire to rise beyond the State he has reached. Through the ages the African appears to have evolved no organized religious creed, and though some tribes appear to believe in a deity, the religious sense seldom rises above pantheistic animalism and seems more often to take the form of a vague dread of the supernatural. (Lugard 1926: 70)

This was the official approach to Africans and consequently the worldview embraced by the news media at the time. Instead of destruction and misery, the white man was reported as bringing progress to the continent in almost every single story of the most influential newspapers of that time. The colonialist's construct, as embedded in the discourse, reduced Africans to a sub-human status. It was not only derisively dismissive of African religious beliefs, it also highlighted two 'perceived' lacks: 'lack of organized religious creed' and 'lack of organisation and management'. The first 'lack' is fundamental in the justification of forceful colonial occupation, and the second is the fulcrum for the rationalisation of current interventions. Lugard makes this point more explicit:

> 'He lacks the power of organization, and is conspicuously deficient in the management and control alike of men or business. He loves the display of power, but fails to realize its responsibility ... he will work hard with less incentive than most races. He has the courage of the fighting animal, an instinct rather than a moral virtue ... In brief, the virtues and defects of this race-type are those of attractive children, whose confidence when it is won is given ungrudgingly as to an older and wiser superior and without envy ... Perhaps the two traits which have impressed me as those most characteristic of the African native are his lack of apprehension and his lack of ability to visualize the future. (Ibid.: 70)

What is exceptionally interesting nevertheless is how those same discourses are reproduced nowadays, but through the use of metaphors and modern euphemisms. The use of terms such as 'lack of good governance', 'humanitarian intervention' and 'failed states' in the media narratives or by 'expert' news sources are in fact modern synonyms for old ideas. The Africans' inability to govern themselves is often inscribed in narratives that use terms such as 'tribal politics', 'lack of modern institutions' and 'corrupt leadership'. Consequently, these political metaphors justify intervention in Africa, as western values and institutions are still paraded as the solution for Africa's problem.

The consensus among western powers since the end of the Second World War has been to talk about improving material well-being as a way of avoiding discussing political rights in Africa (Easterly 2013: 339). Thanks to this post-war agreement, many old colonial myths continue to be recycled by claiming that trade and economic growth will improve the life of millions in Africa, despite overwhelming evidence that current models applied by multilateral organisations such as the World Bank and IMF have, overall, made African people poorer, more unequal and far more excluded from the rest of the world.

However, as this discourse is framed in geopolitical terms, if the trade is with competing and emerging powers, then the reporting becomes critical of the new players. In a *Guardian* article published under the headline 'China says booming trade with Africa is transforming continent', it is pointed out that

China said yesterday its two-way trade with Africa had increased by nearly 45% in a year to hit a record $114.81bn (£75bn), highlighting a trend that could be helping transform the world's poorest continent. Beijing said economic ties with Africa had recovered from a dip in 2009 due to the global financial crisis and would now grow even faster. In 1992 two-way trade between China and Africa stood at just $1bn. But Chinese demand for oil, gas, iron ore and other raw materials for its rapidly growing economy has spurred trade and investments in Africa in recent years. Critics of the relationship accuse China of failing to create local jobs, flooding markets with poor quality goods, and turning a blind eye to human rights abuses in countries such as oil-rich Sudan and diamond-rich Zimbabwe. (Smith 2010)

As in this article, the story is often the same. China is investing in Africa but is doing so in its own interests, by dumping its own products in those countries and destroying their indigenous industries. Hillary Clinton, then US Secretary of State, expressed similar sentiments while speaking during a television interview in Lusaka, Zambia (Reuters 2011). In her response to a question about China's rising influence in Africa, Clinton warns against 'new colonialism' in Africa, 'When people come to Africa to make investments, we want them to do well but also want them to do good,' she said. 'We don't want them to undermine good governance in Africa.'

This narrative might sound correct but is largely hypocritical, as what the Chinese are doing now is not that different from what western governments and corporations have been doing in Africa for the last two hundred years.

In stories related to western investment, on the other hand, we see the use of more positive phrases: 'transfer of technology', 'development of skills' and 'partnership', among others. In these stories, western corporations, having behaved in the past in very similar ways to their Chinese counterparts now, are nevertheless given a much more welcoming treatment by news reporters; the emphasis will be on the opportunities and potential of such investments, highlighting the positive role of both the companies and countries that are investing in Africa. In an article from the Italian news agency ANSA on 12 June 2011 under the headline 'Westwood promotes Ethical Fashion in Africa', we read:

The virtual store Yoox.com has confirmed its ethical approach to fashion and its support for the cause by promoting environmental

Ethical Fashion Africa Project of Vivienne Westwood. YOOXYGEN will make available exclusively online new collection of bags and accessories designed by British designer and created in collaboration with the International Trade Centre (ITC), joint body of the United Nations (UN) and of' World Trade Organization (WTO). (ANSA 2011)

The news report from ANSA makes no mention of how profits are distributed, nor does it looks at the history of the fashion industry and its association with poor working conditions, use of animal fur and environmental degradation. There is no mention either of the fact that Yoox.com sells products from corporations such as Armani, which the majority of Africans would not be able to afford. The only focus in the story is on how charitable the venture seems to be.

In fact, news reports of western corporations investing in Africa are often treated sympathetically and it is only on those occasions when the companies are responsible for major disasters or wrongdoings that they are singled out for criticism in media reports. In an article by the Australian Associated Press (AAP), published by *The Australian* on January 27, 2011 under the headline 'African resources a plus for us, says Foreign Minister Kevin Rudd', we read:

Africa's economic potential spells opportunity for Australia, Foreign Minister Kevin Rudd says. In Ethiopia to open Australia's new embassy in Addis Ababa, Mr Rudd said he was committed to deeper political engagement with Africa on a range of issues. 'Australian investment in Africa's resources sector is about $20 billion, with billions more in prospect. We are determined to use Australian expertise to help African countries … manage their resources so that they spur economic development.'

Foreign Minister Kevin Rudd's determination to use 'Australian expertise' to help Africans 'manage their resources' is simply a modern-day rehash of Lugard's words. In that same speech, he suggests a greater participation and presence of Africa in the United Nations' Security Council but falls short of asking for a permanent seat for an African country.

The article also fails to mention that Australian investment in Africa has mainly gone into mining, with particular emphasis in recent times on extraction of uranium, the residue of which returns to Africa in the form of nuclear waste (Abdullahi 2008). Mining in Africa is one of the primary causes of environmental damage. Degradation of local land and, in the case of Australian mining companies, is directly related to non-compliance with national and international standards of operation. Paradoxically, in 2007, the government of which Rudd was a minister opened the gates for Australian companies to mine uranium in Australia itself, but most Australian state governments banned it.

The fact remains that many multinational corporations operate in Africa under standards that are lower than those in place in the countries where they are headquartered. Organisations such as Royal Dutch Shell have a poor environmental and human rights record in Nigeria, while claiming sustainability and responsibility credentials in Britain and the Netherlands. None the less, in most news reports on trade and investment, the issue of double standards is ignored. Instead, private investment is often associated with growth and progress. The prevalent narratives are packed with neoliberal explanations in which the private sector is often the hero, while the public sector is regularly presented as the corrupt villain preventing Africa's progress.

In effect, the African public sector's media image is often skewed and structured in very problematic ways. Medical aid is often provided, it is reported, by NGOs or western-trained doctors and nurses who are underfunded and work in very difficult conditions while dealing with an overwhelming demand for assistance. This is despite the fact that most African countries have had positive experiences with regards to state-delivered health provisions in spite of the prohibitive costs of drugs and medical technologies caused by the restrictive issue of patents and copyrights, the West's constant poaching of Africa's best doctors and nurses and the historical legacy of colonial rule that left behind crumbling infra-structure and few human resources to support social services in general.

An example of this is a 2001 article from the *Seattle Post-Intelligencer* under the headline 'A breakdown of our primary health care system':

Here in one of the world's top oil-producing countries – fifth-largest supplier to the United States – the wealth is in the hands of a few. On many counts, the average Nigerian is worse off now than when the nation gained independence from Britain 41 years ago. It is no secret that Nigeria is a mess. Ask any Nigerian. Ask, for example, how they're doing when it comes to the basic public-health need to vaccinate their children against diseases such as measles, polio, diphtheria or tetanus.

'We have no immunization system,' said Dr. Benedict Mairiga, the earnest medical director of one of the country's major care centres, Plateau State Hospital in the northern city of Jos. 'We don't even have a surveillance system that can tell us how many are not being vaccinated.' (Paulson 2001)

In this narrative, we find all the elements of traditional discourses in which local voices are ignored, questioned, or dismissed altogether:

In 1990, Nigeria claimed that 90 per cent of its children were immunized with the basic vaccines. The latest figures from the World Health Organization suggest an average 20 per cent coverage, but Mairiga finds even those figures highly optimistic. 'What we're seeing here is the breakdown of our primary health care system,' he said. Nigerians don't mince words. Most will tell you that their country is judged the most corrupt nation on Earth. Just getting through the airport in Lagos is considered a trial. The locals, if they aren't seeking to separate travellers from their money, will at least want to know what they're doing here. (Ibid.)

The reports tends to emphasise the inability of the government to attend to the needs of its people:

One of Bill Gates' top health strategists, Dr. William Foege, thinks Nigeria 'provides an important model for the rest of the developing world' and some key lessons the Gates Foundation must take to heart if it wishes to accomplish any lasting change. Those lessons come from the resilience and resourcefulness of Nigeria's people, not its government. And they can be found in the work of Nigerians like Dr. Emmanuel Miri, who was educated in the United States and has devoted his life to improving the health of his homeland.

In these stories the heroes are normally those educated in the West or working for or in partnership with western NGOs, while the state and government officials are often represented as corrupt, unreliable and constantly undermining western efforts to improve life in that continent.

It is by no means being suggested here that all reports on Africa follow this pattern. However, the prevalent approach in the reporting of Africa is one in which the West is presented as a role model. Because of this, news media reports on poverty in Africa often make explicit and implicit comparisons between the West's efficient, civilised and honest societies and values against the less transparent and uncivilised ways of the African continent. As Valentin Mudimbe points out:

> Although generalizations are of course dangerous, colonialism and colonization basically mean organization, arrangement. The two words derive from the Latin word colére, meaning to cultivate or to design. Indeed the historical colonial experience does not and obviously cannot reflect the peaceful connotations of these words. But it can be admitted that the colonists (those settling a region), as well as the colonialists (those exploiting a territory by dominating a local majority) have all tended to organize and transform non-European areas into fundamentally European constructs. (Mudimbe 1988: 1)

These constructs reflect the aspiration of western societies that perceive themselves to be cohesive and efficient and therefore think that they have the right to intervene in order to improve the lives of Africans.

On the other hand, it is also important to explain that the reference to colonial rule as a 'better time' in journalistic narratives happens because of a binary system in which the colonial is always seen as better against the local; this idea is also widely assumed by the locals thanks to an inculcated atavistic complex of inferiority. In this dichotomised system,

> ...a great number of current paradigmatic oppositions have developed: traditional versus modern; oral versus written and printed; agrarian and customary communities versus urban and industrialized civilization; subsistence economies versus highly productive economies. (Ibid.: 4)

These dichotomies are very present in the journalistic narratives, which use them not only to describe the current situation in Africa, but also to explain poverty as an historical and/or cultural phenomenon. The comparisons allow journalists to render invisible the historical and structural explanations involving the colonial bequest of impoverished people. It also allows them to obviate inherited dependency systems in which the same type of commercial trade is still practiced in the context of global systems that serve only to increase inequality.

Creating Crisis

Overall, it should be clear by now that the news coverage of Africa's poverty is mostly characterised by a neoliberal and post-colonial paradigm in which root causes are ignored and simplistic explanations are provided instead. This is the case even in the face of the most catastrophic events, for example, when terms such as 'famine' are used by the global media. An article in the *Telegraph* from 29 July 2011 with the headline 'Horn of Africa famine spreads' states that 'All of southern Somalia is slipping into famine, the UN warned on Friday as it raised its appeal for urgent funds by a quarter to £1.5 billion' (Pflanz 2011).

The dispatch was sent from Nairobi and therefore it is safe to assume that it was either given as a press release or provided in a press conference. It is not our intention to question the severity of the situation in Somalia. However, it does become clear from reading the dispatch that what is emphasised is the West's ability to dictate who needs help and who does not. This power of the western governments, corporations, multilateral organisations and NGOs to define discourses, terminology and conceptualisations is perhaps the single most important tool in shaping the parameters of news reporting about Africa.

Take for example the calls to support countries in Africa that liberalise their economies when organisations such as the G8 and other multilateral agencies insist on the removal of trade barriers and the infusion of foreign capital as the panacea for development. This was the case when the news media reported extensively on the then Prime Minister Tony Blair and his Commission for Africa proposing a doubling of aid to Africa if it opened its doors for 'free trade', that is, if it removed *all* trade barriers, this despite the fact that western countries such as Britain did exactly the opposite during their early stages of development.

In his book, *Bad Samaritan*, economist Ha-Joon Chang (2007) explains that all G8 and G20 countries historically achieved industrial growth by setting protectionist barriers. Now, he explains, they have co-opted the multilateral agencies to put impediments for Africa to do the same. He calls this phenomenon 'kicking away the ladder' in his book of the same title (2002); that is, once you secure your own competitive advantages you prevent everyone else from getting theirs. Yet the journalistic narrative seems to be one in which trade liberalisation is the *outcome* of economic development and not its *cause*.

The case of foreign aid destined for African countries and how it is presented by the journalistic narrative suffers from a similar paradox. The impression created by the aid discourse would suggest that Africa has received the lion's share of global aid, but the opposite is actually the case. Citing the World Bank Miracle Report of 1993, William Gumede reveals in an article published by the *Guardian* in 2010 that South Korea – just one country in East Asia – from the end of the Second World War until the 1980s received the equivalent of all the aid that the whole of Africa combined received over a similar period (Gumede 2010).

The other paradox in the journalistic narrative about Africa is the lack of connection between patterns of consumption in the West and poverty in that continent. One example of this is the way in which technology – especially high-tech communication – is often presented as a possible 'silver bullet' for poverty. News reports repeatedly claim that mobile phone technology has transformed the lives of millions in the past decade, when in reality all social indicators show instead a marked deterioration of living standards in the same period. Furthermore, poorly researched news reports on how digital technologies are opening a new era of progress for Africans frequently ignore how the West's appetite for African minerals that allowed that digital revolution to take place devours them at very cheap prices while fuelling civil wars in places such as the Democratic Republic of Congo. One exception to this was published by the London-based *Telegraph* in 2008:

> Few people have heard of this rare mineral, known as coltan, even though millions of people in the developed world rely on it. But global demand for the mineral, and a handful of other materials used in everything from cell phones to soup tins, is keeping the armies of Congo's ceaseless wars fighting. More than 80 per cent of the world's coltan is in Africa, and 80 per cent of that lies in territory controlled by Congo's various ragtag rebel groups, armed militia and its corrupt and underfunded national army. (Pflanz 2008)

However, this report is not the norm and it is often the case that these types of links are not established by most journalists. Pflanz's article is also one of the few examples which make the historical link to the Belgian King Leopold's exploitation of rubber and his excesses in that country during the nineteenth century, while providing some sense of some co-responsibility:

But in Congo's anarchic environment, it is impossible for customers to know for sure that the tantalum in their mobile phone, DVD player, PlayStation or desktop computer did not come from a rebel-held mine. Buyers say that ore from these mines is mixed with that from legitimate mines, and they cannot tell which is which. There is no equivalent of the Kimberley Process, the international system which certifies that diamonds are from conflict-free areas. (Ibid.)

Nevertheless, in his report, Pflanz states that the Kimberley Process Certification Scheme (KPCS) is another standard imposed by the West, which in itself is questionable as it omits conflict zones, such as Israel, where diamonds are not extracted, but where they are cut; thus, despite gross violations of human rights, Israel's diamond exports remain untouched.

One could argue that with few exceptions and despite technological advances, the overall coverage of poverty in Africa by the global news media is today no more revealing of the continent's realities than it was a hundred years ago. It is true that for some more progressive media, Africa's story is changing. As an editorial titled 'A fresh chapter is opening in Africa's history', in the *Guardian* in 2011 attested, the African economy is predicted to grow at an average rate of more than 7 per cent over the next two decades – faster than China's; a hundred African companies have revenues greater than $1 billion; the combined GDP of the largest eleven African countries will be bigger than Russia's or China's by 2050; Africa has 60 per cent of the world's total amount of uncultivated arable land, and the rate of return on foreign investment in Africa is greater than in any other developing region. Similarly, according to the *Economist* (in January 2011), six of the ten most rapidly expanding economies over the past decade were in sub-Saharan Africa – this of a continent the news media describes as 'hopeless'.

However, news reporting of Africa is still largely contextualised by the assumptions of neoliberalism, the constant need for economic growth and crisis. Moreover, Africa is still largely presented as a continent in despair and in need of patronising guidance by the West, because the news coverage is still embedded in many of the old ideas that shaped our understanding and perception of the 'Dark Continent' more than a century ago. Indeed, research carried out on the organisation of the 2010 World Cup in South Africa noted, for example, that themes of Afro-pessimism, African essentialism and (neo)colonialism still contributed to problematic and colonial representations of South Africa in the build-up to the tournament (Hammett 2001: 63). Other similar studies have referred to how *Time* magazine represented sub-Saharan African women in its coverage of HIV/AIDS, pointing out that the media continue to rely on older colonial imageries of Africa as the feminised, diseased 'Dark continent' (Brijnath 2007: 371). Looking at this, one can say that the rhetoric of Empire has mutated into new journalistic metaphors that euphemistically try to say different things but in the end mean the same: a dark scar on a 'beautiful' white face.

5

Visual Journalism and Global Poverty

Jairo Lugo-Ocando and Scott Eldridge II[1]

Kevin Carter's photograph of a starving child in Sudan, with a vulture lurking in the background, is one of the most iconic visual depictions of poverty ever made. Published in the *New York Times* in 1993, Carter received the Pulitzer Prize for this photo only months before he committed suicide at the age of 33. The image has become a ubiquitous signifier of famine, that has informed other portrayals of poverty ever since. This particular photo has become referential because certain images, whether stereotypical or unique, carry an ability to express emotions and knowledge (Hariman and Lucaites 2007: 10) in ways that words simply cannot achieve.

To be sure, the modern understanding of poverty owes a great deal to these kinds of images. From Dorothea Lange's 1936 photo of the Migrant Mother, Florence Owens Thompson, as an iconic image of the Great Depression, many of these pictures have become de facto portrayals of poverty-stricken people, portrayals that bring the world of those in poverty to our attention. Whether in the form of pictures, videos, cartoons, or illustrations, they become indelible metaphors for how we see peoples and regions of the world. These images do not, however, represent a singular reality. They rather rely on a series of stereotypes that resonate with the pictures already in our minds, drawing from pre-existing conceptualisations, ideologies and values. Images of poverty through their frames reflect the different layers of both image making and image reception that compose societal knowledge and knowledge production.

Certainly, in order for images to be effective as news – that is, to be able to communicate the story and engage the public with it – they must reflect something from within the existing framework of knowledge and emotions that already shape our societal understanding of the world. In so doing, the classic portrayals of poverty can be seen as channelling familiar icons that 'communicate social knowledge' (Tulloch and Blood 2010: 514). They act as reference points that appeal emotionally to our collective memory, while defining poverty as a socially constructed reality.

These graphic representations stamp indelible images in our minds that then define meaning. For example, the images taken by Walker Evans (1903–75) of an emaciated child in his mother's arms are a modern-day pietà of the Depression-era United States. In relation to this, Susan Sontag (1971) writes about how most of us, lacking direct access to the world outside, rely on images to build our sense of people and events further afield. Sontag gives a nod to Plato's allegory of the cave, and the shadow images of the world outside projected on the cave wall, to describe the power images have to convey a particular kind of reality.

Nevertheless, not even the best photography, taken by the most conscientious journalist, is reality. At its best, it is just representation, and as such it draws on symbolic meaning that tries to simplify for its audience the complex world out there. These visualisations have managed to channel those familiar and human emotions of sorrow, loss and, ultimately, powerlessness. Wrapping complicated situations around familiar and simple frames, these images allows news workers to tell these stories with clarity. But at what cost?

Indeed, one of the key problems that we face when examining the poverty's visual representation is the fact that these images also enable people to contemplate poverty as an aesthetic form. In so doing, the images act as screens that tame our ethical struggle to look real poverty in the eye when we know it is looking back at us. Because of this function, we are able to contemplate, almost morbidly, images of death and famine in distant places with the same aesthetic fascination which we experience when we see other forms of art and in a way which we certainly could not when we pass a beggar in the streets (Franquet dos Santos 2013: 347). We find some grim humour in cartoons that satirise suffering and injustice and aesthetically appreciate artistic representations that convey to us the suffering of others, as we remind ourselves that these images come from another, distant, reality.

Therefore, this chapter examines the role of images in mediating poverty as a socially constructed reality and assesses the impact of that mediation in the creation of the public imaginary. In so doing, it discusses the ethical dimensions and implications of the use of images in the global reporting of poverty and how this resonates and reinforces our own preconceptions in the West. The chapter goes on to remind us that, as Roland Barthes once wrote, 'photography is subversive, not when it frightens, repels, or even stigmatises, but when it is pensive' (1981: 38); in other words, when it makes us think. It explores the relationship between images of poverty in the global news media and the way in which poverty and inequality is imagined among western audiences through these images.

The chapter looks at the problems that derive from visual representations and misrepresentations of certain segments of the population by exploring the visual construction of the news agenda on poverty around gender and race. It does so while discussing how the global media narratives facilitate the creation of heroes, villains and victims. It examines how the news media images have shaped the notions of poverty in the context of popular culture, and discusses why it is important to deconstruct these notions in the face of growing inequality.

What We Know

We should start by asking ourselves why images are important in the discussion about the global media's representation of poverty. The answer is two-fold: because they are a powerful element in shaping public responses and subsequent government policies and approaches (Zelizer 2001: 306), and because they do so by simplifying and dramatising the more complex socio-economic and political factors behind these policies.

Indeed, one factor that has contributed to the persistence of poverty emanates from the repetition of similar societal images that portray the economically deprived in negative ways, while limiting calls for structural changes on their behalf. While the media has the potential to challenge dominant beliefs about the poor and to generate support for progressive anti-poverty movements (Carroll and Ratner 1999: 33), it is equally capable of stifling such calls (Moeller 1999).

What we observe overall with regards to representations of poverty in the visual global media is that its practices tend to adopt the charitable but uncritical tone of its written counterparts in journalism. Consequently, the reproduction of images tends to obscure any calls for change. This is the end result of a particular type of organisational culture which sees photographers in particular as subaltern actors in the process of news gathering and production. Within these organisational dynamics, photojournalists are expected to follow the principles of objectivity and 'capture the suffering of others'. Thus, news images become a systematic effort to reproduce discourses of passivity and reduce their subjects to the 'other'. In this context, the predominant image of a famished women and her child is often 'naturalised', conveying therefore the implicit message that poverty is unavoidable. In this construction of reality, context is often missing, as photographic images carry their meaning through a single moment.

There is nevertheless 'a strong emotional response or identification' (Brennen 2010: 79) to these images in which poverty becomes inextricably tied to its portrayal. Because of this, understanding of poverty among audiences happens by means of these constructions and consequently becomes reality: 'A photograph passes for incontrovertible proof that a given thing happened. The picture may distort; but there is always a presumption that something exists or did exist, which is like what's in the picture' (Sontag 1971: 5).

A person in poverty is shown as idle, their hand outstretched and waiting, against a vast rural setting in the background. To each component of this scenario, any number of images can be imagined or remembered. Nevertheless, these stereotypical images are reproduced endlessly in many formats and in many places precisely because they tell a familiar and identifiable story. In this context, locations such as Africa are presented constantly as a 'vast end endless village' (Dogra 2012: 71).

This concept is not unique to poverty or the developing world. The use of familiar cultural archetypes can be found in the images which news agencies and broadcasters use when they cover their own countries as well. Still, even when addressing 'domestic' issues, the emphasis remains on differentiating between 'us', including both those communicating and those receiving the images, and 'them', that is, those in a state of poverty.

This 'us' and 'them' dynamic reflects also how these news cultures have dominant discourses and prevalent visions in society: 'Emphasize positive things about Us; Emphasize negative things about Them; De-emphasize negative things about Us; De-emphasize positive things about Them' (van Dijk 1998: 44). For poverty overseas, this might include portraying 'Us' as providing aid, and 'Them' as in need of its receipt. It emphasises the care given, and de-emphasises any larger socio-economic or political foundations to the poverty being portrayed.

Domestically, in the US for instance, this remains the case, as race and social dynamics are foregrounded in news images. Several studies have found that poverty is disproportionately portrayed as a 'black' problem, even though black people represent less than one-third of the poor in that country (Gilens 1996; Clawson and Trice 2000). On 29 August 1977, *Time* magazine,[2] in one of its most influential editions, employed these dynamics in a feature on the 'underclass' – the 'minority within a minority'. Throughout that issue, visual images of the urban poor were used to symbolise what poverty 'was' in the United States at the time.

Another important aspect in this duality between the portrayal of poverty abroad and at home is the claim that western audiences are now suffering from 'compassion fatigue' (Moeller 1999), in relation to efforts to alleviate poverty abroad. According to this view, these audiences are asking why should they keep providing aid to developing countries when there is no apparent change. Indeed, given the budgetary cuts at home, these audiences ask, why then so much is being done abroad?

A common element that both realms share is the ability to showcase passivity and helplessness, and therefore the ultimate need for intervention. As long as the image of poverty remains passive, 'othered' and far away (for reasons of geography or other ways of marginalisation), it is safe to contemplate. People in a state of poverty abroad are often portrayed as an 'other' who is a passive recipient of aid, rather than playing an active part in the drama or in the solution (Bullock et al. 2001: 242), in a similar manner to the way in which those who live in poverty at home are portrayed as the passive recipients of benefits, who are 'unwilling' to work.

In these images, poverty is also feminised and infantilised, reinforcing cultural stereotypes of vulnerability and passivity and ultimately the need for intervention. By constructing the way poverty is imagined and conceptualised, the global media direct their audiences to reflect on the plight of others, but ascribe no agency for change. At best, there is a tenuous moral call for voluntary action.

When referring to Latin America in his essay 'The Aesthetics of Hunger', Glauber Rocha suggested that while the Third World laments its general misery, the foreign observer cultivates a taste for that misery, not as a tragic symptom of a wider perverse system, but merely as a formal element in their field of individual interests. The Third World neither communicates its real misery to the 'civilised man', nor does the 'civilised man' truly comprehend the Third World's misery (Rocha 1965: 14).

Overall, images disseminated by the global media come to represent poverty as natural and endemic, as if little can be done about it except for palliative efforts. It is true that sometimes these images also call for urgency and intervention. However, these calls invariably offer audiences a limited range of options for action, usually confined to foreign aid, private-individual donations and/or military intervention. This portrayal legitimates, through passivity and naturalisation of poverty, the notion that it is acceptable for some to be in poverty.

In this comfort zone, poverty and famine continue to be 'associated with a dark non-white world, a place where tragedy and hopelessness reign and where one's success is determined by compassion' (Balaji 2011: 52). In creating this safety buffer, poverty's visual representation becomes opaque: the contrast between 'our' opulence and 'their' deprivation is removed. Instead, images of predominantly black women and children that come into our living rooms seem to have no connection with our own predominantly 'white' reality. They are the image of 'others' with whom we have little or no connection beyond our willingness to give them our leftovers. That is in essence the perverse yet powerful message that most of the images of poverty in the global news media communicate.

Once viewers are saturated with the same images appearing over and over again, then the audience is said to be suffering from 'compassion fatigue'. This thesis mainly blames television for bombarding spectators with images of human misfortune and, consequently, holds television accountable for trivialising suffering and blunting the spectator's charitable sensibility towards distant suffering. It is not only, as Lille Chouliaraki points out, television's inability to represent suffering as deserving of the spectators' emotions and actions, resulting in certain people and places being excluded (2006: 188), or just the fact that this exclusion means that television blocks images that take the spectators away from their comfort zone. What is in play is something more sinister: the way in which these images are standardised like any other market commodity, which the viewers are free to take or leave.

At the heart of this process is the marketisation of visual morality in which 'choice' is inscribed in the neoliberal discourses to denote the supposed ability to 'do something', when in reality it just fosters a different type of passivity and corruption. Indeed, most of the images disseminated by the global media outlets call for donations or pledges, rather than fundamental transformations.

If they were instead to call for such transformations, the images deployed would challenge inequality. In that case, most of the images we would see would reflect the appetite for fur, gold, diamonds, oil and wealth in general in our own societies rather than just the effects of this greed on others. They would put more emphasis on tax havens, military expenditure and corporate greed and link them to the present suffering of our fellow human beings. They would show the increasing degree of inequality in which the world lives, while transmitting a powerful yet very simple message of injustice rather than pity.

However, the global media does not work this way, and more than two decades after Carter's photo of a starving child watched by a vulture, the western world's camera lenses are focusing on Africa once more for an iconic image that can still convey the poverty message in the most traditional terms.

What We Do Not Know

Following Roland Barthes's (1981) concepts of *studium* and *punctum*, we could argue that the editorial dynamics that shape the gathering of images to illustrate, inform and editorialise news of poverty are subject to a widening gap between the *studium*, denoting the cultural, linguistic, and political interpretation of images of the poor, and the *punctum*, or ability to feel real empathy, and hence to relate to, the subject of the photographs.

Indeed, images of poverty in the news are never presented in a vacuum. As with any communicative action, these images are shaped by ideology, the main determinants being news cultures and organisational dynamics, which define the limits of the nature and usage of the images that represent poverty. In this context, photographers and television crews do not have to be told what type of images to look for – they already know this too well. Their work, rather, reflects Pierre Bourdieu's idea of *habitus* and therefore the dominant view of society within the journalistic field.

As Roland Barthes wrote, 'Society is concerned to tame the photograph, to temper the madness which keeps threatening to explode in the face of whoever looks at it' (1981: 119). Society can do this, he argued, through two means. One is to turn photography into art, to deprive it of madness so that by becoming an illusion, it can no longer be used to confront the individual with reality. This is the case with portrayals of poverty, as many of the more compelling and liberating images are found in galleries, not newsstands, or in books, rather than the evening news. The other is to generalise portrayals until they become banal in the eyes of the audience, stripped of their power to shock. No longer provocative, subversive or pensive, one could argue that this banality forms the fundamental basis of compassion fatigue.

Within these controls, it is no wonder that some of the more thought-provoking portrayals of poverty and some of the most captivating images emerge through retrospectives, collaborations with advocacy groups and non-profits, and reach the public outside of the typical editorial structures of traditional news media outlets. This is not to say these images are not finding their way into public discourses, as there are prominent examples of images that go against the norm, but it reflects how such visual journalism is treated as art, or as a niche discipline, or otherwise outside of mainstream news.

The end result of this dynamic is perverse: images that allow us to identify with the victims of poverty as equals and who are present, rather than the 'other' who is safely distant, are often rejected by the traditional media. Instead, the pictures that fit the standardised news values find their way into the global systems of news distribution. The editorial process, therefore, effectively tames the image as a journalistic genre and deprives it of its power to show the irrationality of poverty in a world that has so much wealth.

Not all images are bound by the same specificities. Maverick photographers, cartoonists and illustrators often provide glimpses of an alternative representation of the poor around the world. International news agencies and broadcasters, key players in the dissemination of global news, are none the less reluctant to carry these challenging images, not necessarily because of editorial censorship, but mostly due to procedural systems that impose limitations in the name of objectivity, taste and the market. For many photographers and camera people working for the global news media and trying to present a different aspect of poverty, the experience is similar: certain images will just not get through.

It is instead through other paths that alternative images manage to get through to the public. In the past, these included the creation of photographic cooperatives such as Magnum Photos, funded by Henri Cartier-Bresson, which included among others Robert Capa, David 'Chim' Seymour, George Rodger and William Vandivert, Rita Vandivert and Maria Eisner. In fact, the great majority of the challenging images on poverty are brought to us by photographers who operate outside the news-gathering systems and manage to sell their pictures to cooperatives and intermediaries who are capable of working beyond the usual editorial criteria.

More recently, there have been important efforts to disseminate alternative images of poverty, such as the case of AmericanPoverty.org. This is a project of the 'In Our Own Backyard' collective of photojournalists that has been capturing images of poverty across the United States. In doing so, the project tries to break through the normalised portrayal of poverty as a problem of 'others'. With poignant images of children, and photo series that reflect race and poverty but do not rely on racial stereotypes or clichéd portrayals, the AmericanPoverty.org project has adopted an unabashed social justice component to its work, and its mission: 'To use visual media to raise awareness about poverty in the United States, dispel inaccurate and destructive stereotypes about poor people and encourage action to alleviate poverty.'[3]

Their work resonates strongly with the work of photographers during the Great Depression of the late 1920s and '30s, and recognises the way images can convey an understanding of 'how the other half lives', to borrow from Jacob Riis's (1849–1914) work on New York slums. Their work does not suggest passivity, but embeds a call for change. However, while the project has received substantial news coverage, the images themselves are not filtered into regular news discourses; they remain the subject of books, gallery shows and travelling exhibitions.

The key for presenting alternative and more imaginative ways of visually representing poverty has been shown to be linked to the ability of photographers, camera people and news editors to detach themselves from the notion of objectivity. As Barbie Zelizer points out, one of the reasons photography rose to fill the space of chaos and confusion on September 11 was precisely because it deviated from the normal journalistic routines (in Zelizer and Allan 2002: 55).

Indeed, in the process of gathering images of poverty, objectivity has no place in modern journalism,[4] a principle perhaps best expressed in Milton Rogovin's words when he said, 'All my life I've focused on the poor. The rich ones have their own photographers' (Collins 2011). He also said: 'I wanted to make sympathetic portraits of the poorest of the poor that showed them as decent humans struggling to get by … that they were people just like us and should not be looked down upon.'[5]

In taking this approach, Rogovin, who was blacklisted by the House Un-American Activities Committee in the 1950s, gave an extraordinary lesson to all those who want to bring an understanding of poverty into the living room in alternative ways; that is, any photograph, video, or metaphor should honour the subject with the simple yet powerful idea of equality and respect.

It is a lesson that also reminds us that the gathering and dissemination of images require a dose of humility. Images, videos and metaphors, even with the most precise lens, can never truly capture the reality of poverty. It is too mobile, dynamic and changeable to be encapsulated in a short take or drawing. It is also a reminder of the fact that those holding a camera or a pen should have a 'unique responsibility' (Chouliaraki 2010: 520) to set themselves free from the idea of objectivity and to make symbolic representations of the world, its news and events.

Image Gathering

There are of course important exceptions to the standardised way in which global news media presents poverty. Some of the most interesting photographs of poverty in recent times were taken by Pulitzer Prize-winner Patrick Farrell during the hurricane season in Haiti in 2009. In one photo, a young boy retrieves a battered pushchair near his family's flooded home in Gonaives, just days after tropical storm Hannah hit that country. The boy is pushing the buggy through the mud, perhaps in an attempt to rescue what is left of a shattered life. The boy is almost naked and covered in mud. It is one of the few pictures disseminated by the global news media that actually presents a different face and one in which aesthetics are not as important as the powerful message the picture transmits.[6]

The picture suggests in a very subtle way the huge gap between the lives of people in that part of the world and our lives. What we would normally throw away, the buggy, is being rescued by the child. He is actively putting together a life torn apart by the disaster, pushing with resolution and determination. The image encapsulates the real story of the poor: survival and resistance, not passivity. Farrell, who works for the *Miami Herald*, describes one of the reasons why he was able to capture such a scene: 'I was on one side of a river that flooded. Suddenly, I saw this boy pushing the pushchair. I had a lot of empathy with the people in Haiti as I myself had seen some of my relatives and friends losing their homes also to hurricanes' (interview with the author, 12 November 2011).

He also explains why so many of his photos about the poor tend to be very different from other photographers in that they capture his subjects' dignity:

I have been asked many times how come my pictures are able to depict despair with such respect. When I was young and had started to work as a photographer I did not think a lot about it. However, now I know.

I treat them with respect. I only take the picture if I feel I am not intruding. No picture is worth taking if it disrespects the subject; after all it is their tragedy. (Ibid.)

Steve McCurry, despite being also a mainstream photographer, is another example of someone who captures images of poverty that present a more accurate and dignified semblance of people and places. When it comes to reflecting poverty, McCurry is one of the finest photographers today, as his work captures the essence of human struggle and joy. His work in Afghanistan is both powerful and revealing. In one of the photographs in his collection *In the Shadow of the Mountains*, titled 'School room in a ruined building',[7] he captures a group of children in a lesson at school. Boys and girls listen to one of their classmates reading, while the teacher writes something on what is left of a blackboard. The school has almost no walls and no roof whatsoever. Despite this, the children sit there on a locally made carpet, taking notes. It is the sense of dignified normality that seems so impressive, were it not for a man in the background looking over a wall at a soldier who seems to give instructions (McCurry 2007).

McCurry has a hard-earned reputation for amazing visuals of people all over the world, most of whom live in conditions of poverty. What McCurry has done, though, is show the humanity and dignity of the people he portrays, and the stunning beauty and vibrancy of the people and places he photographs. Amid rubble and poverty, his images try not to dehumanise. His strong portraiture work does not shy away from depictions of poverty and human suffering, but he does not emphasise or use clichéd images of poverty. Where McCurry shines, in his images of poverty, is through his positive reflections of humanity.[8] That we can talk about McCurry suggests, perhaps, there is another way.

Indeed, many photographers working directly for the mainstream media often produce interesting and challenging images of poverty. However, sub-editing processes are designed to standardise news content so it is easier to interchange content as a commodity in the international news market, and as a result most of these great pieces are lost or ignored. It is to the credit of the powerful images taken by photographers and the very few mavericks in editorial positions that, almost miraculously, we get to see a distinctive view of poverty in the international media landscape.

The fact is that 'most media material circulating across the continent is produced by Euro-American media organisations' (van Ginneken 1998: 71) and these organisations tend to apply editorial standards that reinforce prevalent views on poverty. The end result is that those in poverty are presented as passive and 'dependent' on other people (Kendall 2005: 93). News media organisations such as news agencies, which still control most of the systems of news content and material distribution, operate in ways that systematically demand a certain type of picture. This means that the news editors must re-code news material so that it fits the demands of global news markets.

Very few news agencies make room for 'balanced representation' in their coverage (Bielsa and Bassnett 2009: 81), while most rely on a set criteria in the selection of images to be used and distributed. This situation is made worse because photographers working for the agencies are in competition with each other, so most of them steer their work towards the mono-thematic commercial standards set by the decreasing number of buyers.

More importantly, not all photojournalists compete on a level playing field. Those working directly for the news agencies have precedence, making it harder to make a living from this profession. For those working independently, Latin American-based freelance photographer Gustavo Bauer points out:

> Once a group of pictures have been selected, then they are allocated in a database that is available for subscribers round the world. To some, it might appear surprising that at the end, news editors of media outlets all around the world tend to choose similar images, and very often even the same images despite having available a wide repository of pictures.[9]

In reality, news cultures that define the selection of news material are very similar across the world. In this context, the distribution systems tend to give indications as to which images are being used by other media outlets. As in most other areas of the news market, competition mostly promotes standardisation, as any photo taken or purchased needs to be re-sold to as many customers as possible. This means buying and then distributing pictures that respond to the expectations of the organisation and its clients. The inevitable outcome is that we get to see the pictures that are already in our heads.

Cartoons

Another area of visual journalism that plays an important part in the construction of the imaginary of poverty is the cartoon. However, the term 'cartoon' is now so widely used that an exact definition is elusive. Nevertheless, cartoons constitute one of the most important forms of political discourse in the media (Greenberg 2002: 181). Generally, a cartoon means a humorous or satirical drawing that tells a story or makes a statement in one or more pictures. One of the first publications to use cartoons to editorialise about poverty was *Punch* magazine in London, established in 1841 by Henry Mayhew and Ebenezer Landells. The magazine introduced the idea of a 'cartoon' as a comic drawing. The poor who appeared in the early cartoons were shown as 'labouring poor, dressed in rags and rejected by the authorities' (Reiss 2006: 394).

Over the years, cartoons that deal with poverty have developed more sophisticated ways of expressing and satirising the contradictions that surround it. Newspapers and magazines use cartoons to editorialise, and, contrary to photo-journalists, cartoonists are often given enough freedom to produce illustrations that simplify and satirise complex situations in the news. Nowadays, most cartoons tend to reflect the current affairs being discussed in the news agenda and therefore poverty is depicted only in those occasions in which it becomes news (for example, during famines and natural disasters, or in special feature articles).

However, on some occasions, cartoonists are able to introduce poverty in very creative and challenging ways into situations that apparently have nothing to do with poverty. One of these occasions was Mike Keefe's cartoon published in the *Denver Post* on 8 June 2011,[10] where we see what seem to be Wall Street executives running in despair, some jumping from buildings, reminiscent of the 1929 crash; one of them in the background is giving a dollar to a beggar who is asking for money besides a placard saying 'my portfolio is holding steady, ask me how' and wearing a T-shirt bearing the phrase 'chronic jobless'. The cartoon captures perfectly the paradox of the financial crisis, where the fall in wealth of the very few has taken over the news agenda. The real poor in this case, the beggar, is represented as calm and giving advice to the rich, as he knows what poverty means.

Zapiro, the pen name for South African cartoonist Jonathan Shapiro, has done this with great tact. Honing a career in a still-recovering post-apartheid country, Zapiro has brought humanity into his portrayals of the politics and often-fractious dynamics of South African society. His cartoons depicting corruption emphasise the cost to the populace of lavish spending.[11] His portrayal of inequality never shies away from the legacy that underpins the imbalance.[12] What Zapiro's work shows is a close relationship between the politics that editorial cartoonists so often emphasise and the societal and historic dynamics from which those politics emerge. It argues, through its symbolism, that the resonant image depicting the dynamics of 'today' is not confined to that moment, but reflective of its background. Work like Zapiro's shows that within even the most contemporary news topics around inequality and poverty there is a deep history that warrants recalling.

Even when working for the most partisan print media, cartoonists enjoy a freedom that very few photographers or illustrators can share. It is not only that they are given a wider range of options from which to select, but the editorial constraints and limits to their work are minimal: taste and the highest moral standards. Indeed, as Steve Bell, political cartoonist for the *Guardian* puts it: 'I'm always coming up against the problem of taste and I freely admit, I do transgress … I step over the line quite a lot but I think, well, you have to. It's almost your duty to do it if you can' (Preston SF Group 1995). Bell explains that he has had very little editorial interference:

> Generally I do my own editing. I don't submit roughs to the paper. I couldn't stand that, it would take years off my life. David Austin who does the Pocket cartoon, he goes in to the paper as he just lives round the corner. He, as a matter of course will submit six ideas and they'll use two. I said, what are you doing that for, you mad fool. He just says he likes to work that way. Some people do, but I couldn't stand it, I'll do my own editing and I decide what I'm going to do and do it, generally it goes in. Sometimes there's a problem with libel. (Ibid.)

There seem to be certain limits, but they are few and far between. Bell says that in the past he has 'once or twice' had a cartoon rejected and on a few occasions been asked to modify it:

> It doesn't happen very often. Recently I had to amend a couple. There was one about Aitken I had to paint out a couple of things I put at the bottom. Because he is actually suing them so they are very, very sensitive about that at the moment. Anything you do can jeopardise their position. The lawyers are very hot on that sort of thing. The other thing is that politicians do not generally sue for libel. I hope they don't anyway. (Ibid.)

In well-established newspapers and magazines, this degree of editorial freedom is the common experience of cartoonists. The two-time Pulitzer Prize winner, Michael Ramirez, whose cartoons are syndicated in more than four hundred newspapers, explains:

> Editorial cartoons should be smart and substantive, provocative and informative. They should stir passions and deep emotions. Editorial cartoons should be the catalyst for thought, and frankly speaking, if you can make politicians think, that is an accomplishment in itself. (Ramirez 2013)

For many cartoonists, despite their political preference, freedom to use satire is crucial in providing a strong message to the public. Signe Wilkinson, who was the first female cartoonist to win a Pulitzer Prize in 1992, points out that

> There are no limitations for cartoonists, there are limitations on what various publications are willing to print. I have an on-going relationship with my readers, which to me means that I don't take them for granted, and I don't insult their intelligence by avoiding certain topics. My strand is this: If any group of people, whether political, ethnic or religious wants the government to do something that will affect my life (laws, taxes, editorial freedom, whatever), that group has wandered into the political sphere and should be treated as any other political operative. (Heller 2002: 44)

Wilkinson's own work became controversial in November 2005 when she produced a cartoon on violence between black people in the *Philadelphia Daily News*. Her response was that she was only depicting reality and that 85 per cent of the homicide rate in that city was committed by blacks against other blacks. However, facts do not match in this case with satire, as in Philadelphia it is poverty and not race that is the defining feature regarding violence. Indeed, when it comes to poverty, and despite the levels of freedom enjoyed by cartoonists, they can also suffer from the same blind spots as news reporters and editors and also use 'objectivity' to justify their blindness.

As we suggested previously, the driving force in selecting the theme of the cartoon is often what is on the front page or has been the most important headline of the week. Therefore, if there is little or no coverage of poverty, cartoons will then tend also to minimise or ignore the subject altogether. Looking at the five newspapers with the highest circulation in the United States and their five counterparts in Britain between June and August 2011, we can see that had it not been for Somalia, the representations of poverty in cartoons would had been almost non-existent. From a total of 749 editorial cartoons from that period, only 67 were about poverty or inequality, of which 32 were about Somalia. Moreover, considering that the issue of Somalia only became a predominant feature of the news agenda in mid-July of that year, we could infer that this figure is low for the rest of the year.

Indeed, explicit news about poverty can be absent from print media for long periods of time. For example, looking at the work of Jeff Danziger, a *New York Times* political cartoonist we can observe that he had one cartoon on poverty published in the period described above.[13] This is not to suggest that this absence is somehow a deliberate action on the part of the cartoonists, but to remind ourselves of how closely the work of the editorial cartoonists is determined – and constrained – by the news agenda itself.

Despite the apparent freedom to 'create' representations of poverty that could in theory synthesise and denounce the inherent contradictions of inequality that lead to poverty, cartoonists are instead restrained from using cartoons that go too far from existing paradigms of understanding. In these paradigms, readers must work out the cartoonist's interpretation of events, the evaluation given to these events and their opinion. This is because editorial cartoons work 'principally by comparison and imagery', therefore requiring a specific context in which to be interpreted (Streicher 1967).

In terms of the representation of poverty and producing a satire of inequality to awaken the political conscience, the cartoonist's work will be often defined by a historical range of images which have remained 'strikingly consistent over at least the last hundred years' (Seymour-Ure 2008: 77). As with any other news media content used to report on or to depict poverty, the lesson is clear: despite its apparent editorial independence, cartoons do not operate in a vacuum.

Poor Television

In his work on representations of poverty on Irish television, Eoin Devereux points out that poverty is almost invisible on the screens, which is 'symptomatic of a greater invisibility, namely the lack of transparency of the social structure' (1998: 146). This conclusion could be easily extended to international networks such as the BBC and CNN, where the presence of poverty as a news item is structurally absent. While most networks have correspondents and editors for sports, politics, economics and, more recently, the environment, none of the leading networks from the US or Europe have 'poverty/inequality' correspondents.

The result is, as expected, that video images on poverty will only be made available when there is a media event that 'justifies' mobilising camera crews and equipment where poverty 'takes place', which is often far away. As discussed previously here, in places such as Africa this can mean that the availability of television images of poverty will be highly dependent on support from multilateral organisations, governments and NGOs. Gustavo Valdivieso, a former official working as the press coordinator for the Office of the United Nations High Commissioner for Refugees in Colombia suggests:

> Unless we provided all the logistics and support, it was very difficult to get the television crew of a major international broadcaster into a crisis area to see the appalling conditions in which people were living. My guess is that costs associated with the logistics play an important part in that decision. (Interview with the author, 12 March 2012)

Indeed, television is a complex and costly operation which is becoming increasingly dependent on using NGOs and the military to cover events in certain places, thereby compromising the 'objectivity' of its news reports (Aday et al. 2005: 3). In this context, covering poverty is not always the first choice for news editors when it comes to mobilising the tremendous logistics required to film in distant places.

Few crews from CNN International, Fox News, or the BBC will be mobilised to report about poverty 'in-house', unless it is related to media events such as natural disasters or riots, as exemplified by Hurricane Katrina in 2005 and the Tottenham riots in London in 2011. These, of course, are not the only priorities in deciding which events to cover. In a study of television coverage of strikes, Harmon and Lee argue that there is an element of social class that also may be at play in the selection of which event to cover, which calls for a more nuanced understanding of news coverage 'beyond points raised by political economy theory and declining resources' (2010: 501).

In addition, and against the backdrop of print media, television offers little background or context to the issues it reports, with detrimental effects to the way it presents images about poverty to its audiences. From studies carried out in the United States, we know that television news is slightly less likely than newspapers to provide structural reasons as the root causes of and possible solutions to poverty (Kim et al. 2010: 563).

Other determinants include editorial policy, which, as we have already discussed, tends to follow foreign policy. Hence, crude images such as those shown by CNN in its piece 'Famine widespread in Zimbabwe' broadcast on 10 October 2008 had completely disappeared by the following year, once there was a unity government in place with pro-Western allies in the cabinet. The famine or threat of famine had not disappeared but what *had* vanished was the willingness to show images that could undermine the new political arrangement, sanctioned by the West.

The other main issue is the nature of the images shown on television. Overall, those in poverty are rarely used as news sources by journalists. They do appear on the screens, but as inarticulate and hopeless people in which black women and children feature as symbolising poverty. Television news formats, which by nature are problematic in terms of a comprehensive communication of news, tend to focus on the manifestations of poverty and only provide an emotional but limited understanding of the problem.

The Power of Images

Arguably, visual representation of poverty is perhaps the single most influential factor in defining how the general public imagines poverty. Indeed, the way we think about poverty is shown to be dependent on how the issue is framed. When news media presentations frame poverty as a general outcome, responsibility for poverty is assigned to society-at-large; when news presentations frame poverty as the particular situation of a poor person, responsibility is assigned to the individual (Iyengar 1990: 19).

Nevertheless, we ought to remember that, in most cases, those images do not represent the reality they claim to have captured. As Susan Sontag pointed out, reality has always been interpreted through the reports that are associated with images:

But when in the mid-nineteenth century, the standard seemed finally attainable, the retreat of old religious and political illusions before the advance of humanistic and scientific thinking did not – as anticipated – create mass defections to the real. On the contrary, the new age of unbelief strengthened the allegiance to images. (Sontag 1971: 153)

In terms of the modern history of the media, the twentieth century was with little doubt the era of the image. However, while in the nineteenth century, painters such as John Martin allowed the public to re-imagine poverty in more critical ways, the subsequent century fixed our imagination to paradigmatic and static photographic images which supplanted reality and became reality in themselves.

The advent of film, photography and ultimately television standardised the imagery of poverty in a manner that allowed objective detachment from it, while providing a comfort zone between inequality and poverty as if they were not connected. For the first time in human history, we were able to see suffering without the fear or shame of our gaze being returned. With the benefit of news images as a screen that filters out and tames our responsibility for our fellow human beings, the moral connection between 'their' hunger and 'our' wealth disappears and is supplanted instead by the ethics of charity which assigned the western audiences voluntarism rather than responsibility.

However, the twentieth century also showed us that this is not the only thing that modern ways of capturing news images can offer us. They can also be a powerful tool to change perceptions and ideas on poverty in ways that translate into political mobilisation and action. Lewis Wickes Hine (1874–1940) once said that the great social peril is darkness and ignorance and that therefore we require light in floods. Hine, one of the most extraordinary photographers of poverty of all times, used his camera and the images he brought to the public as a tool for social reform (Freedman and Hine 1998).[14]

Hine's work became instrumental in mobilising the public and pressing legislators to change the child labour laws in the United States (Ang 2005: 89). His most influential photographs were those of child workers taken between 1908 and 1921. His photos were employed by the National Child Labour Commission to document children working in factories, mills, mines, canneries, farms and on the urban streets of the United States. More than 5,000 photographs – from his first diptychs and triptychs to the more interpretive and lyrical photo montages of 'Time Exposures' in 1914–15 – secured Hine's role as the 'Crusader with a Camera'. As Hine's reputation as a reformer grew, so did his status as a pioneer of documentary style, and Hine's admirers embraced and emulated both his courage and artistic vision (Pace 2002: 324). He died penniless and homeless, but left one of the most enduring legacies for those capturing and disseminating images of the poor.

In the tradition of such photographers, we should point out the greatest lesson of all in his legacy: that images of the poor in the news should incite and encourage social reform and not merely reflect suffering. As Julianne Newton writes of photojournalists, at their best, they are 'Covert artist[s] with an acute social conscience, intent on naming the nameless, revealing the contradictions of life, and exposing the emotions people would rather ignore or suppress beneath our supposedly rational culture' (Newton 2000: 50).

Conversely, it is important to remember that the type of work that Hine displayed requires re-assessing the prevalent news cultures and re-engaging with the notion of journalism's commitment to social justice. If we look back to the traditions of Walker Evans, or Jacob Riis, or the modern work of Steve Liss at AmericanPoverty.org, or of James Nachtwey, or Steve McCurry, we see a tradition of photojournalism as social justice. With their work and others mentioned in this chapter, there is a recognition that news images need not follow the same stereotypical frames and clichés they have, and that the stories images tell can do so with an embrace of humanity that provides an opportunity for captivating images to provoke change, and inspire equality.

6

Spinning Poverty!

On 4 January 1890, the *Leeds Mercury* newspaper in England published an article calling for donations with the headline 'The China Famine of 1888–89' (Issue 16,145). It was a news story based on what, by modern standards, would have been a press release sent to the paper by the North China Famine Relief Committee. It quoted a letter from W.V. Drummond, chairman of the committee, in which he explained how bad the situation was in that country and how much difference the help already given had made to the people experiencing the famine. The article then quoted another letter from Chang Yaoa, a local governor, whom Drummond introduces to the readers 'as a fine man'. In it, Chang appeals for additional aid, while also thanking the people in Britain for the donations already made.

The *Leeds Mercury* article shows not only how far anti-poverty campaigns go back in time, but also reminds us of how little things have changed. Indeed, this article has all the elements of today's modern public relations press releases, often sent by anti-poverty NGOs to media outlets in the West (van Leuven et al. 2013: 1). First, the issue or crisis is introduced by a westerner, who then goes on to select and confer legitimacy on the 'indigenous' voices and later explains the dilemma, while calling for humanitarian assistance and financial aid. Indeed, despite the fact that media campaigns have nowadays become far more sophisticated and a much better-funded exercise in political communication, they retain, nevertheless, a similar structure and many of the same features as their nineteenth-century predecessors.

Today, multilateral agencies, NGOs, think tanks and corporations invest heavily in media campaigns to establish relationships with stakeholders (Shumate and O'Connor 2010: 580) and to influence people's perception of poverty and development (Rideout 2011: 25); this is because these campaigns are instrumental in the articulation of news agendas, framing narratives and defining media representations of those in poverty.

These orchestrated efforts deployed by NGOs and intergovernmental organisations (IGOs) are crucial in determining not only which issues will become news stories, but also the subsequent public perception of those issues. These campaigns are part of propaganda efforts to influence, convince and mobilise the public towards supporting and funding specific anti-poverty actions. The reference to 'propaganda' is because it denotes unity in communication and action (Miller and Dinan 2007: 5), which describes better what is happening in the field. Hence, propaganda is more comprehensive as a term when it comes to describing and explaining what those promoting anti-poverty awareness and actions are doing, from the United Nations High Commissioner for Refugees in Colombia to children's charities operating in the Congo.

It also explains why, for example, events such as the 2010 earthquake in Haiti received so much coverage in the first week afterwards, compared to other similar tragedies, because many NGOs with access to the global media were already operating there. In fact, looking at news sources quoted by journalists over a sample of 63 articles published in January of that year in seven international newspapers, it is clear that many NGOs and international organisations capable of activating a media campaign were already in Haiti before the earthquake happened. As a result, the media found news sources and news shapers who were in the right place and who had in the eyes of the media the necessary authority to tell them the story. They also shared the same worldview, resources and in many instances and at many levels similar ideologies and discourses.

However, because of its intrinsic link with intentionality, the notion of propaganda has limited value as an explanatory framework when it comes to understanding efforts at mobilisation that seem to 'just happen' in the context of anti-poverty media campaigns. For this, we need to look instead at specific communicative and relational theory that deals with wider areas such as media campaigns, public relations and lobbying.

The other limitation imposed by propaganda in allowing us to examine the role of media campaigns in defining news coverage and media representation of poverty is the assumption of ideological coherence and unity of purpose (Ellul 1965; Domenach 1969). Although it might be argued that these are also propaganda, many anti-poverty efforts are not necessarily driven by ideology, at least not in the crudest sense, as there is no 'community' managing these campaigns with a homogeneous worldview. Instead, what the empirical data indicate is that these groups are made up of individuals and groups that in many cases not only do not share principles and values, but moreover deploy distinctive ideological agendas (Cullen 2010: 317) and compete for resources while nevertheless colluding with each other at certain times.

Therefore, in order to provide a critical and comprehensive assessment of the campaigns that promote anti-poverty actions, encourage mobilisation and that are also instrumental in the process of agenda setting, we need to study them in the context of the wider subject area of political communication, with particular emphasis on the role of public relations in manufacturing news stories about poverty that are effectively appealing to the news agenda. That is, we need to look at anti-poverty media campaigns as professional practices that relate to contesting agendas trying to provide distinctive directions to the themes being discussed in the media sphere.

Over the past hundred years, public relations have become one of the most influential forces in shaping public opinion (Miller and Dinan 2007). As a discipline, it includes both communicative and relational elements (L'Etang 2008: 18). In the realm of communicative elements, anti-poverty campaigns focus on developing news agenda themes and messages that are picked up by the mainstream media, which then bring the wider issues behind the campaign to their audiences' attention. In the jurisdiction of relational elements, media campaigns seek to foster, among other things, networks of individuals that promote a cause or idea and that provide framing to the news, for example, as news sources. In both cases, the intention is not only to pinpoint the subject or theme, but also to provide specific angles and perceptions so as to mobilise public opinion in a certain way, while triggering action in the form of policy making or fundraising.

This chapter discusses how these campaigns are designed and implemented, who is behind them and how they affect the media's coverage of poverty. In so doing, the chapter will look at the broader concept of 'media campaigns' (Lugo 2007: 26) and explore the role of public relations and lobbying in the articulation of poverty in media narratives. In so doing, it aims to understand the role of thematic orchestration in the agenda setting of anti-poverty campaigns and how these efforts are carried out by organisations and individuals.

Why Media Campaigns?

Multilateral organisations, government agencies, NGOs and other third-sector organisations have for a long time been well aware of how important propaganda in general and media campaigns in particular are in the context of achieving their goals and selling their policies. For example, when the United Nations (UN) civil service was established in 1946, the first UN Secretary General Trygve Lie appointed eight assistant secretaries-general, one of them an assistant secretary-general in charge of the Department of Public Information (DPI). This meant that the UN effectively gave 'public information' the same status as the other branches of the organisation (Alleyne 2003: 1).

In the modern era, these organisations are conscious that to achieve their targets it is crucial that they convince politicians and the public in the metropolitan 'centres' of power to divert resources to the urban and rural 'periphery' of developing countries, especially when it comes to legitimising and sustaining the bureaucracies that deliver these resources. These efforts are even more important when it comes to mobilising the public towards anti-poverty alleviation actions, especially in situations of crisis such as famines, natural disasters and pandemics.

The fact that many of these media campaigns are set up and managed by third-sector organisations is very relevant in this analysis. These organisations' propaganda efforts mainly focus on delivering messages using the mainstream media. As Martin Shaw observes, because of the limitations of other civil society institutions in the representations of global crises to wider audiences, the mass media plays an exceptionally critical role (1996: 72). This is a role that nevertheless requires first, the promotion of the theme or issue to guarantee media attention and, subsequently, the display of orchestrated efforts to 'manage' a specific type of coverage and representation to produce the angle and narrative required to mobilise the elites and the public.

These propaganda efforts can be categorised under the banner of media campaigns, which have been defined as orchestrated, but temporary, efforts to promote specific political goals by means of a given media outlet (Arterton 1987: 40). William Paisley points out two quite different but complementary definitions of public communication campaigns that can be found in the academic literature. One refers to the intention to influence other groups' beliefs and the other focuses on the methods employed, such as the use of promotional messages through mass channels to target audiences (cited in Dearing and Rogers 1996: 16). However, this last definition tends not to take completely into account the way in which agenda-setting and media campaigns are inherently part of the same political process (Lugo-Ocando 2011: 100).

Furthermore, as a process of communicative action, media campaigns go beyond the objective of affecting audiences and news agendas as they also pursue influence and political power. Therefore, anti-poverty media campaigns cannot be seen solely as extensions of marketing communication for fundraising, as they are political in every sense, with a clear and defined aim of providing power and influence to the bureaucracies that deploy them. More importantly, it is in this last context that these campaigns define and help shape the coverage of poverty by the global news media. The logistics, analysis and overall conceptualisation they provide to journalists who cover poverty is pivotal in defining their work.

This is because when a media campaign is launched, the aim of multilateral organisations, government agencies and NGOs is not only to mobilise support towards anti-poverty efforts and set a particular orientation for the news agenda, but also to acquire political influence that can be capitalised upon in terms of that organisation's worldly objectives, such as influence in the process of decision making, public policy design and access to resources.

Certainly, those organisations which manage these anti-poverty campaigns often become a 'point of reference' for the media, both as news sources and enablers of coverage, providing content and logistical support to media outlets. They are also a reference point for politicians who rely on them for general advice, designing policy, mobilising the public and helping stage-managed interventions. This additional leverage is nothing but power in its most traditional sense and, despite the genuine charitable status of many of these organisations, at the end of the day, they need to be mediators in the transaction of power and resources if they are to survive in an increasingly competitive environment.

It is against this background that anti-poverty media campaigns are designed and deployed by a series of institutions and organisations around the world such as the UN, multilateral organisations, government agencies, NGOs and other third-party organisations. In some cases, these are relatively well-funded organisations, such as USAID from the US and the Department for International Development (DFID) from Britain, in which case, the media campaigns tend to become part of a wider public diplomacy strategy. In others, such as Oxfam, Save the Children and the Red Cross, they have a widespread network of supporters that guarantee some stable income. Media campaigns here fulfil the purpose of enabling corporative action by these organisations and their internal bureaucracies in delivering aid, sustaining existing programmes and providing intervention capabilities and influence over policy making. Finally, there is a multiplicity of medium and small organisations that deal with poverty or related issues that are completely dependent on public appeals or that receive public resources and which tend to focus on very timely and particular issues, for example, eye operations for children in the developing world, access to a clean water supply and women's education. Hence, one cannot underestimate the function of these campaigns in legitimising the same organisations that articulate them.

Despite the fact that many of these organisations pursue different types of outcomes, alleviation of poverty is nevertheless the common denominator for most of them. Therefore, the key media strategy is to generate a news agenda that a) raises awareness about poverty and b) provides a sense of direction in the development and implementation of effective anti-poverty efforts. Fundraising campaigns can, however, take very different forms according to the issues and areas with which the organisation is involved. Furthermore, as access to public resources and donation has become increasingly limited, the inevitable consequence is competition among these organisations.

From the United Nations' High Commissioner for Refugees (UNHCR) to the charity Save the Children, they all compete in a market, not only for resources in the face of budget allocation and fundraising, but also for branding, as this ultimately guarantees the survival of the bureaucracy. Indeed, despite collaboration between the different organisations, each poverty crisis is still a race for media attention, fundraising and political leverage. The ultimate measure of their effectiveness is the amount of funds raised and which organisation received the most media attention for their own particular cause.

Exploring the Basics

Despite major contributions in the field (Dogra 2012; Naude et al. 2004; Sisco et al. 2010; Swanger and Rodger 2013), more research in the area of anti-poverty media campaigns is needed before we can fully understand their nature and characteristics. The fact remains that there is still a great deal we do not understand about the nature of media campaigns, especially about those that concentrate on anti-poverty efforts. We know very little about the frameworks in which they are designed and the details of ideological networks that articulate common action. There is an overall need for a more comprehensive and deep critical theory that can assess their role in society, one that can provide understanding of their strategic importance in the set of political communications of anti-poverty agendas in the construction of social reality. This, however, goes beyond the scope of this book and would certainly merit a monograph on its own, such as the extraordinary volume *Representations of Global Poverty* by Nandita Dogra (2012). Let us say for now that they are one of the most important communicative resources shaping the global news agenda about poverty.

To this day, the epistemology on media campaigns has mostly concentrated on how they can affect public debate and audiences' attitudes towards poverty during election campaigns (Arterton 1987; Manheim 2011), but we still do not understand fully how they articulate and enable political mobilisation for other causes. The concept of 'media campaigns' has largely been defined by political communication studies (Arterton 1987; McNair 1995; Negrine and Lilleker 2002) and public relations literature (Grunig 1992; L'Etang and Pieczka 1996; Parkinson and Ekachai 2006). In both areas, the epistemology on media campaigns has included both normative and critical approaches. Nevertheless, there is general agreement on the defining characteristic features of these campaigns, such as orchestration, emphasis and intentionality.

These campaigns to fundraise or mobilise public opinion and politicians in favour of a humanitarian cause have been conceptualised as either public relations media campaigns, when launched by a group or organisation for the purpose of image-management/relational networking/reputation, or as media advocacy, when they are based on favourable orchestrated efforts, delivered by the media itself in order to address an issue which seemingly concerns the community (Dearing and Rogers 1996: 4).

The aim of media advocacy is to create awareness, thereby triggering action and ultimately promoting the public good (Lloyd 1973; Seib and Fitzpatrick 1994; Sallot et al. 1998; and Somerville 2001). Hence, campaigns should be considered as discursive acts and as such they are constituted in a variety of ways so as to maintain or restore the status quo (Wodak 2004: 8).

According to this alternative framework, a wide variety of media reportage can then be categorised as a media campaign, frequently taking on a discursive function that constructs misrepresentations of poverty, race and immigration, even where the main players have no intention of doing so (Lugo 2007: 23). This is not to say that these campaigns are not primarily designed and implemented in order to encourage donations and financial support; but to emphasise that, they also serve a wider range of interests as discussed above.

Dealing with Poverty

Jonathan Benthall begins his book *Disasters, Relief and the Media* by citing a senior aid official interviewed by *The Times* of London about a disaster in which a boat from Somalia was hijacked by an armed gang that raped and slaughtered seventy passengers who were trying to escape from Mogadishu. The official in question said that such a tragedy was in a way 'good news' as it would help divert attention from the media to the wider crisis confronted by that country, which the official described in the report as the 'worst holocaust since the second world war' (1993: 1).

The episode illustrates two key issues that require further discussion. One is the need to attract media attention; the other is the official's tone and words. With regards to the first, we have already mentioned several of the reasons why organisations would want to orchestrate and amplify anti-poverty campaigns, which in many cases have little to do with the poor themselves but with the bureaucracy's desire to perpetuate itself. These include fundraising, political leverage and public diplomacy.

During the crisis in Somalia in 2011, for example, USAID went out of its way to inform the media about how the rebels had blocked their efforts to deliver food and medical assistance to the people. This was a crude way of using these types of crises to exercise power. Nevertheless, many other organisations went about things quietly, using the crisis as an appeal for fundraising.

The second issue is far more complex and problematic, because it makes us question these organisations' legitimacy in the context of what should be an act of media transparency. It also goes to show that overall they have an excessive influence in shaping news and too much power in determining which images and voices we are allowed to see and hear. Their ability to provide logistics, access to news sources and knowledge with regards to poverty is so overwhelming that, in the end, they contribute to the distortion of the news on poverty while feeding upon this same dynamic.

There are several reasons why these organisations have become so important in setting the news agenda internationally over the years, especially in the light of where and when news on poverty is manufactured.

About 80 per cent of the world's population lives in developing countries, marked by low incomes and high poverty, high unemployment and low levels of education (Stiglitz 2006: 26). Furthermore, disasters hit the poorest parts of the globe the hardest because more often than not the infrastructure is simply not there to resist the disaster's impact or to support the victims after the event. Of those killed or affected by disasters each year, 98 per cent come from the developing world. The average disaster toll in the poorer countries is over a thousand deaths per incident, whereas when disasters happen in wealthier countries, the average death toll is 23. The impact of disasters is extremely uneven, as is their reporting and perception (Franks 2006: 281; Franks 2013: 51).

Therefore, it is almost inevitable that the global news outlets' coverage concentrates on the developing nations as it is there that these phenomena mostly occur. Nevertheless, the numbers of correspondents and news bureaus in developing countries has shrunk at a remarkable speed in the past twenty years or so (Harding 2009). Facing these constraints, and despite the good intentions of some working within the news organisations, dispatches on poverty are now almost always limited to tragedies, media events and to the occasional celebrity visiting a country to 'adopt' a child, promote a noble cause, or draw attention to a crisis of biblical proportions.

In an increasing number of cases, news stories in the 'poor world' are covered only because someone else is footing the bill, what some authors have called 'news subsidy' (Berkowitz and Adams 1990; Kiousis et al. 2009; Lewis et al. 2008b). In many cases, media packages are produced and distributed to the media without a journalist setting foot in the place being reported on, while logistical support is provided to media covering specific events. Therefore, poverty is managed like any other topic by spin doctors, who deliver both media attention and tone, while the media becomes more and more embedded in supporting organisations' narratives, subsequently embracing their discourses on poverty in their own news.

What is happening with the news coverage of global poverty is exactly what is happening in the rest of the media sector, described eloquently and in detail by Nick Davis in Flat Earth News (2008) and studied in depth by Justin Lewis, Andy Williams and Bob Franklin (2008a): the increasing presence in the media space of public relations-generated content in the face of diminishing resources in the newsroom. Indeed, while many newsrooms around the world are dramatically reducing resources and personnel, the anti-poverty organisations are dedicating more to the dissemination of their own agendas.

Furthermore, as Linda Polman points out, a significant proportion of aid organisations' budgets is devoted to press and publicity. It is a vicious circle in which these agencies depend increasingly upon the media for publicity, while the media depends more and more upon the agencies to tell them where the stories are (2010: 39), provide quotes and embed them into their next mission. One could argue that while in the 1980s, the aid agencies would jump onto the media bandwagon to try to gain exposure, today not only do they drive the bandwagon, but they also decide where the horses should go.

Not all global media outlets rely entirely on the logistics of multilateral organisations or third parties to reach those places where tragedies are unfolding. News agencies such as Associated Press, Thomson Reuters, AFP, Bloomberg, EFE and ANSA still have a widespread network of correspondents and stringers who produce an important amount of news and who are relatively easy to move into these zones; as other media outlets pull out from certain places, news agencies are then requested to do more. These agencies provide the international news content which is published and broadcast by the mainstream media in the western world.

In light of decreasing coverage on poverty and in the face of humanitarian tragedies, some news agencies have fostered very important initiatives that allow the use of news about impending disasters to raise awareness about humanitarian issues in a proactive way, allowing authorities and the public to mobilise before it is too late. AlertNet, for example, is a free news service run by the Thomson Reuters Foundation covering crises worldwide, providing information on natural disasters, conflicts, refugees, hunger, diseases and climate change. The website is directed at relief workers, donors, policymakers, researchers, students, journalists and the general public. This is one of the types of services that continue to highlight the so-called 'forgotten emergencies', while providing NGOs and third-party sector with news material that they can use in their media campaigns.

Having said that, the nature of the stories on poverty and the places in which famines and other tragedies, such as remote places in Africa and Asia, often requires a logistical effort to mobilise people and equipment that is so demanding that the global news media is dependent on the support of the military (including forces such as the UN blue helmets, NATO and even local militias), multilateral organisations such as the

WHO, UNICEF and, increasingly, on NGOs such as Oxfam, the Red Cross and *Médecins Sans Frontières* to get to the places where these disasters and tragedies are happening. The problem is that each of these institutions has its own agenda and competing ideology, which in turn defines and frames the news stories.

Operation Poverty

In his defence of P.I. Coblenz in the *Gaceta Renana*, Karl Marx observed:

> When a part of the people, and the most numerous by the way, see itself affected by a sudden and terrible calamity and no one even talks about this calamity or considers it as an issue for consideration and discussion, then the majority of the people will inevitably reach the conclusion that the others are unable or unwilling to talk about this tragedy. (1841: 175)

Tragedies such as famines and earthquakes receive coverage because they represent events that are newsworthy for both the media and their audiences. Nevertheless, not all tragedies receive the same amount of attention and most of the media tend to retreat and ignore the aftermaths (Smith et al. 2006; Harding 2009; Moore 2010). Issues such as proximity, possible historical links between the events and a former colonial power and the presence of westerners define what is covered in the periphery, especially with regards to poverty. Occasionally there might be a remembrance programme after one year and that would usually be the end of the story, but mostly after the initial media attention, the people and places affected disappear under the radar.

So let us start by recognising the important and, in many cases, very useful role of humanitarian media campaigns launched and managed by multilateral institutions, NGOs, third-party organisations and media outlets. These campaigns are a beacon in the often overcrowded media space, which is dominated by black holes that swallow the attention, resources and energy of editors and journalists around the world. It is because of some of these media campaigns that not only do we get to know about famines, disasters and tragedies in many parts of this planet, but also that some attention is still directed towards the people and places affected in the aftermath of these tragedies.

In helping to bring such issues to the attention of the public, these campaigns have been instrumental in disseminating news, raising awareness and encouraging both governments and the public to engage with the matter. For example, it was NGOs who brought to the attention of news media issues relating to poverty and social exclusion in the context of technological innovation such as the issue of a 'digital divide' (Kovacs 2006: 431). It is, on the other hand, campaigns about refugees from the UNHCR that keep reminding us about ongoing conflicts, such as in the Congo or Colombia which would otherwise be likely to be dropped from the radar.

Media campaigns on poverty differentiate from public campaigns in that they are mainly directed towards getting the attention of the news media and using this to convey specific messages. They can be part of wider campaigns that include advertising and lobbying; however, because of budgetary constraints, many media campaigns have little or no resources for paid advertisements about specific events and, therefore, are almost wholly dependent on public relations efforts to gain media space and airtime. There is, therefore an important relational element in these efforts, which often require not only close links with journalists and editors in order to access this space, but also a provision of accessible news sources and news shapers in the form of a network of 'experts' made available to the media.

Humanitarian campaigns operate mostly on a temporary basis, although they sometimes relate to structural issues. This is in the sense that they are designed and implemented to gain media attention in the framework of a specific time period, either to raise awareness about an event or to use this event to promote a cause or an objective. Public relations officials and press officers, many of them former journalists, understand the dynamics of newsrooms around the world and they exploit this knowledge to effectively target stories in the global media. They are aware that media outlets tend to prioritise hard news stories and will only provide feature stories, which require far more time and space, when they have some sort of exclusivity in relation to them. As a former officer for Oxfam puts it:

> The effort to provide elements and content revolving around issues that can translate into hard news will attract the attention of several media outlets at the time, even if the space and attention span is less. Hence, to focus the resources on issues that can lead to hard news pays off. (Interview with the author, 12 September 2011; identity withheld)

The campaigns are carefully planned and they include developing media information packs, organising press conferences, providing experts to be interviewed and logistical support to mobilise journalists to 'poor areas', where tragedies such as famine take place. They also perform media monitoring, visits to the media, events for journalists and editors and general support for reporters trying to produce a story on the issue.

In every single sense, media campaigns deployed and managed by the anti-poverty community are very professional operations that emulate public relations exercises carried out in the corporate private sector, whether this is raising funding for children in Africa or trying to promote workers' rights in Central America (Armbruster-Sandoval 2003: 553). The image they project is that they need to intervene; they sell a product: the idea that resources allocated to them in the form of budget and donations, and western intervention in general, will make things better. In a manner of speaking, these campaigns do improve things, although only as temporary palliatives to structural pain and suffering.

However, by focusing almost entirely on alleviation efforts and aid, these campaigns reinforce the worst features of the news coverage of poverty. They also help frame the news stories in ways that appeal for help and somehow facilitate intervention. Experts used as sources will generally concentrate on impending dangers, and only infrequently discuss the structural inequalities that led to the situation in the first place. For fear of offending or upsetting potential donors, these campaigns generally tend to obviate critical analysis, and try to avoid discussing issues such as inequality, in particular.

Another problem with these campaigns is that most people behind them have a very similar background to the journalists covering the same issues. For example, NGOs are generally staffed by well-educated, white upper- and middle-class professionals, often adept in policy analysis and legal issues (Wall 2003: 37). Public relations managers and press officers from multilateral organisations will be former journalists and people educated in similar institutions to those in the newsroom. The result is a natural reinforcement of the pack mentality, which encourages similar views and approaches.

Justifying Spin

Another important consideration is the fact that most media campaigns on poverty are normally organised around crises such as famines or natural disasters. Some are also launched to coincide with particular events such as the G7 gatherings or the Davos summit meetings of world leaders. Others use instead commemorative events, such as the anniversary of a particular famine, to highlight the issues which they want to address. The intentions, directions and focus vary from issue to issue depending on the organisation or institutions which launch them and the broad areas in which they operate. However, these campaigns have some things in common, as they are both thematic and temporary.

Having a theme upon which to focus allows these campaigns to pitch the content they produce and to frame the news about it in a certain way. For some organisations with a well-defined function such as UNICEF, Save the Children or Operation Smile, the theme is, generally speaking, straightforward; in this case, the welfare of children. Some other organisations might find it more difficult to determine the focus around which to build their media campaigns.

Overall, the fundamental quest by those managing these campaigns is making poverty news. Nevertheless, the aim is not to raise awareness about the issue per se, although this is often stated in their principles and written objectives, but to trigger actions and responses in the form of resources and policies. Hence, media campaigns use poverty as a theme to mobilise the public and elites, to gather resources and to gain influence among those who develop policy and make decisions.

The other important aspect of these types of media campaigns is that, since they are thematic, they tend to operate on a temporary basis. This means that they concentrate on certain events and use them to promote their objectives, lasting for only a specific period of time. In so doing, they get on top of the news waves created by certain events and ride on them to disseminate their messages. Famines, hurricanes, earthquakes and conflicts, among others, are often used by multilateral organisations and NGOs to provide content on poverty to the media and frame the news. Overall, one could say that non-governmental players have become increasingly effective in advancing their agendas and disseminating their messages in international affairs (Zhang and Swartz 2009: 47).

A few campaigns, such as Make Poverty History (MPH), have tried, with mixed results, to deal with more structural issues. In the strict sense of what is being discussed here, MPH was an advocacy campaign, which contained some media elements. It was launched from 2005 onwards in various countries by aid and development agencies to raise awareness of global poverty and achieve policy change by the government as part of the wider initiative 'Global Call to Action Against Poverty'.

One of the most interesting features of this campaign was that it aimed to bring into the debate tangible commitments for cosmopolitan solidarity by 'creating obligations towards people suffering outside the nations taking part in it'. In order to do so, the MPH campaign created public spaces within national media for the formation of consensus to extend citizenship beyond national borders (Nash 2008: 168).

This campaign had at its core issues of inequality and debt reduction and used a series of themes to bring these issues to the attention of the audiences and overall to mobilise public opinion to change policy regarding debt. Depending on the country, the different campaigns under the umbrella of MPH in each country focused on different issues according to the specific circumstances, although most of these campaigns related to issues such as the Millennium Development Goal, foreign aid, trade and inequality.

These campaigns, however, had limited success and after a while they lost impetus as some of their key supporters withdrew. Criticising the disbandment of the MPH campaign in Britain: Alex Callinicos points out,

> I suspect that the disbanding of MPH has a lot to do with the interests of the big NGOs that dominated it. A permanent coalition would have got in the way of their own fundraising and recruitment activities. Off the back of MPH, Oxfam has launched a campaign for a million pledges to 'help end poverty once and for all'. I hope people do sign up to Oxfam's campaign. But it's a pity Oxfam doesn't have the democratic internal procedures that would give its supporters a say in major policy decisions such as this one. For the truth is that scrapping MPH was an utterly shameful decision. It can only promote the belief that those who currently dominate the world are benevolent figures who will, with a few pushes from below, continue to take 'small steady steps forwards'. But this is a lie that helps to kill millions every year. (Callinicos 2006)

Another key problem of these campaigns was that instead of focusing on the idea of poverty and growing inequality as a global problem, they embrace instead the traditional view of the 'problem' of Africa and 'we' as Africa's possible saviours:

It is certainly the case that MPH was not based on the propagation of derivative African images. Nevertheless, when one looks at the small number of campaign images of poverty that were employed, and when one considers the literatures – spoken and written – of MPH and its spokespeople, it is clear that Africa was the reference point for almost all campaign material. The MPH website had four images of people from the Global South, three of which were African – and all of the three were children. (Graham 2010: 398)

In the end, the MPH campaign became a year-long effort which had only limited success, as debt reduction was offset against already reduced credit accounts. Only a few poor countries could claim that they were any better off after the campaign. The MPH campaign did, however, introduce the idea of 'justice and not charity'; it attempted to create a frame of global responsibilities by building a new type of imagined community (Nash 2008: 172), but not without great opposition and struggle.

Despite these campaigns' limitations, global news media are particularly prone to be influenced by them 'as only a few news organisation are capable of financially sustaining a vast network of reporters and correspondents around the world' (van Ginneken 1998: 130).[1] Africa is in fact one of the worst covered areas in the world in terms of the number of news bureaus and correspondents assigned to the region. Therefore, media campaigns fill an information deficit when it comes to bringing issues relating to poverty to the public's attention. It is not only the media that are reminded about poverty by these campaigns, but also key institutions on the world stage. For example, as Sarah Babb points out:

> By the end of the 1980s, after half a decade of downplaying poverty, the World Bank suddenly rediscovered the issue of poverty. The apparent impetus for this revival was a new alliance between anti-poverty NGOs and sympathetic members of the US Congress who had warned of the dire consequence of the structural adjustment programmes in developing countries. (2009: 164)

This seemed at the time a clear indication of how campaigns, in a wider sense, could help focus the agenda on poverty. Looking back, however, one could also argue that the World Bank was more interested in gaining the support of Democrats in Congress in their effort to convince a reluctant

US government to recapitalise the bank as an explanation for the Bank's new interest in poverty.

Another crucial way of understanding how these media campaigns operate is to examine the way in which they find and target interlocutors in the mainstream media. Few global news organisations have correspondents exclusively dedicated to issues such as poverty, social exclusion, or development. Therefore, NGOs and multilateral organisations hire staff who deal exclusively or mainly with the subject and provide content that is then picked up by the media or logistical support for non-specialist journalists who are covering these issues. These organisations have specialised databases to know who to contact and what to offer which creates a particularly effective interaction between their organisations and the news media.

The X Factor

With so many challenges and limitations, including the fact that poverty in itself seems to be rarely appealing as a news item, it is difficult to understand how these campaigns have any success at all in promoting anti-poverty agendas. Indeed, most press officers interviewed say that it is becoming more difficult to access media space, unless these organisations invest heavily in public relations. Decreasing newspaper sales, audience fragmentation and news 'tabloidisation' in general have made poverty a difficult theme to 'sell', especially when there are no catastrophic events to justify sending a correspondent, let alone a television crew, to far-flung places. In this context, traditional correspondents become more and more 'parachutists' (Sambrook 2010: 18), while in order to save money, news desks move them around constantly to cover complex realities; their presence in those places must be financially justified in terms of ratings and sales.

It is important also to highlight that multilateral organisations, NGOs and third-sector groups are increasingly resorting to celebrity culture to tap into the media agenda (Cooper 2008: 11). By appointing celebrities as good-will ambassadors, these organisations not only obtain media exposure but, in some cases, manage also to get support from the public relations machinery behind these celebrities. Music concerts, television appeals by movie stars and news coverage around well-publicised child adoption have become, over the years, a common feature of promoting poverty issues. Another important aspect in the use of celebrities is that their intervention takes place within media events that are 'staged and broadcast live' (Negrine 1996: 172). One of the best-known and more successful of these cases was Band Aid, founded in 1984 by Bob Geldof and Midge Ure to raise money for famine relief in Ethiopia. Indeed, as some authors have already pointed out, the 1984 Ethiopian famine was not picked up by the western news media until very late, despite urgent warnings from different sources (Philo 1993: 106). Among the several elements that mobilise the news media to highlight a story such as this is of course the presence of a celebrity who can organise media events and use their own public appeal to attract media attention. These media events allow promoters to manage and benefit from news content as the celebrities' presence confers legitimacy to the message and validates the role of the organisations, institutions and charities behind the event.

None the less, the problem with media campaigns that use celebrities to create and commodify news audiences is that celebrities create a false linkage between consumption and the need for aid. In so doing, they legitimise not only consumption but also their own lifestyles as presumably having a positive impact on poverty relief. For example, in looking at the Product RED campaign launched by the singer Bono, some scholarly research has found that it gave a lower priority to treating disease than to the social and environmental relations that underpin the production and trade of the goods sold under the campaign's umbrella. This process, also known as 'commodity fetishism' – a term first used by Marx – is not new in capitalist relationships. However, what is new in the context of the Product RED campaign was its deployment by celebrities in connecting consumption and aid (Richey and Ponte 2008: 722).

New media campaigns on poverty now tend to be designed as show business, which is made explicit by the use of celebrities. Media campaigns are now being constructed as dramas, 'intended to elicit strong emotions and to create emotional involvement' (Nash 2008: 173). However, in placing the emphasis on theatricality, they not only reinforce superficial views on poverty in news coverage but also undermine the public's ability to rationalise the issue in ways that can really address a structural solution rather than just palliative measures.

Moreover, celebrity culture promotes social inequality under the guise of charity, in which the powerful and famous become 'heroes' as they bring relief and hope to the excluded and dispossessed. The higher up the social scale, the more recognition the celebrity receives when they make a philanthropic gesture, despite the fact that their lavish lifestyle contrasts abysmally with the aid recipients', something that is rarely mentioned in news reports. This is another main problem with media campaigns using celebrities: by promoting consumption of celebrity culture and lifestyle without questioning the structural issues that make this lifestyle of excess possible, these campaigns make inequality not only acceptable but also desirable.

In this narrative, what it is important is the elites' good deeds, not the enormous inequality that characterises their relationship with the recipients of those deeds. When celebrities visit a place to promote a cause, the campaign managers often make sure that difficult questions are not asked and press conferences usually happen in tightly controlled environments.

When the singer Madonna travelled to Africa in 2006 with her then-husband film-maker Guy Ritchie, 'to help fight poverty and the problem of HIV and AIDS', the couple ended up adopting a child from Malawi. According to media reports at the time, 'the boy's father, Yohane Banda, told the media: "I know he will be very happy in America."' (BBC, 11 October 2006). The parents were supposedly unable to look after him because they were poor. Instead of the media asking why the parents felt obliged to give their son to strangers who would take him away to a foreign country, the reports simply focus on the celebrity's generosity in bringing that child to the West and providing him with a living standard that his siblings could never dream of. Neither did the media question why, if the couple was so concerned about this child, they did not give money to help the whole family so the child could stay with his parents and siblings. Many celebrity adoptions are subject to very similar questions and are equally problematic.

Most of the media are silent, uncritical and on the whole complacent in their coverage of celebrities paying visits to disaster areas, only to return shortly afterwards to the comfort zone of their own lives. This is because this coverage tends to be staged by media campaigners as media events in the context of the celebrities' private life, whose engagements are supposedly carried out in 'their own time'. Research shows that celebrity humanitarian interventions with regards to poverty are well received by the public, precisely because celebrities' luxurious private lives are often omitted in the news reports (Van den Bulcka and Panis 2010: 242). By framing these events as public events while setting strict access barriers to the celebrities' private lives, the campaigners secure overwhelmingly favourable and uncritical news coverage that does not question the overall context of inequality.

Some scholars have called this the 'celebrity–consumption–compassion complex' (Goodmana and Barnessa 2011), which refers to the behaviour of 'development celebrities' (those using their image to deal with issues of poverty and development policy). However, these issues are as much about everyday events, materials, technologies, emotions and consumer acts as they are about the mediated constructions of the stars who now 'market' development:

> Moreover, this complex is constructed by and constructs what we are calling 'star/poverty space' that works to facilitate the 'expertise' and 'authenticity' and, thus, elevated voice and authority, of development celebrities through poverty tours, photoshoots, textual and visual diaries, websites and tweets. In short, the creation of star/poverty space is performed through a kind of 'materiality of authenticity' that is at the centre of the networks of development celebrity. (Ibid.: 82)

This 'celebrity–consumption–compassion complex' is not limited to movie stars or sport personalities. Increasingly we see other members of the elites receiving comparable treatment as their image managers employ similar public relations tactics, for example, philanthropist millionaires such as Melinda and Bill Gates, who are now beyond the criticism of the media.

To be sure, the celebrity-driven campaign not only includes the use of famous people but also the 'celebritisation' of institutions and themes which problematises the way western publics are informed, by staging narratives that are superficial and which tend to focus on victims and saviours. It makes it also more difficult for critical journalists to question the legitimacy of sources and what they say. More important, this 'celebrity cult' which now is embraced by many NGOs (Verma 2003: 150), seems to have further usurped the true voices of those in poverty and to have been designed to appease genuine protest.

This celebrity treatment is of course not gratuitous, as it transfers responsibilities regarding poverty to the private sphere while depoliticising the debate, as it provides the appearance of neutrality so as to be able to achieve 'consensus' in the face of donation, adoption and many other voluntary actions. It also allows a news coverage of poverty that not only bypasses the inequality issue, but that seems to settle any further confrontational debate and commit it to a specific and very safe realm. This is the real danger of such celebrity campaigns: setting ground rules for superficial and uncritical news coverage of poverty.

The Real Limitations

Overall, the main problem with anti-poverty propaganda is that, in general, it follows similar patterns to those trailed by the news coverage of news media. In concentrating on the manifestations and not the root cause of poverty (which, we have argued, is inequality), anti-poverty propaganda tends to reinforce current trends on reporting poverty rather than helping to create an alternative matrix in order to foster critical thinking and action. Instead, humanitarian campaigns aggravate the situation because they reinforce mainstream discourses of poverty that fail to question inequality – as we have seen in the case of celebrities.

The fact that so many humanitarian campaigns have the interests of the campaigners and not of the people at their heart means that the framing and news content derived from them often reinforce the worst features already present in the news coverage of poverty. With some important exceptions, they tend to rely on providing support to cover issues such as famines, earthquakes and other tragedies, which becomes an exercise in which the 'urgent' kills the 'important'.

Indeed, critical examination of policy and structural issues by media analysis is relegated to second place by the urgent need to persuade rich donors to address the urgency of the situation. Because of this, humanitarian media campaigns contribute to reinforcing this lack of criticism by postponing the discussion of controversial issues, this despite the fact that many of them do make reference to fair trade and changes in legislation. Nevertheless, in the majority of cases, it is the campaigns that deal with specific events that occur more frequently and are better resourced, that end up being more influential in this vast group of campaigns. Critiques of the structural issues that lead to those crises in the first place are suppressed, to avoid upsetting and alienating potential donors.

Moreover, as these media campaigns are managed by multilateral organisations and third-party players, they tend to convey the same discourses that highlight poverty as the issue rather than inequality. In so doing, references to inequality have become even less visible in the debate and this is precisely not the type of spin that anti-poverty thinking and action requires.

7

The Emergence of
Alternative Voices

Since the publication of UNESCO's report *One World, Many Voices* (MacBride 1980), there has been a growing consensus among scholars, news people and the international community in general about the need for developing nations to have their own voice on the world media stage. This consensus has been reached in part because of a growing awareness about the requirement to empower those in poverty so they can articulate their own responses, in their own terms, to the challenges they face.

Where there is not so much agreement is in defining the form and nature of the media provisions these countries and societies ought to have. For example, there is still reluctance in some sectors to accept that due to market failure, the state has a fundamental role in the creation, promotion and sustainability of public service news media outlets (Garnham 1994; Jakubowicz 2007; Morris and Waisbord 2001; Ward 2005) that can offer somehow a less ethnocentric reporting.

Indeed, beyond narrow neoliberal preconceptions, most of the more successful media provisions for international news relied and still depend upon the active presence of the state with important support from public finances, from the state-owned and taxpayer-funded BBC in London to the state-owned and largely state-subsidised Al-Jazeera network in Doha.[1] Other state-sponsored news media outlets include France 24, Euronews, Russian Television, CCTV from China, Prensa Latina from Cuba and Telesur from Venezuela, while news agencies such as Inter-Press Services (IPS) would not have survived in their current form without support from governments, the United Nations and other multilateral institutions. The point being, that contrary to the prevalent neoliberal assumption, the facts on the ground tell us that alternative media provisions would not be viable without public investment.

Consequently, at the centre of the discussion about what type of provision should the developing world embrace is the dichotomy between privately owned media against government-owned media. Until the 1960s, UNESCO and other international bodies continued to make the distinction between news and official government information (Tatarian 1978: 9). In the context of the Cold War, this translated into a distinction between 'free' and 'authoritarian' media. This is why it became so important for media scholars in the developing world to debunk the neoliberal corporative argument that it was only through the private sector, by means of capital and technology, that the so-called 'Third World' could obtain its own voice in an objective, balanced and credible manner (Ford 1999: 16).

The criticism coming from the developing countries highlighted the distorted views provided by the global media about the South (Diaz Rangel 1966; Raghavan 1993; Mattelart 1994; Kivikuru 2001). The overall exercise reflected calls made by leaders such as Kwame Nkrumah (1909–72), who asked for a new kind of journalism, which could provide an alternative to the colonial narrative. This criticism was not simply an exercise of 'geopolitics' as some authors have suggested (Sparks 2007: 108), since many of the aspirations for a more balanced system of information were valid and legitimate, even if in many cases they were used as propaganda during the Cold War or by self-proclaimed left-wing dictatorships to legitimise censorship and abuse.

This was no small achievement, as the predominant view until then in most international forums during the Cold War – imposed by the US hegemony – was that the free flow of information and privately owned media were the only way of guaranteeing media freedom from state intervention and propaganda. The end result of the UNESCO debate was overwhelmingly in favour of a new information order that would legitimise the participation of the state in the gathering, production and dissemination of news.

The tensions generated by this debate and the final outcome (*Many Voices, One World*, also known as the *MacBride Report*) resulted in the United States and Britain withdrawing from UNESCO in 1984.[2] Both the US and Britain claimed that the new information world order would give a free hand to authoritarian governments to use state resources to fund propaganda. Indeed, during the Cold War, any media outlet in the developing world that was linked to the government would have been treated with suspicion (Norris 1995: 357) and the content provided to the newsrooms would have been dismissed or quarantined as suspected propaganda. For example, the attempt of the then Venezuelan government to buy United Press International (UPI) in the late 1970s met with extraordinary resistance from its shareholders and subscribers in the United States and Europe, to the point that the Venezuelan government had to pull out of the deal (Lugo-Ocando 1998: 76).

Many decades after the *MacBride Report*, the media landscape has changed dramatically. The emergence of alternative broadcast news networks and the increasing use of the Internet to gather and disseminate news have enabled many countries to project a different worldview across the globe (Seib 2008: 12). International broadcasters, such as Al-Jazeera, Al-Arabiya and Telesur, and alternative news media outlets such as Democracy Now!, Radio Pacifica and IPS, have all brought new perspectives to reporting on the poor and have pushed for a wider and more comprehensive news coverage with regards to inequality. These media experiences have also influenced changes across the whole of the media landscape as other more traditional and commercially driven media outlets have adopted many of their conventions and practices. In the past few years, we have started to see new formats such as *Inside Africa* on CNN and organisations such as the BBC making more use of local talent in the places from which they report rather than just parachuting in people from London as they did in the past.

I am not suggesting that there is already a new alternative to the old media system and conventions; although I do believe it is definitively under construction. Instead, I want to assess the impact of this new media landscape in the articulation of poverty as a news item, while asking if the emerging media landscape has contributed to improving news coverage of the subject or has affected somehow the traditional media landscape's ecology. This section examines to what degree it is possible to argue that the new media outlets from alternative sectors in the developing countries, together with the Internet, have transformed the way in which poverty is treated in news narratives.

In so doing, the chapter discusses the role of these media outlets in the news coverage of poverty in light of theoretical contributions and how this relates overall to the debates for a New World Information and Communication Order (NWICO). By looking at current media developments in the historical context of promises and aspirations made during the 1980s, I enquire whether these media outlets are reaching out for a truly alternative agenda with regards to poverty or if they are merely reproducing the same types of schemes and practices as their counterparts in the industrialised nations have done thus far. 真的替代 or 复生物）

A Tale of Two Towns

There seems to be a general assumption that despite the fact that there are different journalistic practices across different countries and societies, journalism standards are somehow 'universal' (Fuller 1996; Kovach and Rosenstiel 2003; Randall 2000). The problem with this assumption is that by 'universal', what is really meant is a notion of professionalism that carries deeply embedded within it a particular western ideal. These standards have been widely described in scholarly literature, which have referred to them as the modern journalistic form that has emerged alongside liberal democracy and which embodies the principles of intellectual freedom and pluralism (McNair 1998: 84), while claiming balance and neutrality in the reporting of news.

Today, the dominance of a specific understanding of what journalism is has translated into a monopoly on its conceptualisation, definition and measurement. This idea is reflected in narratives that portray a model of journalism that was created in the centre and exported to the periphery as a gift from the Enlightenment and contextualised in the same discourses that spread the ideas of empire and colonialism's benevolent legacy. This idea is artificial but nevertheless prevalent in the post-Enlightenment narrative and embraces objectivity and balance as its defining ideological categories. This narrative is often recycled in scholarly work and among practitioners to perpetuate a myth that gives credibility and power to construct and deconstruct journalism as a universal profession around the world. As with all myths that are backed by resources and power, the notion of a universal journalist has been evangelised and absorbed as a quasi-religious phenomenon in which values and views need to be accepted in order to call oneself a true journalist.

As with other professions and professional practices which have managed to erase diversity from the myth of their origins, the cult of western journalism has managed to establish itself as the superior and only acceptable form of journalism. Because of this, mainstream journalism in the so-called 'developing world' constantly aspires to be a mirror image of the West, partly due to its own colonial legacy and partly to its own atavistic inferiority complex. The end result is the same: journalistic practices and the basic structure of the news cultures are imported and implanted in newsrooms around the world and with them the way in which these media outlets approach poverty as a news item.

The standardisation process has not always gone unchallenged. The western commercial media model has sometimes encountered cases in which local media have refused to be neutral and have instead committed explicitly to anti-colonial and progressive narratives. In places such as Nigeria, the local media in the 1950s sided with the independence movement of the time (Oso 1990: 41). However, globalisation, having brought deregulation and concentration of media ownership, has made it difficult to resist a type of universality driven by market-oriented thinking and has pushed news editors and journalists to embrace single-minded worldviews about poverty and exclusion around the planet. In places such as Argentina and Kenya, national news media outlets that provided some degree of diversity of interpretations of the facts, are now owned by multinational conglomerates that impose single ways of doing journalism and follow more homogenous editorial policies.

Practices and approaches are central in defining organisational cultures and editorial policies in the newsrooms around the globe with regards to poverty. News media are after all part of more structured power systems that are deeply embedded in the geopolitics and political economy at stake. Acting as 'modern missionaries of corporate capitalism' (Herman and McChesney 1997), the media is a global entity that responds to ideological driving forces that encourage homogeneous practices and approaches; this consequently streams narratives and views about all issues in society including poverty. Therefore, coverage of poverty by the media systems in the developing world, as expected, has taken on many of the same traits as its counterparts in the North. In reality, and in despite of some resistance, the privately owned mainstream media in the South have become very like their role models in the US and western Europe.

Media research in Latin America, for example, reveals that many shortcomings observed in the European and American media with regards to the news coverage of poverty can also be recognized in Latin America (Kitzberger and Pérez 2009). This study looked at 2,853 articles from seven different countries (Argentina, Bolivia, Brazil, Chile, Mexico, Peru and Venezuela) over a period of six months, while undertaking both qualitative and quantitative analysis of the two newspapers in each country with the largest circulation. Generally speaking, poverty occupied an average of just 0.68 per cent of these newspapers' printed space during the first half of 2006. Mexico's newspapers devoted the most space to news of poverty, while Peru's media were the least interested in the subject (see Table 7.1).

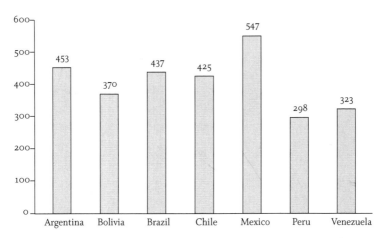

Table 7.1   Latin American newspapers' coverage of poverty, by number of articles

Source: GlobalNews 2007.

To give an idea of how bad this situation is with the Latin America news media, we only have to compare it with the space devoted to other 'news' items, such as articles about the sportswear company Adidas which, in that same period, was allocated 0.31 per cent of the space in these newspapers (this figure excludes paid advertisement).

Moreover, 71 per cent of news reports about poverty in Latin American newspapers referred to it only indirectly; that is, they only referred to poverty as a collateral aspect of the story. This is a very similar finding to comparable studies in Britain, where poverty appears mostly as an indirect issue in news reports (Seymour 2009; Devereux 1986; Golding and Middelton 1982). In places such as Venezuela, where the news media has become a political opponent to a government that promotes wealth redistribution (Lugo-Ocando and Romero 2003), mention of poverty is almost minimal – although comparatively so, based on the region's total – and when it does appear it is overwhelmingly in an indirect manner (90 per cent). Furthermore, over 80 per cent of the news coverage on poverty across newspapers in Latin America appeared as hard news, while only 3 per cent were in-depth reportages.

A related study carried out by the Argentina-based media analysis firm Global News in 2005 shows that most news stories on poverty in places such as Argentina, Mexico and Peru failed to mention the causes. In places such as Brazil, 82 per cent of the stories failed to mention any cause or to assess policies and situations which might have pushed people into poverty. Instead, most stories simply reflected the situation of the people facing exclusion without providing a context to understand why they had become impoverished. According to the study, across South America, it is only in Peru that we find that 40 per cent of the news stories on poverty contained some explanatory framework about the root causes; the downside is that Peru's media is also the least interested in the issue.

This same research indicates that despite being societies with very high levels of poverty, inequality and social exclusion, only a fraction of the editorial pages were dedicated to the subject. In places such as Mexico, the two main newspapers sampled had not one single opinion piece on poverty written by a politician during the six first months of 2006, while in the other countries, articles on poverty amounted to less than 1 per cent of the editorial pages; in the region as a whole, there was a tiny proportion of opinion pieces dedicated to poverty, which reached an average of only 11 per cent in all editorial pages.

The meagre news coverage of poverty by newspapers in Latin America is completely unjustifiable as they have far more resources and space (in terms of the number of pages) than media outlets in other parts of the developing world and they are thriving in what is still a significant print-media market in the world of newspapers and magazines. The fact that news on poverty in these countries manages to make only 2 per cent of the front pages is, on all counts, a remarkable failure in terms of journalistic engagement with society.

There is also some indication that in Asia and Africa the news coverage of poverty is similarly neglected as 'contradictions tend to be sharpest on the peripheries' (Tomaselli 2009). Colin Bickler, a Fellow in International Journalism at City University in London and former Reuters correspondent in both Asia and Africa, recalls:

> The news services did produce lots of material on poverty, but it was rarely used by the newsrooms in the developing countries I worked in. Our work about issues such as famine, health, inequality and deprivation in general was often wasted as they would simply not pick it up. (Interview with the author, 1 June 2011)

One of the reasons for such neglect, it has been suggested, is that there is no market for this type of story in that part of the world, mainly, because that same inequality makes quality media inaccessible and unaffordable for the majority of the people (Nyamnjoh 2005: 22). Therefore, the media in these places tend to reflect more the views of the wealthy audiences they intend to reach, which allow the news media to 'commodify' and sell it to the advertisers which fund their operations. This explains in part why the media organisations in that part of the world tend to emphasise other issues such as sports, while making a predominant display of 'infotainment' rather than serious news about the state of poverty suffered by a great part of their own constituents.

This lack of coverage of poverty in the developing world happens despite the fact that the underlying roots of most of the issues reported by the news media organisations in those countries are poverty, social exclusion and overall inequality. Nevertheless, the coverage in developing countries rarely seems to reflect this and only rarely does it deal with the issue of inequality and wealth distribution. One important reason is that news cultures in many developing countries continue to be bound by post-colonial legacies.

Indeed, Peter Golding's influential piece on the transferral of ideology and the professionalisation of journalists in the Third World (1977) is still one of the most plausible reasons as to why the media in places such as Africa, Asia and Latin America adopt similar approaches and practices when covering the outside world; that is, they adopt similar values to those of their counterparts in the developed world. More recent research has supported this view by pointing out that in many countries 'traditional Western ideals of detachment and being a watchdog still flourish among the standards accepted by journalists' (Hanitzsch et al. 2011: 280).

These same voices have suggested that interventionist aspects of journalism do not enjoy wide support among journalists and that they tend to stay away from influencing public opinion and advocating social change. None the less, if some of these values, such as public transparency, free speech, people's involvement, journalistic independence, truthfulness and fair reporting seem to be regarded as 'non-negotiable' by most journalists in their own cases, they are rarely considered as rights and obligations that apply to society as a whole (Skjerdal 2009: 32).

The end result is that journalists working in the news media in developing countries tend to appropriate these values in a particular way in order to justify a lack of commitment to structural change and wealth redistribution. Indeed, one of the key problems in the coverage of poverty, as we have identified in earlier chapters, is the ideological 'ritual of objectivity' (Tuchman 1972) and its consequence for the assessment of the causes of poverty, namely inequality. This happens on a greater scale in places where there are sharper class divisions and in which the elites, in some cases the same people, control all the media, the political institutions and the means of production. Golding's explanation remains, nevertheless, insufficient in light of recent developments in North Africa and the Middle East, during the so-called 'Arab Spring', where many media outlets did not conform to the ideological notion of detachment and objectivity.

The reporting of poverty by the media in developing countries is overall a by-product of the colonial legacy: journalists' background, training and education remain important aspects of the configuration of news (Jimada 1992: 366). This is not limited to post-colonial countries but to most developing countries which see western journalism as a paradigm. Indeed, many journalists' experience in developing countries is that poverty is one of the most difficult subjects to cover and also one of the hardest to sell in the newsroom. Denis Ocwich, for example, has identified issues concerning the ability of journalists in Africa, where poverty is widespread, to reach rural people, both as audiences and as the subjects of news reporting (2010: 242). Hernán Lugo Galicia, from *El Nacional* in Venezuela points out:

> It is not that we lack commitment; it is that we lack resources and scope. Poverty is all around us, so it is very difficult to convince our editors and readers that poverty in itself is newsworthy. Because of this, it is also very difficult to convince the managers to provide the resources to go to places in which there is a story on poverty. Priorities in the agenda always make news stories on poverty secondary. You know the old saying in journalism: the urgent always kills the important. (Interview with the author, 14 September 2012)

Lugo Galicia's views are shared by others who have had similar experiences in other parts of the world. The fact is that the type of cash-strapped newsrooms described by Nick Davis (2008) in Britain, where journalists from the mainstream media now struggle to cover even the most basic stories and must rely on PR, has been a chronic situation in many newsrooms in the developing world for many decades.

Other important constraints come from news cultures in which self-censorship is well-established and poverty is seen as a hot political topic. In Central Asia, for example, political and economic factors have derailed many attempts to challenge existing structures of power that perpetuate poverty and inequality. In places such as Kazakhstan and Uzbekistan:

> Journalism is in worse shape than the rest of the post-Communist world, largely because the socioeconomic and political situations in this relatively remote region remain in flux from a backwardness that modernity is only of late and slowly affecting. One of the most confounding elements that stymie the evolution of Central Asia journalism is a culture that drives the new post-Communist institutions and the mentalities of the region's socio-political, economic, and cultural elites. (Kenny and Gross 2008: 515)

Moreover, while many governments around the world are reluctant to draw attention to the poverty in their own countries, most governments in the developing world are actively trying to remove it from public debate altogether. The Brazilian government's efforts to 'cleanse' its shanty-towns in the build-up to the 2014 World Cup were a clear example of this (*Daily Mail* 2014). News media, in many cases, collude in this effort by ignoring the subject or framing it in ways in which those in a state of poverty seem wholly responsible for their own situation. Slums in Mexico City, Rio de Janeiro, Rangoon, Beijing and Johannesburg are rendered invisible by politicians with the news media's active support, particularly during state visits and events such as the Olympic Games. In some cases, these slums have been literally fenced off and their inhabitants temporarily evicted (Davis 2006: 107), without a single report in the local media on the suffering and exclusion that these actions have provoked, or the hypocrisy of the authorities. This is, I argue, an extension of what have become trends in which gated communities are created both physically within states and metaphorically by the media.

The gated communities are justified by the need for protection. Their existence as a disruption of public life is rarely brought to light and more often than not the excluding nature and inequality that brings them about is ignored in media reports. The concept of gated communities in the news imaginary is pivotal to understand a key narrative, that of the need to sacrifice freedom and rights for security (something that became even more evident after 9/11). It is also one of the underlying reasons why news reports can 'other' those in poverty. Furthermore, this pervasive logic of security versus rights justifies the 'geopolitics of oppression'. In this context, the wall erected in the occupied Palestinian territories by the Israeli government is justified to stop possible attacks, even though it really serves to hide poverty and exclusion. Gated communities in Johannesburg or in Caracas are no different: they are erected to hide poverty, exclusion and inequality, but are justified on the basis of security. Poverty is therefore 'eradicated' from public spaces by making people invisible. In places such as Nigeria, Haiti and Pakistan, entire parks and other public places are now closed to the general public for the enjoyment of the very few. In some cases, the barriers surround the wealthy and at other times, they are there to imprison those in poverty. However, in both cases, they send an unequivocal message of power and control while reinforcing a sense of division.

The 'gated-community' mentality allows the media to define the people affected in simplistic narratives of good and bad, religion or race. An example of this was the media frenzy that followed the fatal shooting of Trayvon Martin by George Zimmerman on 26 February 2012 in a gated community in Sanford, Florida. In this case, the media reports mostly ignored class issues and inequality, concentrating instead on race as a decoy.

In countries with high levels of inequality, the coverage of poverty tends to be problematic and politically sensitive. In these places, inequality is a no-go area for many journalists who otherwise would face harsh censorship. For Andrés Cañizález, coordinator of the Political Communication and Freedom of Speech programme at the Universidad Católica Andrés Bello in Venezuela:

> Some governments do not want to recognise that they have failed in the area of poverty, especially when they have come to power under the promises of a better life for all. To acknowledge poverty is to admit failure and to some extent defeat. That is a fact in the developing world as in the industrialised nations. (Interview with the author, 12 July 2011)

In places such as Equatorial Guinea and Burma, brutal repression against journalists has been documented for merely reporting basic facts about poverty that would have been commonplace in any other part of the world (Ogbondah 1997; Michnik 1998). In other places, such as China, Russia and Brazil, the situation is not much better; even when governments are less brutal, censorship and self-censorship on poverty is still rife.

There are important consequences for the lack of news coverage of poverty in the developing world as the mass media have a crucial role in shaping policy and action towards the poor, by ensuring that citizens' needs, preferences and expectations are translated into policy, resource allocation and wealth redistribution. Research carried out in India, for example, reveals that governments are far more responsive to potential famines and food shortages where newspaper circulation is higher and where there is ample news coverage of the subject (Besley et al. 2001).

As noted by Amartya Kumar Sen (1981) with regards to the role of democratic media and famines, the national and local news media can make a big difference to the situation of the poor in their own countries, and are the first line of public consciousness regarding poverty. However they are also, with few exceptions, the least prepared to confront the issue, often lacking the resources and, in many cases, the editorial will to do so.

Overall, the emerging news agenda on poverty, one that could potentially be more promising and that could focus on wealth redistribution, has not yet come from traditional media outlets in poor countries as they tend, as we have seen here, to replicate the behaviour and habits of their former colonial masters. Instead, hopes are now being placed in transnational networks and news agencies also from the developing world. Their initial success has made the news media in the world's powerful capitals, and to no lesser extent the local media in the developing world, more aware of the challenges. Because of this, many media outlets have opened up spaces for news coverage of poverty in terms and formats that did not exist before. They have also, to some degree, pushed for an incipient alternative agenda on the issue.

A Whole New World

The arrival of networks such as Al-Jazeera has cross-pollinated territory which had been fertilised for years by the offspring from the debates surrounding NWICO and the subsequent creation of smaller news agencies such as Inter-Press Service. Until their arrival, however, the mainstream global media virtually ignored poverty and social exclusion as a by-product of inequality. News coverage of famines, as we have discussed already in this book, were routinely carried out as pre-formatted rituals in which the causes of poverty were often attributed to corrupt dictators, too much state intervention and too little liberalisation of markets.

The situation in Somalia in 2010–11 is emblematic of this type of coverage. In presenting it as a 'crisis', news media outlets such as CNN, the BBC and the *New York Times* reduced these events to a temporary status in which natural forces and political evils, such as drought and corruption – even when they were recognised as endemic – were to be blamed. In fact, as Maryan Qasim, former minister for women's development and family affairs and adviser in the Transitional Federal Government of Somalia points out:

> This famine, however, did not occur overnight. It was not unexpected. The international community was warned nearly two years ago that livestock were perishing, food prices were rising and that the conflict was creating a devastating situation for an overwhelming number of Somalis. In September 2009, Andrej Mahecic, a spokesman for the UN refugee agency, UNHCR, said more than 50,000 Somalis had fled to Kenya in the start of 2009 alone, and in the same year the UN estimated that there were 3.8 million Somalis in urgent need of humanitarian assistance. This famine, like most, has been a gradual process that the international community has chosen to ignore. (Qasim 2011)

In reality, hunger in Somalia is a structural issue which exemplifies the abysmal divisions between the North and the South. It also provides an acute picture of a legacy of interventions and persistent negligence by the so-called 'international community' which has used Somalia for decades as a dumping ground for weapons and toxic waste (Clapp 1994: 17). However, few of these facts are ever included in the western media's news coverage. Consequently, public awareness in the West regarding direct responsibilities in the current crisis is almost non-existent.

Furthermore, European and US news agencies and broadcast networks were reporting that rebel forces were preventing all forms of aid from reaching the people, while in fact the ban was only against the United Nations, which had played an unlawful political role in supporting one of the sides in the conflict. In a *Guardian* article, 'Somali rebels deny lifting ban on foreign aid groups', correspondent Xan Rice wrote:

The rebel group al-Shabab, which controls much of southern Somalia, had said earlier this month that it would allow all humanitarian groups access to assist with the drought response. But al-Shabab spokesman Sheikh Ali Mohamud Rage has told a local radio station that the ban on specific aid agencies, which was imposed in 2009 and 2010, still stands. At the time, the rebels accused various humanitarian groups, including the UN's World Food Programme (WFP), which is expected to lead the current drought response, of damaging the local economy, being anti-Muslim, and of spying for the government. (Rice 2011)

At the time of sending this dispatch, Rice was based in Nairobi and had no way of confirming the situation on the ground. The report was based on a local radio intervention in Somalia itself, which could not have been heard in Nairobi: it is possible to assume then that a 'third party' could have provided the information to the *Guardian*'s journalist.[3] Foreign aid is often used as a tool of geopolitics and public diplomacy, endorsed by the media that collude, deliberately or not, with the donor countries' foreign policy (Benthall 1993; Polman 2010). These types of bias in news reports are a classic example of geopolitical games and propaganda and the type of framing is very common in media outlets on both sides of the North Atlantic (Bantimaroudis and Ban 2001: 184).

Inter-Press Service, in contrast, provided a more comprehensive and distinctive coverage of the issue, despite having fewer resources on the ground than news agencies such as Reuters, Associated Press, or AFP. In a report, 'Armed Militia Grab the Famine Business', dispatched from Mogadishu, correspondent Abdurrahman Warsameh highlights, 'Armed groups are withholding aid and preventing Somali famine refugees from leaving camps to ensure the continued supply of food by aid agencies that they are presently selling on the open market' (Warsameh 2011).

The report uses voices that are articulate and express very clearly their own needs, challenging western narratives and doing so without intermediaries, something that is rarely seen in news reports from traditional news media outlets:

Since Mohamed Elmi, 69, and his family arrived at a camp for famine refugees in Mogadishu they have barely had enough to eat. Armed gunmen running the camp steal their food and prevent them from leaving to search for aid elsewhere, he says. Elmi told IPS that this happens because aid agencies deliver food to the people running the camp for distribution and not to the famine victims themselves. And they are prevented from leaving because aid will no longer be delivered to the camps if they do. 'I don't know who is running this, but we have said time and again that we are never, never given anything by the foremen running [the camp]. Let them kill me if they want ... We cannot leave here to find a better place,' Elmi told IPS.

One key difference between IPS and other news agencies when reporting poverty 'is that since it started operations it was conceived more as a cooperative of journalists rather than a news corporation', says Ramesh Jura, former Regional Director for IPS Europe:

> Over the years, we have had to adapt and change and it has not been easy to penetrate the mainstream media and sell our services, but we have had, I would say, a relative success in providing alternative views about the developing world. The agency is also dependent on grants from sponsors, which gives us some additional freedom in terms of commercial prerogatives. Our correspondents live and more often than not were born in the places from which they report. Their news beat is their homeland and that accounts a lot for a more comprehensive understanding of the context in which news in those places happens. (Interview with the author, 2 November 2009)

IPS has correspondents only in certain countries; in most cases, they are their own managers and operate under a sort of franchise. Therefore, the living standards of IPS correspondents are very similar to an ordinary middle-class citizen of the place in which they are based. Unlike many foreign aid officials and correspondents from major news agencies and broadcasters, they are not parachuted into the places from which they are reporting. They live in similar conditions to other local journalists and ordinary people. They shop in the same markets and endure the electricity blackouts, the crime and the traffic jams and feel the overwhelming anxiety that most citizens of the developing world feel about making ends meet.

Paradoxically, this type of coverage has been criticised in the past by senior correspondents from the global media who have defended 'parachute' journalism by claiming that 'impartiality' is compromised when reporters are locally recruited, because that makes them vulnerable to national and local pressures (Halliday 2011). However, over the years, IPS has had mixed results in trying to publicise poverty as a news item and it is only since the mid-1990s, with the growth in the use of the Internet, that the agency has been capable of reaching a wider audience, especially with regards to gaining more recognition in a media landscape which is still basically dominated by a couple of key players.

The real breakthrough in terms of news coverage of the South has come with the arrival of Al-Jazeera; both directly in terms of reaching audiences with alternative coverage as well as indirectly by making other media outlets change or at least modify their news format so as to offer more coverage of issues related to poverty and inequality. There is already a vast scholarly literature on the Al-Jazeera phenomenon – its history, its appearance on the world stage and the role it plays in the geopolitics of the media (El-Nawawy and Iskandar 2003; Mellor 2011; Miles 2006; Seib 2008; Zayani 2005).

To start with, traditional framing research techniques used by scholars is challenged by the type of news coverage produced by Al-Jazeera as the network tends to operate outside traditional US/UK hegemonic discourses. This indicates that something particularly different is happening in the Al-Jazeera newsroom that allows the network to provide a different output. The global broadcaster seems to have far more autonomy from domestic media regulations, corporate prerogatives and national power structures, and therefore so far it has been able to challenge 'dominant social discourse and the existing political order' (Wojcieszak 2007: 115). With regard to reporting poverty, insufficient research has been carried out and more comparative analysis is required to establish with more certainty the degree of differentiated coverage that is being offered in media outlets such as Al-Jazeera, although Mellor (2005) has provided us with an excellent overview of the distinctive coverage from the Arab world media with regards to news on 9/11.

Our own analysis of news programmes and schedules during March, April, May and June of 2011 suggests that Al-Jazeera in English provided over 17 per cent more airtime than CNN International and almost 21 per cent more than the World Service of the BBC to issues in which the word 'poverty' was mentioned. The pilot research also indicates that had it not been for the crisis in Somalia of that year, the difference would have been even greater. We have attributed the difference to the location of Al-Jazeera's bureaus which tend to cover more areas in the global South than its counterparts in Europe and the US. A more in-depth part of this study also reveals a very distinctive type of coverage, which differs greatly in the choice of words used in the reports and in the nature of the context provided when reporting these issues. More important, in this same sample, the frequency in the use of words 'poverty' and 'inequality' is far greater in Al-Jazeera than in CNN and the BBC. Although these findings are not sufficiently representative, they do suggest a very important shift in the coverage of poverty.

Since the creation of Al-Jazeera, other networks such as CNN International have begun to offer more airtime to programmes on poverty and have created broadcast magazines such as *Inside Africa*. These programmes often devote far more time to poverty and related issues, going far beyond the traditional news approaches. However, the BBC management's responses in London to the challenges posed by Al-Jazeera seem instead to outsiders as perhaps rushed and clumsy and more of a tragedy than a strategy on how to lose influence in the developing world.

Indeed, the BBC World Service, which, in contrast to the rest of the BBC, was until recently dependent on the Foreign and Commonwealth Office for funding (officially making it a propaganda arm of the government), proceeded to dismantle its Spanish, Latin America and Caribbean services, as well as its Portuguese service for Africa, which served some of the poorest people in that continent who still have little access to the Internet. The cuts also affected several services in other languages and involved a substantial reduction in the overall budgets for news coverage, especially the deployment of correspondents and resources to generate news content. Paradoxically, at the same time, the government announced it would give the BBC World Service an extra £2.2 million per year over the next three years to strengthen its Arab service and to develop a partnership with a local broadcaster that could compete with Al-Jazeera.[4]

These moves on the part of traditional western broadcasters confirm to some that the Arab network's presence poses a particular challenge to their traditional hegemony. In fact, Al-Jazeera has proven to have gained credibility by not only investing more in better news coverage of the developing world but also by associating itself with those better placed to cover parts of the world where the network has limited reach. For example, a very interesting development in Al-Jazeera's coverage is that it has developed a close relationship with the IPS news agency and other networks such as TeleSur in Latin America. As a result of this, Al-Jazeera has been able to amplify its reach and make links with logistical provision in the South, establishing an effective monitoring network that allows broadcaster to learn, very quickly, about 'hot' topics before other outlets do. This is happening at a time when quasi-equival services that could help western media to explore new agendas, such as BBC Monitoring, are facing severe cuts.

The association between Al-Jazeera and IPS also provides a particularly distinctive and wide-ranging approach to reporting on poverty, which transcends traditional ideological frameworks in news reporting from both the left and the right. Indeed, both bring their networks of journalists together to shed light on stories in places which the traditional global media cannot reach independently. These news stories often highlight inequality at the core of the news narratives and undertake a more critical news agenda on poverty, which makes a huge difference in demonstrating that alternative coverage of the poor is possible.

By no means does this imply that coverage of poverty by Al-Jazeera has fulfilled the aspirations of what news reporting of the poor should be, but it does represent a vast improvement to traditional coverage. However, the greater impact of the news channel upon the global media landscape has been on the type of competition it has created in terms of trust and legitimacy;[5] something that has obliged competitors to start making space for alternative types of reporting and practices (for example, over the past few years, organisations such as the BBC and CNN have started to hire local reporters rather than parachuting in people as correspondents). Al-Jazeera's ability to open up spaces, to set bureaus in places often ignored by others and to articulate alternative narratives about exclusion is in itself a great achievement and should be welcome.

Looking for a Voice

It is also important to emphasise that the experience of Al-Jazeera is not a technologically deterministic one. Instead, it has been a combination of good journalism and sustained investment facilitated by a satellite platform that was already there. Nevertheless, some continue to argue that recent developments in the Arab world are a by-product of the dissemination of interactive and digital technologies. In a recent article, Mexican writer ˉlos Fuentes argued that the tools used by those rising up against the ˉships in the Arab world were 'civilisational' technologies ˉˉitter and iPhone (Aristegui 2012). Fuentes echoes a ccording to which these technologies have created htened political sensitivity in which interconnec- change.

Some have tried to provide similar explanations for the riots in England in 2011, maintaining that social network technologies allowed the protesters to bypass the security forces and create anarchy. In an article, 'London Riots: how BlackBerry Messenger played a Key Role', published in the *Guardian*, Josh Halliday wrote that the British police had been misled by looking on Facebook and Twitter for signs of spreading unrest; instead, he argued, 'they should have watched BBM [Blackberry]' (Halliday 8 August 2011). The British government even went on to suggest the possibility of banning social networks during the riots and at least two individuals were arrested and sentenced for using their Facebook accounts to incite protests.

However, as some authors have already pointed out, it would be naïve to conclude that the increasing liberalisation and civic engagement in the Middle East can be attributable mainly to the dissemination of information and communication technologies; the Arab uprising involves a far more complex set of explanations (Aouragh and Alexander 2011; Joffé 2011; Khondker 2011). For Asharq Al-Awsat-Samir Aita, editor-in-chief of the Arabic edition of *Le Monde Diplomatique*, the so-called 'Arab Spring' is a result of twenty years of demographic changes,

> It is the same forces that led to the May of 1968 in France and the anti-war movement in the US that now shape the changes in the Middle East. It is a generation that demands its rights but who are jobless and facing a deteriorating economy due to neoliberal policies who have gone to the streets of the Arab world to demand changes. (Interview with the author, 13 March 2012)

According to him, 'there were very objective material causes for the uprising in the Middle East and the riots in Europe; they are called injustice, exclusion and inequality.'

In countries such as Tunisia, Libya and Egypt, data from the Organisation for Economic Co-operation and Development (OECD) and the World Bank show that despite years of economic growth, there had been no reduction in household poverty and what is worse, there was a fall in per capita consumption (Davis 2006: 164). Similar data also suggest that riots in France in 2005 and in England in 2011 are manifestations of unfairness and increasing inequality.

These events are also a continuum of history. Riots, protests and uprisings have always been historical manifestations of resistance against exclusion and growing disparities. From Spartacus's well-known struggle against the Roman Empire, often seen as oppressed people fighting for their freedom against a slave-owning aristocracy, to the 1989 protests in Tiananmen Square, passing through the hundreds of rebellions which occurred in the New World during the centuries of oppression and slavery and the hundreds of thousands of uprisings in recent history against power and oppression, the history of the world is the history of resistance against inequality. Technologies could perhaps have helped trigger the explosion, but the objective conditions were certainly there already. That should be the focus of the news story. Moreover, as it is simplistic to attribute social unrest to technologies to which relatively so few people have access.

This is not to say that the technology has played no part in this. On the contrary, the broader processes in which the transnational media operates have to some degree facilitated the international flow of information and increased openness in society (Wojcieszak 2007: 123). Today, citizens are able to compare their lives to those of their peers in the rest of the world and want to articulate comparable demands. They are rapidly becoming conscious that not only can they aspire to a decent life, but that they also have a right to one. These audiences in Africa, Asia and Latin America are conscious of the enormous injustice in the world and the apathetic indifference to which they and their societies have been subjected by the global media. However, the fact remains that it is inequality itself, especially during times of demographic changes, that creates the conditions for revolutions and upheavals.

A Final Lesson

Overall, the phenomenon of Al-Jazeera is a valuable lesson because it shows that different agendas can be successful in creating a different cognitive environment and that the media in the developing world can reflect different realities in the news by taking different approaches to the news. However, its accomplishments also reinforce some of the *MacBride Report*'s original calls for state intervention. Al-Jazeera would not have been possible without the initial involvement of the taxpayer-funded BBC and the financial endorsement of the Qatari government. The experience is also true in other parts of the world in which influential media outlets with a clear agenda on inequality have managed to go mainstream.

The case of the Catholic media outlets in Latin America such as the radio network Fe y Alegria, or the Bolivian news agency Fides, are eloquent examples of what is possible and achievable on a regional and national scale. Fe y Alegria has made poverty a core theme in all its news magazines, highlighting the issue of inequality and the need for wealth redistribution, while keeping high ratings among the audiences and a portfolio of advertisers and sponsors, including the state (Lugo-Ocando et al. 2010: 150). The Bolivian news agency Fides, for its part, has become one of the most trusted media outlets in that country, supplying news content to many mainstream news media outlets despite the distinctive editorial policies, political preferences and ideological stances of its clients.

The conclusion is that those in poverty can have a voice, but it may not be as uniform as one might desire. It will instead reflect the diversity that characterises the rest of humanity, although it might find some uniformity in underlining class issues and inequality. However, one thing all these societies do have in common is that to find that voice, they must look not only at organisations and complex structures of news gathering, production and dissemination, they should also demand the ethical individual contribution of each and every journalist, as they can, at the end of the day, make a real difference.

It might have been naïve to expect this to happen thirty years ago, when the world appeared to be dominated by two superpowers. None the less, the 'cultural chaos' (McNair 2006) brought about by communications globalisation has opened a space to formulate a new world information order. Let us just hope that the contradictions apparent to so many also become self-evident to those behind the news desks in both the North and South, who will then have to either adapt or step aside in the face of the incoming changes.

Conclusion
Beyond the Unsustainable News Agenda

In the past decade, the world has seen major tragedies around the globe, among them the disastrous 2004 Indian Ocean earthquake and tsunami, the fatal floods provoked by Hurricane Katrina in the US in 2005, and the 2011 massive earthquake and tsunami leading to nuclear disaster in Fukushima, Japan. We saw the US, the remaining superpower, almost incapable of dealing with a major natural disaster (Townsend 2006) and Japan become one of the major recipients of aid, after being one of the main donors, as aid to poor countries was being severely cut, despite record profits from Japan's main corporations and sustained military expenditure (Kyodo News 2013).

Dispersed through these events, we witnessed several major scandals that completely undermined the idea that some countries in the developing world are poor because they have corrupt governments, as the Irish singer Bono continues to insist in his travels around the world (Elliott 2006). In Iraq, for example, corruption among US forces was not just linked to the illegality of the decision to go to war in 2003 or to the blunt and deliberate lies told by US Secretary Colin Powell and ambassador to the UN John Bolton about weapons of mass destruction (WMD), but also reflected in the loss of US$12 billion in cash sent by the US government to Iraq, which simply 'vanished into thin air' (Pallister 2007).

It was also during this time that the British government under Tony Blair's premiership halted an investigation into bribes of US$1.2 billion to a member of the Saudi royal family in exchange for weapons contracts (Leigh and Evans 2007). The neo-conservative Paul Wolfowitz, who often referred to corruption as the developing world's most pressing problem, resigned as president of the World Bank because of corruption and abuse of power (Goodman 2007). In this same period, the then director general of the International Monetary Fund and French presidential contender, Dominique Strauss-Kahn, was apprehended by police for the alleged rape of a maid in his US$3,000 per night hotel bedroom in New York. It was in these times that we witnessed large-scale corruption among members of the British Parliament who illegally over-claimed on their expenses (Martin 2014), received cash in exchange for awarding honours and for arranging private meetings between the Prime Minister David Cameron and tax-evading corporations in return for party donations (Holt 2011).

We watched the top officers of Scotland Yard receiving bribes in exchange for passing information about people's private lives and ongoing police cases to Rupert Murdoch's newspapers and turning a blind eye to the illegal hacking of people's mobile phones (Doward 2012). We saw widespread cases of corruption, abuse of power and simple theft in Canada, Japan, Spain and the United States among high-ranking politicians and public servants. What we have learned from these events is that we should be under no illusion that corruption is solely to be blamed for poverty. What we can see instead is that countries in the West can be as corrupt as anywhere else and none the less still be considered 'developed' and wealthy.

The other aspect that we need to acknowledge is that many of these events are brought to us instantly in our living rooms thanks to the enhanced capability of global news to spotlight struggles for human rights and democracy around the world, an advance which affects both the forces of reaction and progressive change (Cottle 2010: 474). Indeed, despite the limitations described in this book, there is the potential for global journalism to facilitate structural change. Technological developments and new political conditions offer journalists as a collective professional body a unique opportunity to cultivate 'a distinctive form of knowledge' in relation to poverty and inequality (Waisbord 2013: 200).

The media is operating in a world news environment in which no longer is it possible to sustain the patronising and hyper-colonial tone undertaken in relation to those in a state of poverty while ignoring the structural causes of exclusion. The global news media and particularly journalists, therefore, need to embrace a more dialectical understanding of poverty so they can focus more on inequality and wealth redistribution as the driving agenda. What is needed, consequently, is an interconnected view of the issues that recognises that wealth redistribution is a priority, and that no amount of aid will make up for the fact that poverty is a direct result of historical inequalities and structural conditions.

It is no longer possible to sustain a news agenda where poverty is treated as an exotic news item which we in the West can simply contemplate with apathy. As Chris Woods, an award-winning investigative journalist and documentary film-maker attached to the Bureau of Investigative Journalism in London points out:

> Poverty is right in front of our nose and perhaps that is why it is not properly investigated. We see it as a natural and prevalent reality. We just don't want to deal with it, perhaps because it is overwhelming and too challenging. Therefore, what I think really needs to be investigated is our own indifference towards poverty. (Interview with the author, 15 March 2012)

To challenge this indifference, we 'need to democratise the media' (Hackett 2005). This will not of course be an easy task as the news coverage of poverty by the global media is, after all, a reflection of current power structures, class interests and systems of capital ownership. That is why it is so important to bear in mind that journalists, as individuals and as a collective body, can make a difference inside these systems, despite their backgrounds and the constraints and limitations imposed upon them.

In this respect, many journalists and editors around the world are becoming far more conscientious about their role and their ability to challenge traditional conceptions of poverty and highlight the structural inequalities that drive hundreds of millions to the global periphery. Far from Fukuyama's predictions in *The End of History and the Last Man* (1992), the construction of a new type of journalism will demand educating ideologically committed individuals who are aware, reflective and critical of their own agency and power in the articulation of news.

This type of journalistic practice will require a new media environment in which the old and new will coexist and where there will be the need for state-supported alternatives that can provide provisions for some of these journalists to produce and disseminate their work. Not only in state-owned or state-controlled media outlets as it has been until now, but also by providing a multiplicity of paths in which society – as the ultimate element of the state – can subsidise spaces for freedom, dialogue and encounter. This could mean supporting transnational and collective news bodies, cooperative networks and individual initiatives. In relation to this last option it is worth highlighting the case of Dahr Jamail, who was one of the few unembedded journalists to report extensively from Iraq during the 2003 Iraq invasion. Originally a mountaineer, Jamail set up a news blog which rapidly became very popular. At the outbreak of war in Iraq, Jamail's followers – feeling let down by the traditional media – funded him to go to that country to cover the conflict.

I adopt here, of course, an understanding of the state that incorporates the Gramscian view that the state is intrinsically linked to civil society. As such, it can and should be at the core of new structures gathering and disseminating news about poverty in different ways. News is after all part of our common welfare, bringing us together through the collective sum of humanitarian moralities.

What is also clear is that the traditional commercial media landscape is no longer sufficient or perhaps even viable as a provider of the type of news that society needs. It is no coincidence that in Britain, the media outlets that provide more coverage on poverty and that speak more constantly about inequality are precisely those operating under a different type of ownership such as the *Guardian* and Channel 4.

However, beyond media ownership, the pivotal task for those wanting to change the news agenda on poverty and provide a voice for the excluded is to rethink the manuals on how to produce good journalism. This implies getting rid once and for all of the ideological ritual of objectivity and being able to bypass the constraints of self-interest and privilege.

Journalists also need to step aside from the prevalent discourses dominated by the notions of progress, market forces and infinite growth as the panacea for poverty. Let us remember that this is a paradigm in which globalisation solves the problem by denying it (Ris, 1997: 236). Growth, one of the key drivers of journalistic narratives about poverty, in itself is not the solution, as evidence from Africa shows, where growth of 5 and 6 per cent per year has made very little difference to poverty levels or people's quality of life (Mosley 2013: 3). Moreover, as the United Nations Report on the World Social Situation clearly points out, 'global poverty levels have changed very little over the past two decades' (2009: 33). In Africa, parts of Asia and Latin America, the same report argues, things have become even worse, with significant deterioration in the living standards of the poor compared to the 1970s. People in the West appear dismayed when they find out that there are far more people living under slavery today than ever before in human history (Bales et al. 2009: 18); they seem shocked to discover that in one of London's most luxurious areas, an Indonesian maid 'drank acid to kill herself after being treated like a slave' for years (Razaq 2010). Or take the example of the 'ghost ships' that enslave and even kill workers while meeting the global demand for prawns, as revealed in a recent *Guardian* investigation (Hodal et al. 2014). Hi-tech products, such as the popular iPhone, are made by workers in China who are not allowed even to talk to each other so as to keep productivity high (Moore, Malcolm 2010). These are not isolated cases – much of what we wear, use and eat is produced by people working under modern conditions of slavery or semi-slavery.

The prevalent idea that we, as a global society, are defeating poverty and making conditions better for all is an illusion that still dominates most news narratives. It is a perverse notion that makes it even harder to develop a new type of agenda and consequently hinders real policy change. Because of this false optimism, audiences have become less concerned about a problem that is supposedly being solved by their own consumption habits – as this would fuel growth in poor countries– while being led to believe that they, as individuals, are incapable of doing anything except for making the occasional donation. Consequently, poverty appears in the news as a sporadic setback in the overall triumphant advance of progress. Detachment from the public then follows, as people assume that these isolated 'setbacks' will be corrected by the system's professional bodies and technocrats.

Despite all this, one after the other, news articles and other global media reports seem to spread, from the pulpit of fundamentalist market-driven economics, the belief in growth, consumption and global trade as the answer against poverty. These reports continue to embrace, at least with regards to poverty abroad, the same type of arguments that have miserably failed in the past thirty or so years, citing the same news sources, quoting the same news shapers and overall echoing similar discourses in the news on poverty.

In the light of this monumental failure, journalists should question the type of thinking that creates the very damaging policies that dominate ideas of progress. If in doubt, they only need to look back at the endless stories of mining industries, dams and other infrastructure built in the name of growth and progress that literally destroyed the livelihoods of the people they were supposed to benefit. This should account for an empirical questioning of liberal economics, growth and infinite consumption as the 'silver bullets' against exclusion.

Journalists should question this last even from the point of view of their own personal experience, as very few journalists covering world poverty would say hand on heart that things have improved since the 1980s for all the fellows at the bottom. Their own daily beat in the cities shows bigger slums, poorer rural areas, while they themselves, as middle-class professionals, are having to work harder for comparatively far less money. As the United Nations report mentioned above highlights:

> The mixed record of poverty reduction calls into question the efficiency of conventional approaches involving economic liberalisation and privatisation. Instead, Governments need to play a development role, with implementation of integrated economic and social policies designed to support inclusive output and employment growth as well as to reduce inequality and promote justice in society. (2009: 34)

Why then does the media still push for the idea of progress according to which 'things are getting better'? In part, the answer is because their reporters are still embedded with news sources and news shapers that have a vested interest in denying the colossal failure of the post-1980s neoliberal setting. For these sources, closely associated with the owners and commercial partners of the corporative news media, to pay more taxes, promote land redistribution, democratise and further regulate the financial system, subsidise and protect local infant industries, nationalise certain services and to re-balance the distribution of wealth globally and nationally are not particularly desirable options.

Another reason for this constant recycling of bad ideas is that journalists have been made to pretend that their reporting must be non-ideological and cannot be shaped by their own values and worldviews. This ideology of objectivity prevents many journalists from advocating for social change, while having to produce their stories by means of an authorial structure that mostly reflects the ideas of those in power and the utilitarian rationale of their professional practice. Instead, journalists should be more explicit and openly encourage social change by exposing situations such as inequality, structural injustice, tax evasion and the need to reconsider systems and structures of production and distribution of wealth.

Journalism is after all a process that constantly creates and reinforces social reality. In so doing, it provides an ideological framework for how we see and interpret the world around us. Therefore, the interpretation of poverty as a human creation and as a by-product of the way we have decided to organise ourselves as a society is the top priority of journalism.

This change of focus from reporting the manifestations of poverty to one that highlights inequality and its causes will not be an easy one, as it will confront the challenges posed by the economic prerogatives of the commercial model upon which the media has thrived up to now. It is not, however, an impossible task, and the current crisis in the traditional media model is an opportunity for a real change in the ways in which journalism approaches poverty as a news item.

The Risk of Empathy

Up to now, news coverage of poverty in the global media has predominantly reflected the views and perceptions of the wealthy, consequently reproducing discourses of power. This coverage has looked at famines, earthquakes, destitution and poverty in general with sorrow and as such, it has encouraged regimes of pity. The audiences' response to the theatricality of suffering has translated into occasional donations, reinforcing the sense of power of those flipping channels, tuning in a station and, more recently, clicking on a hyperlink. While watching and listening to these news reports, these audiences are told that they can 'do something about it' by giving a couple of dollars a month or signing up to a variety of donation schemes.

This is a perfect situation for those at the top of the pyramid as it plays to all the narratives they want to perpetuate. It makes people think that charity is sufficient in terms of their own responsibility, while failing to question the inherent causes of that situation and their own patterns of consumption. It happens because news coverage of poverty emanates mostly from the comfort zone of power that uses pity as a substitute for solidarity, hence it rarely needs to face critically the issue of inequality.

The question is, therefore, how to engage with the public in a way that it can trigger real change and create the type of solidarity and understanding that in the past led workers to create unions and people to mobilise against oppression. Some authors have argued that 'empathy is necessary but it does not always assist understanding':

> News must alert us to the difficult things we would prefer not to have to admit – and give us the grounds for gruelling toleration, not just the cosy belief of similarity. The democratic expectation is that news, unlike tragedy, will move beyond feeling to action – or at least willed pressure and change. Indeed, if audiences are passive and uninterested, sometimes the media have to stand in for them, and agitate on their behalf. (Seaton 2005: 286)

However, I am not convinced by this 'standing in' for the audience, as in practice it has become nothing more than another exercise of power and pseudo-action. In fact, the way I see it, the audiences who are asked to donate are just being allowed to emulate the power of those who intervene with foreign aid. What is needed instead is a type of news coverage that creates real empathy and political solidarity, which makes individuals on both sides of the screen see each other as equals, and as having the same rights.

To do this, journalism needs to articulate empathy in terms of the possibility that those on the screen could be one of us. Consequently, journalism needs to set aside the sense of power that destroys humility in the newsroom and embrace a view of 'shared risk', in which all people share the same concerns about the future. At this point, it is useful to recall the late John Rawls (1921–2002) and his classical contribution *A Theory of Justice* (1971), where he defended the principle of average utility – that is, that institutions should be arranged so as to try to maximise the average utility (per capita), rather than the absolute weighted sum of the expectations of the individuals (1971: 162). To justify this, Rawls uses the example of an individual who will enter a world in which they neither know if the knowledge and skills they have will allow then to have a decent life, nor do they know into which particular group they'll be born. As a result, the individual will be reluctant to give privileges to any group and will instead opt for a society in which individuals have fairer positions and that overall offers them a wider safety net, which was his argument in favour of the welfare state.

This is, of course, a simplification of Rawls's theory, which is far more complex. However, what is important about it for our particular discussion is what it tells us about the need for fairness in a world of risk. Indeed, only by providing individuals in the West with a sense of what it is to be in a state of poverty and by making audiences face the risks of being socially excluded, can we start mobilising public debate towards a system of policies that rebalances wealth and creates a more sustainable and fair society.

As Silvio Waisbord has eloquently highlighted, journalism that deals with development needs a sober re-assessment to determine both its theoretical and its pragmatic validity (2012: 155). This means, I suggest, to rethink journalism practice in relation to the news coverage of poverty in two fundamental dimensions. One is the need to reassess the utilitarian rationale that underpins journalism as a professional practice, while the other is to contest its normative claims that it is there just to inform. Instead make journalists explore the propagation of ideas of uncertainty and risk as possible narratives in their day-to-day work.

On the first point, it is important to acknowledge that journalism, as other modern professions born from the Enlightenment, has mostly embraced since the mid-nineteenth century a predominantly positivist philosophy and a utilitarian rationale. However, contrary to other professions and practices that emerged in or were shaped by the Industrial Revolution and the British Empire such as travel writing, anthropology and sociology, journalism has so far not come to terms with its positivist and utilitarian nature.

From this perspective, news coverage has limited itself to describing the manifestations of poverty in the context of boosting sales and increasing ratings in order to satisfy the demands of the commercial model in which it operates. Using objectivity as a normative claim, commercially funded journalism therefore is able to operate under the disguise of neutrality to avoid questioning the structural reasons for poverty.

Journalists then, in their daily practice, try to maximise their gains and minimise their suffering by focusing on the news elements that makes them successful within the given commercial sets of the profession. Most forget that journalism is also about assigning responsibilities and helping to articulate possible scenarios and structural solutions to those issues that it covers.

The response in relation to this first point is for journalists to depart from this pretension of neutrality and objectivity. Instead, they need to openly embed their own experiences in each one of their stories. What I am suggesting is nothing less than to bring into journalism practice the notion that all human experience shares certain essential structural features and to accept that reason and emotions cannot be clearly separated as a source of morality in their stories about poverty.

This brings me to the second point, which is the need of news coverage of poverty to be able to tell a story in which audiences are able to understand empathically the risk and uncertainty those suffering are going through. Let me start by clarifying that I am not implying the simplistic assumption that human beings are only responsive to fear to accept change or be empathic with those who suffer. On the contrary, my point is that journalism needs to narrativise news on poverty in the context of risk and uncertainty as rational aspects that shape our ability to make decisions.

Indeed, despite the common association of risk with fear, the fact remains that risk is instead one of the most important rationales in our logical processes of decision making. Moreover, as Niklas Luhmann highlighted, the evaluation of risk and the willingness to accept risk is not only a psychological dilemma but also a social one (1993: 3). This being the case, journalists' narrative need to incorporate risk as an element of their stories about poverty and the only way I can see that happening is by changing the position of those who suffer from the distant 'other' to one of 'us'. This implies not only a different rhetoric of the way journalism tells stories altogether but also, and above all, a re-examination of the most basic tools and practice that journalists undertake to gather and produce news.

Unequal News

So, if contemporary journalism intends to cover poverty in a different manner, it will need, for example, to construct its discursive rhetoric around equality. It must understand that equality matters and it matters a lot (Davis 1998; Dorling 2010; Wilkinson and Pickett 2009). This rhetoric must place at its heart the eradication of poverty and replacement of the structures and systems that perpetuate inequality with other ones. Journalism cannot continue to portray a situation in which inequality is tolerable as long as economic growth keeps pulling people out of destitution.

Therefore, the challenge is to bring back inequality as the core theme in public debates on poverty. This is now possible as, in many ways, journalists operate in a healthier environment for discussion, in which they no longer must face the false dichotomies of totalitarian states claiming socialism or are constrained by Cold War imperatives. This effort will also demand that we contextualise the quest for equality in the much wider picture of environmentalism.

This is by no means naïve or unachievable as modern journalists and editors have the resources and are better placed than their predecessors to develop a kind of reporting of poverty which exposes inequality, even within the constraints of the corporative walls that have until now narrowly defined the news agenda. Contrary to the works of Henry Matthew in the nineteenth century, journalists today are not bound to views that see those in poverty as lacking skill or will. They can see instead that there are structural systems in place that are making all of us ever more unequal.

The task will also demand a different news culture, one that is fully committed to exploring ways in which humanity can reorganise itself as a society of equals. This means a journalism that assumes citizenship as an inherent condition of all human beings, not in the decontextualised terms of patriotism or cosmopolitanism, but as a practice which sees us and them as the same by recognising our differences and diversities. To do so, journalism will have to progress back to its 'pamphletarian' roots, that is, as an activity in which practitioners morally seek to deliver justice in the broadest moral terms. This is what the news coverage of poverty should be all about.

Notes

Introduction

1. I am using here the term 'imaginary' as the articulation of reality through the messages and images provided by the media. The notion is widely used in academia (Castoriadis 1997; Pérez 1999) and is inspired by the conception of Benedict Anderson's imagined communities (1983).

Chapter 2   The Poverty of Ideas in the Newsroom

1. Steven Harkins is a PhD candidate in the Department of Journalism Studies at the University of Sheffield. He holds a BA (Hons) in Politics and Journalism Studies from the University of Stirling and an MSc in Media and Communications Research from the University of Strathclyde. He is author of several academic journal articles. His research examines representations of poverty and inequality in the British media.
2. Although some newspapers such as the *Daily Mail* did change the editorial stance they had before the war, in which they openly supported Hitler and the Nazi Party.

Chapter 3   What Lies Beneath?

1. To be fair, this situation has changed slightly over the years and more and more news organisations are employing local journalists, but the majority of these news organisations' correspondents are still westerners.
2. Another interesting case is immigration, where cosmopolitan journalism often operates using double standards by supporting discourses that speak out against immigration but are committed to boosting birth rates in their own countries (Dettmer 2013).
3. Which is perhaps similar to what some countries have done when trying to improve women's rights by creating a 'Ministry of Women' that only deals with 'women's issues', thereby effectively creating another policy ghetto.

Chapter 4   Africa, That Scar on Our Face

1. Patrick O. Malaolu, PhD is a Nigerian journalist and former newspaper editor. His journalistic work led him to be imprisoned by the last Nigerian dictatorship. Today he combines his academic activities with being the funder

and CEO of RockCity 101.9 FM, the first private radio station in Abeokuta, Ogun State. He is author of several academic articles and books.

2. Some funders from the corporate sector include ENI (Italy), Royal Dutch Shell (UK/Netherlands), Ernst & Young (UK), Kohlberg Kravis Roberts & Co (US), Thomson Reuters (Canada/UK) and Microsoft (US), among others.

Chapter 5   Visual Journalism and Global Poverty

1. Scott Eldridge II, PhD, is a Lecturer in Journalism Studies at the University of Sheffield (UK). His research explores online media and journalism's reactions to change, journalistic identity, and the language and images of news. He has authored several journal articles on changing journalism dynamics and is Reviews Editor for the journal *Digital Journalism*.

2. Details can be found at http://content.time.com/time/covers/0,16641, 19770829,00.html (accessed 12 May 2014).

3. Details of the project can be seen at http://americanpoverty.org/partners/ about-us/ (accessed 1 June 2014).

4. James Nachtwey, who has worked as a photojournalist for decades covering conflict and human suffering around the world, refers to his role as 'witnessing' and seeking to interpret events while remaining 'invisible'. He identifies his work as one that aims to speak for those he portrays. In his view, this is a form of civic activism, which is subjective. Nachtwey, in a 2007 talk as part of the TED series, describes his work as a 'testimony' that sets out 'to do as much justice as possible to the experience of the people'. He embraces Chouliaraki's idea of 'unique responsibility' (2010), while recognising his images as 'bearers of meanings, enduring carriers of ideals and myths' (Adatto 2008: 243).

5. *The Forgotten Ones* (2003) http://www.miltonrogovin.com/forgottenones. html (accessed 4 March 2013).

6. The picture can be seen in detail at http://www.pulitzer.org/works/2009-Breaking-News-Photography with the caption 'A young boy struggles to rescue a stroller from the wreck of his family's home after Tropical Storm Hanna struck Gonaives'; Patrick Farrell, *Miami Herald*, 5 September 2008, Picture No. 6 (accessed 1 September 2014).

7. Which can be seen at http://www.magnumphotos.com/image/NYC65453. html (accessed 22 August 2014).

8. This work can be seen at http://fadedandblurred.com/spotlight/steve-mccurry/ (accessed 22 August 2014).

9. Interview with the author on 20 July 2011.

10. This can be seen at http://cagle.com/working/110806/keefe.jpg (accessed 22 August 2014).

11. That can be seen at http://www.zapiro.com/cartoon/1460933-130214tt (accessed 22 August 2014).

12. That can be seen at http://www.zapiro.com/cartoon/1313364-121120tt (accessed 22 August 2014).

13. Which can be seen at http://danzigercartoons.com/?p=3393&akst_action=share-this (accessed 22 August 2014).

14. His work can be seen at http://www.getty.edu/art/gettyguide/artMakerDetails? maker=1601 (accessed 22 August 2014).

Chapter 6   Spinning Poverty!

1. Government-sponsored international news services, primarily international broadcasters, have been one of the most important communication vehicles of public diplomacy (Signitzer and Coombs 1992: 137). However, this medium has seen numerous challenges in recent years from advances in technology, changes to the size and nature of audiences, and from overall government intervention.

Chapter 7   The Emergence of Alternative Voices

1. The fact that there is no real distinction between public and private finances in Qatar allows us to claim that Emir Sheikh Hamad bin Khalifa's initial US$137 million loan to set up the station and his subsequent direct and indirect financial contributions can be considered as state-sponsored support.

2. After rejoining the organisation, the United States again withdrew funding from UNESCO in 2011, after the organisation recognised Palestinian statehood.

3. I must reiterate here that the *Guardian* is one of the most proactive media outlets in highlighting issues regarding poverty and inequality, which is why I use it across the book as a standard. I am all too well aware of the restrictions on resources and the editorial policy restraints so at no point should this be read as a criticism of their individual journalists, but rather as an indictment of the system that shapes this type of news coverage.

4. To add insult to injury, in the face of government budget cuts to the BBC World Service, senior management in the corporation denounced the fact that while cuts were being made to the news service, with its consequent loss of 'British influence', the government had nevertheless decided to keep up the levels of funding to foreign aid programmes in the Third World. The *Daily Telegraph* in London, traditionally hostile to the way the BBC is funded, published an article with the headline 'BBC wants taxpayers' money from fund used to help starving in Africa' on 30 January 2011. In it, Jonathan Wynne-Jones, the *Telegraph*'s media correspondent wrote that BBC executives are trying to raid government funds intended to tackle world poverty in an attempt to lessen the impact of cuts on the World Service. A secret memo leaked to the *Telegraph* shows that the state-funded broadcaster has lobbied ministers

to divert £25 million out of the budget of the Department for International Development (DfID) and into its own finances. The corporation claims that the move would be justified because World Service broadcasts can 'contribute to the stabilisation of Pakistan and Afghanistan'.

5. This change will become even more relevant now that Al-Jazeera has bought the US network Current TV, which will give Al-Jazeera access to over 40 million US households.

References

Abdullahi, Najad (2008). '"Toxic waste" behind Somali piracy', *Al-Jazeera Online*, 11 October http://www.aljazeera.com/news/africa/2008/10/2008109174223218644. html (accessed 24 June 2014).

Abelson, Donald E. (2002). *Do Think Tanks Matter? Assessing the Impact of Public Policy Institutes*. Montreal: McGill-Queen's University Press.

Adatto, K. (2008). *Picture Perfect: Life in the Age of the Photo Op*. Princeton, NJ: Princeton University Press.

Aday, Sean, Livingston, Steven and Hebert, Maeve (2005). 'Embedding the truth. A cross-cultural analysis of objectivity and television coverage of the Iraq War', *The International Journal of Press/Politics*, 10(1): 3–21.

Adhikari, G. (2000). 'From the press to the media', *Journal of Democracy*, 11(1): 56–63.

Aggarwala, Narinder K. (1979). 'What is development news?', *Journal of Communication*, 29(2): 180–85.

Alcock, P. (1993 [1997]). *Understanding Poverty*. London: Macmillan.

Allan, K. (1998). *The Meaning of Culture: Moving the Postmodern Critique Forward*. Westport, CT: Greenwood Publishing Group.

Allan, S. (2010). *The Routledge Companion to News and Journalism*. London: Routledge.

Allan, Stuart (2010). 'Journalism and the culture of othering', *Socieda de Brasileira de Pesquisa em Jornalismo* http://www.bjr.sbpjor.org.br/bjr/article/download/15/16 (accessed 16 March 2013).

—— (editor) (2005). *Journalism: Critical Issues*. Buckingham: Open University Press.

—— (1999a). *News Culture*. Buckingham: Open University Press.

—— (1999b). 'News and the public sphere: Towards a history of objectivity and impartiality', in M. Bromley and T. O'Malley (eds) (1997). *A Journalism Reader*. London: Routledge, pp. 297–329.

Alleyne, Mark (2003). *Global Lies? Propaganda, the UN and World Order*. Basingstoke, Hampshire: Palgrave Macmillan.

Alterman, E. and Zornick, G. (2008). 'Think again: Poor coverage on poverty', *Center for American Progress*. http://www.americanprogress.org/issues/2008/08/poverty_coverage.html (accessed 12 October 2011).

Altschull, Herbert (1995). *Agents of Power*. New York: Longman.

Anand, D. (2007). 'Western colonial representation of the Other: The case of Exotica Tibet', *New Political Science*, 29:1: 1–23.

Anderson, Amanda (2001). *The Power of Distance. Cosmopolitanism and the Cultivation of Detachment*. Princeton, NJ: Princeton University Press.

Anderson, B. (1983 [1991]). *Imagined Communities*. London: Verso.

Ang, Tom (2005). *Photography*. London: Dorling Kindersley Limited.

ANSA (2011). 'Westwood promuove Ethical Fashion Africa. Su store Yoox la linea stilista inglese promossa da Onu e Omc', 12 July http://www.ansa.it/web/notizie/rubriche/cultura/2011/06/12/visualizza_new.html_818455560.html (accessed 21 January 2014).

Aouragh, M. and Alexander, A. (2011). 'The Arab Spring – the Egyptian experience: Sense and nonsense of the internet revolution', *International Journal of Communication*, 5(15): 1344–58 http://ijoc.org/index.php/ijoc/article/view/1191/610 (accessed on 1 June 2014).

Aristegui, Carmen (2012). Las revueltas árabes iniciaron un cambio en la civilización, dice Fuentes. *CNN Mexico*, 18 January http://mexico.cnn.com/nacional/2012/01/18/las-revueltas-arabes-iniciaron-un-cambio-en-la-civilizacion-dice-fuentes (accessed March 16, 2013).

Armbruster-Sandoval, R (2003). 'Globalization and transnational labor organizing – The Honduran maquiladora industry and the Kimi campaign', *Social Science History*, 27(4): 551–76.

Arterton, Christopher (1987). *Las estrategias informativas de las campañas presidenciales.* Editorial Ateneo de Caracas: Caracas, Venezuela.

Ashoka (1994). *Palagummi Sainath* http://www.ashoka.org/fellows/viewprofile1.cfm?PersonId=750 (accessed 25 March 2003).

Avery, J. (1997). *Progress, Poverty and Population: Re-reading Condorcet, Godwin and Malthus.* London: Frank Cass.

Babb, Sarah (2009). *Behind the Development Banks.* Chicago, IL: University of Chicago Press.

Bailey, Olga Guedes, and Harindranath, R. (2005). 'Racialized "othering"', in Stuart Allan (ed.), *Journalism: Critical issues.* Buckingham: Open University Press, pp. 274–86.

Balaji, Murali (2011). 'Racializing pity: The Haiti earthquake and the plight of "others"', *Critical Studies in Media Communication*, 28(1): 50–67.

Bales, Kevin, Trodd, Zoe and Williamson, Alex (2009). *Modern Slavery. The Secret World of 27 Million People.* Oxford: Oneworld.

Bantimaroudis, P. and Ban, H (2001). 'Covering the crisis in Somalia: Framing choices by the *New York Times* and the *Manchester Guardian*', in S. Reese, O. Gandy and A. Grant (eds), *Framing Public Life: Perspectives on Media and Our Understanding of the Social World.* London: Lawrence Erlbaum.

Bardoel, J. (1996). 'Beyond journalism: a profession between information society and civil society', *European Journal of Communication*, 11(3): 283–302.

Barkin, Steve M. (1984). 'The journalist as storyteller: An interdisciplinary perspective', *American Journalism*, 1(2): 27–34.

Barnard, Rita (1995). *The Great Depression and the Culture of Abundance: Kenneth Fearing, Nathanael West, and Mass Culture in the 1930s* (Vol. 87). Cambridge: Cambridge University Press.

Barthes, Roland (1981 [2000]). *Camera Lucida.* New York: Hill and Wang.

Baudrillard, J. (1994). *Simulacra and Simulation*, 15th edn. Ann Arbor, MI: University of Michigan Press.

BBC (23 September 2011). 'Has Western capitalism failed?', *BBC News Business* <http://www.bbc.co.uk/news/business-14972015?utm_source=twitterfeed&utm_medium=twitter> (accessed 23 September 2011).

BBC (7 August 2006). 'World Bank in corruption amnesty', *BBC News Channel*, http://news.bbc.co.uk/1/hi/business/5252336.stm (on 1 June 2011).

—— (11 October 2006). 'Madonna "adopts child in Africa"', *BBC News Online* http://news.bbc.co.uk/1/hi/entertainment/6039380.stm (accessed 21 July 2013).

BBC (2005a). 'Niger leader denies hunger claims', *BBC Online* http://news.bbc.co.uk/1/hi/world/africa/4133374.stm (accessed 12 March 2011).

Benthall, Jonathan (1993). *Disasters, Relief and the Media*. London: I.B. Tauris.

Berger, Guy (2000). 'Grave new world? Democratic journalism enters the global twenty-first century', *Journalism Studies*, 1(1): 81–99.

Berger, G.G. (2003). 'The journalism of poverty and the poverty of journalism', Paper for International Communications Forum, Cape Town, 5–9 April 2003 http://www.sarpn.org/documents/d0000311/P262_Berger.pdf (accessed 8 October 2011).

Berger, P. and Luckmann, T. (1966 [1971]). *The Social Construction of Reality: A Treatise in the Sociology of Knowledge*. New York: Anchor Books.

Berkowitz, Dan, and Adams, Douglas B. (1990). 'Information subsidy and agenda-building in local television news', *Journalism & Mass Communication Quarterly*, 67(4): 723–31.

Besley, Timothy, and Burgess, Robin (2001). 'Political agency, government responsiveness and the role of the media', *European Economic Review*, 45: 629–40.

—— (2000). 'The political economy of government responsiveness: theory and evidence from India', Development Economics discussion paper; DEDPS 28. *Suntory and Toyota International Centres for Economics and Related Disciplines*. London: London School of Economics.

——, Banerjee, A., Coate, S., Dreze, J., Dußo, E. and, La Ferrara, E. (2001). 'The Political Economy of Government Responsiveness: Theory and Evidence from India', LSE Papers http://citeseerx.ist.psu.edu/viewdoc/summary?doi=10.1.1.25.195 (accessed 20 March 2011).

Besteman, Catherine (1996). 'Representing violence and "othering" Somalia', *Cultural Anthropology*, 11(1): 120–33.

Bielsa, Esperança and Bassnett, Susan (2009). *Translation in Global News*. London: Routledge.

Biressi, A. and Nunn, H. (2013). *Class and Contemporary British Culture*. London: Palgrave Macmillan.

Boltanski, L. (1999). *Distant Suffering. Politics, Morality and the Media*. Cambridge: Cambridge University Press.

Botes, Janeske (2011). *The Hopeless Continent?: 2007/2008 Local and International Media Representations of Africa*. Saarbrücken, Germany: VDM Verlag.

Bourgault, Louise (1995). *Mass Media in Subsaharan Africa*. Bloomington and Indianapolis: Indiana State University Press.

Boyd-Barrett, Oliver (1997). 'Global news wholesalers as agents of globalization', in A. Sreberny-Mohammadi, D. Winseck, J. McKenna and O. Boyd-Barrett (eds), *Media in Global Context: A Reader*. London: Arnold, pp. 133–44.

—— (1980). *The International News Agencies*. London: Constable & Company Ltd.

—— and Braham, P. (1987). *Media, Knowledge & Power*. London: Croom Helm.

—— and Rantanen, T. (eds). (1998). *The Globalization of News*. London: Sage.

Boydstun, A.E., 2008. 'How policy issues become front-page news', PhD dissertation, Pennsylvania State University.

Boyle, Raymond (2006). 'Running away from the circus', *British Journalism Review*, 17(3): 12–17.

Brake, Laurel, Jones, A. and Madden, L. (1990). *Investigating Victorian Journalism*. London: Palgrave Macmillan.

Brandenburg, Heinz (2007). 'Embedding journalists as a superior strategy to military censorship', *Journalism Studies*, 8(6): 948–63.

Braun, J.A. (no date). 'News Values', in R.K. Nielsen et al. (eds), *International Collaborative Dictionary of Communications* http://mediaresearchhub.ssrc.org/icdc-content-folder/news-values/ (accessed 9 October 2011).

Bratton, Michael and Mattes, Robert (2003). 'Support for economic reform? popular attitudes in Southern Africa', *World Development*, 31(2): 303–23.

Brennen, B. (2010). 'Photojournalism: Historical dimensions to contemporary debates', in Stuart Allen (ed.), *The Routledge Companion to News & Journalism*. London: Routledge, pp. 71–81.

Brijnath, Bianca (2007). 'It's about TIME: Engendering AIDS in Africa', *Culture, Health & Sexuality*, 9(4): 371–86.

Brogan, Benedict (2005). 'It's time to celebrate the Empire, says Brown', *Daily Mail*, 15 January http://www.dailymail.co.uk/news/article-334208/Its-time-celebrate-Empire-says-Brown.html (accessed 23 March 2011).

Bromley, M. (1997). 'The end of journalism? Changes in the workplace practices in the press and broadcasting in the 90s', in M. Bromley and T O'Malley (eds), *A Journalism Reader*. London: Routledge.

Brown, P. and Minty, J. (2006). 'Media coverage and charitable giving after the 2004 tsunami', William Davidson Institute Working Paper Number 855. [online] University of Michigan http://wdi.umich.edu/files/publications/workingpapers/wp855.pdf (acessed 26 October 2011).

Bryant, J. and Zillmann, D. (2002). *Media Effects – Advances in Theory and Research*. Hillsdale, NJ: Lawrence Erlbaum Associates.

Buchanan, J. M., and Gordon, T. (1962 [2010]). *The Calculus of Consent: Logical Foundations of Constitutional Democracy*. Ann Arbor: University of Michigan Press.

Bullock, Heather E., Wyche, Karen Fraser and Williams, Wendy R. (2001). 'Media images of the poor', *Journal of Social Issues*, 57(2): 229–46.

Burns, Lynette Sheridan (2002). *Understanding Journalism*. London: SAGE.

Cabrera, Luis (2010). *The Practice of Global Citizenship*. Cambridge: Cambridge University Press.

Cagé, Julia (2009). 'Asymmetric information, rent extraction and aid efficiency', Paris School of Economics. Working Paper No. 2009-45 http://halshs.archives-ouvertes.fr/docs/00/57/50/55/PDF/wp200945.pdf (accessed 12 July 2011).

Callinicos, Alex (February 18, 2006). 'Winding up Make Poverty History', *Socialist Worker Online*, 18 February, Issue 1988 http://www.socialistworker.co.uk/article.php?article_id=8290 (accessed 8 January 2011.

Campbell, G. (1989). 'Top of the evening', *New Zealand Listener*, 6 May, pp. 18–21.

Campbell, W. Joseph (2003). *Yellow Journalism: Puncturing the Myths, Defining the Legacies*. Westport, CT: Praeger Publishers.

Campbella, Richard and Reevesa, Jimmie L. (1989). 'Covering the homeless: The Joyce Brown story', *Critical Studies in Mass Communication*, 6(1): 21–42.

Capps, G. (2005). 'Redesigning the debt trap', *International Socialism*, 27 June, Issue 107.

Carey, James W. (1986). 'The dark continent of American journalism', in R.K. Manoff and M. Schudson (eds), *Reading the News*, New York: Pantheon, pp. 146–96.

CARMA International (2006). *The CARMA Report on Western media coverage of Humanitarian Disasters*. CARMA. http://www.carma.com/display/Search?searchQuery=disasters&moduleId=7236731 (accessed 20 February 2011).

Carroll, J. (2007). 'Foreign news coverage: the U.S. media's undervalued asset', Joan Shorenstein Center on the Press, Politics and Public Policy Working Paper Series. Harvard University, JFK School of Government. #2007-1 http://www.hks.harvard.edu/presspol/publications/papers/working_papers/2007_01_carroll.pdf (accessed 11 October 2011).

Carroll, W.K. and Ratner, R.S. (1999). 'Media strategies and political projects: A comparative study of social movements', *Canadian Journal of Sociology*, 24(1): 1–34.

Carruthers, Susan L. (2000). *The Media at War: Communication and Conflict in the Twentieth Century*. Basingstoke: Macmillan.

Castoriadis, C. (1997). *The Imaginary Institution of Society: Creativity and Autonomy in the Social-historical World*. Cambridge, MA: MIT Press.

Chafel, Judith A. (1997). 'Societal images of poverty child and adult beliefs', *Youth Society*, 28(4): 432–63.

Chang, Ha-Joon (2011). *23 Things They Don't Tell You about Capitalism*. New York: Bloomsbury Press.

—— (2007). *Bad Samaritans: The Guilty Secrets of Rich Nations and Their Threat to Global Prosperity*. London: Random House.

—— (2002). *Kicking Away the Ladder: Development Strategy in Historical Perspective: Policies and Institutions for Economic Development in Historical Perspective*. London: Anthem Press.

Chavis, Rod (1998). 'Africa in the Western Media'. Paper presented at the Sixth Annual African Studies Consortium Workshop, 2 October http://www.africa. upenn.edu/Workshop/chavis98.html (accessed 12 March 2011).

Chomsky, Noam (1989). *Necessary Illusions: Thought Control in Democratic Societies*. London: Pluto Press.

Chouliaraki, Lille (2013). *The Ironic Spectator*. Cambridge: Polity Press.

—— (2006). *The Spectatorship of Suffering*. London: Sage.

—— and Fairclough, N. (1999). *Discourse in Late Modernity: Rethinking Critical Discourse Analysis*. Edinburgh: Edinburgh University Press.

Christians, C.G. (1996). 'Common grounds and future hopes', in P.M. Lester (ed.), *Images That Injure: Pictorial Stereotypes in the Media*. Westport, CT: Praeger Publishers, pp. 237–43.

Cimoli, M., Dosi, G. and Stiglitz, J. (2009). *Industrial Policy and Development*. Oxford: Oxford Press University.

Clapp, Jennifer (1994). 'Africa, NGOs, and the international toxic waste trade', *Journal of Environment Development*, 3(2): 17–46.

Clawson, Rosalee A. and Trice, Rakuya (2000). 'Poverty as we know it. media portrayals of the poor', *Public Opinion Quarterly*, 64(1): 53–64.

Coatman, J. (1951). 'The BBC, government and politics', *Public Opinion Quarterly*, 15(2): 287–98.

Cobb, M.D. and Jenkins, J.A. (2001). 'Race and the representation of Blacks' interests during Reconstruction', *Political Research Quarterly*, 54: 181–204.

Cockett, R. (1995). *Thinking the Unthinkable: Think-tanks and the Economic Counter-revolution: 1931–1983*. London: HarperCollins Publishers.

Cohen, Bernard (1963). *The Press and Foreign Policy*. Princeton, NJ: Princeton University Press.

Cohen, S. and Young, J. (eds) (1973). *The Manufacture of News*. London: Constable.

Collins, Michael (2011). 'Milton Rogovin obituary photographer whose documentary work chronicled the lives of America's poor', *Guardian*, 1 February http://www. guardian.co.uk/artanddesign/2011/feb/01/milton-rogovin-obituary (accessed 12 May 2011).

Colmery, B., Diaz, A., Gann, E., Heacock, R., Hulland, J. and Kircher-Allen, E. (2009). *There will be Ink: A Study of Journalism Training and the Extractive Industries in Ghana, Nigeria and Uganda*. New York: Revenue Watch Institute and Columbia University's School of International and Public Affairs http://adventures inmediadevelopment.com/there-will-be-ink-a-study-of-journalism-training-and-the-extractive-industries-in-nigeria-ghana-and-uganda/ (accessed 1 September 2011).

Conboy, Martin (2004). *Journalism: A Critical History*. London: Sage.

——, Lugo-Ocando, Jairo and Eldridge, Scott (2014). 'Livingstone and the legacy of Empire in the journalistic imagination', *Ecquid Novi: African Journalism Studies*, 35(1): 3–8.

Connelly, Matthew (2010). *Fatal Misconception. The Struggle to Control World Population*. Cambridge, MA: Harvard University Press.

Coonan, Clifford (2011). 'Chinese vow to keep red flag flying on party's 90th birthday', *Independent*, 2 July http://www.independent.co.uk/news/world/asia/chinese-vow-to-keep-red-flag-flying-on-partys-90th-birthday-2305621.html (accessed 2 July 2011).

Cooper, Andrew F. (2008). *Celebrity Diplomacy*. Boulder, CO.: Paradigm Publisher.

Cooper, K. (1969). *Barriers Down: The Story of the News Agency Epoch*. Ann Arbor: University of Michigan.

Cottle, Simon (2010 [2012]). 'Global crisis and world news ecology', in Stuart Allan (ed.), *The Routledge Companion to News and Journalism*. London: Routledge.

—— (2009). *Global Crisis Reporting*. Berkshire: Open University Press/McGraw-Hill Education.

—— (2006). *Mediatized Conflict*. Maidenhead: Open University Press.

—— (1993). *The News, Urban Conflict and the Inner City*. London: Leicester University Press.

Cullen, Pauline (2010). 'The platform of European social NGOs: ideology, division and coalition', *Journal of Political Ideologies*, 15(3): 317–31.

Curran, James (ed.) (2000). *Media Organisations in Society*. London: Arnold.

—— (1995). *Media, Power & Politics*. London: Routledge.

—— and Seaton, J. (1997). *Power without Responsibility*. London: Routledge.

Daily Mail (3 May 2014). 'Brazil police accused of "cleansing" favelas before World Cup football carnival rolls into town', *Daily Mail Online* http://www.dailymail.co.uk/news/article-2619722/Brazil-police-accused-cleansing-favelas-World-Cup-football-carnival-rolls-town.html (accessed 17 June 2014).

Davis, Mark (2006). *Planet of Slums*. London: Verso Books.

—— (2002). *Late Victorian Holocausts: El Nino Famines and the Making of the Third World*. London: Verso Books.

Davis, Nick (2008). *Flat Earth News*. London: Chatto and Windus.

—— (1998). *Dark Heart, the Shocking Truth about Hidden Britain*. London: Vintage.

Dawson, John A. and Thomas, D. (1975). *Man and His World: An Introduction to Human Geography*. London: Nelson.

Dearing, James W. and Rogers, Everett M. (1996). *Agenda-Setting*. London and Thousand Oaks, CA: Sage.

Delanty, Gerard (2000). *Citizenship in a Global Age. Society, Culture, Politics*. Buckingham: Open University Press.

Department of Economic and Social Affairs of the United Nations (2010). *Report on the World Social Situation 2010: Rethinking Poverty*. New York: The United Nations.

Deuze, M. (2006). 'Liquid and zombie journalism studies', *Newsletter of the ICA Journalism Studies Interest Group*: 2–3.

Devereux, Eoin (1998). *Devils and Angels. Television Ideology and the Coverage of Poverty*. Luton: University of Luton Press.

Diaz Rangel, Eleazar (1966 [1976]). *Pueblos Sub-Informados*. Caracas: Monte Avila Editores.

Dogra, Nandita (2012). *Representations of Global Poverty*. London: I.B. Tauris.

Domenach, Jean-Marie (1969). *La propaganda Política*. Buenos Aires: Talgraf.

Dominick, J. (1977). 'Geographic bias in national TV', *Journal of Communication*, 27: 94–9.

Dorfman, Ariel and Mattelart, Armand (1970). *Para leer al pato Donald. Comunicación de masa y colonialismo*. Buenos Aires: Siglo XXI Editores.

Dorling, Daniel (2010). *Injustice. Why Social Inequality Persists*. Bristol: The Policy Press.

Doward, Jamie (2012). 'Four Sun journalists arrested in investigation into police bribery', *Guardian Online*, 28 January http://www.theguardian.com/media/2012/jan/28/sun-arrests-rebekah-brooks (accessed 13 January 2014).

Drucker, Peter (1994). *Post-Capitalist Society*. London: Butterworth-Heinemann.

Duncan, David (1908 [2000]). *The Life and Letters of Herbert Spencer*. Boston, MA: Adamant Media Corporation.

Easterly, William (2013). *The Tyranny of Experts. Economists, Dictators, and the Forgotten Rights of the Poor*. New York: Basic Books.

—— (2006). *The White Man's Burden: Why the West's Efforts to Aid the Rest Have Done So Much Ill and So Little Good*. New York: The Penguin Press.

—— (2002). 'The cartel of good intentions: The problem of bureaucracy in foreign aid', *Journal of Policy Reform*, 5(4): 223–50.

The Economist (2009). 'A double strike: Africa's 2nd-largest economy has home-grown problems, too', 3 December http://www.economist.com/node/13278805 (accessed 3 September 2011).

—— (2003). 'A place for capital controls', 3 May: 16 http://www.economist.com/node/1748890 (accessed 2 September 2014).

—— (2000) 'Hopeless Africa', 11 May: 1 http://www.economist.com/node/333429 (accessed 11 March 2011).

EFE (2011) '1.000 Millones de personas se van cada día a la cama con hambre', *MMR Globovisión*, 22 September http://www.globovision.com/news.php?nid=203300, (accessed 22 September 2011).

Elliott, Chris (2011). 'Open door', *Guardian*, 30 May, p. 27.

Elliott, Larry (2011). 'Developing world's star nations need more than money to escape poverty, says report', *Observer*, 12 June, Business, p. 43.

—— (2006). 'Bono urges action on corruption in Africa', *Guardian*, 21 May http://www.guardian.co.uk/business/2006/may/21/g8.debt (accessed 12 November 2011).

Ellul, Jacques (1965 [1973]). *Propaganda. The Formation of Men's Attitudes*. New York: Vintage Books.

Ellwood, Wayne (2001 [2009]). *The Non-Sense Guide to Globalisation*. Oxford: New Internationalist Publications Ltd.

El-Nawawy, Mohammed and Iskandar, Adel (2003). *Al-Jazeera: The Story of the Network that is Rattling Governments and Redefining Modern Journalism*. New York: Basic Books.

Encabo, M.N. (1995). 'The ethics of journalism and democracy', *European Journal of Communication*, 10(4): 513–26.

Entman, R.M. (1995). 'Television, democratic theory and the visual construction of poverty', *Research in Political Sociology*, 7: 139–60.

Escobar, Arturo (1995). *Encountering Development. The Making and Unmaking of the Third World*. Princeton, NJ: Princeton University Press.

Ettema, James S. and Glasser, Theodore L. (1998). *Custodians of Conscience: Investigative Journalism and Public Virtue*. New York: Columbia University Press.

Fair, J.E. (1993). 'War, famine, and poverty: Race in the construction of Africa's media image', *Journal of Communication Inquiry*, 17(2): 5–22.

FAIR (2007). 'The poor will always be with us – just not on TV news', *FAIR Study*, October http://www.fair.org/index.php?page=3172 (accessed 12 October 2011).

Fairclough, N. (1995). *Critical Discourse Analysis: The Critical study of Language* (Language in Social Life Series). Harlow: Longman.

—— (1992). *Language and Social Change*. London: Polity Press.

—— (1989). *Language and Power*. London: Longman.

Fishkin, Shelley Fisher (1985). *From Fact to Fiction: Journalism and Imaginative Writing in America*. New York: Oxford University Press.

Fitzgerald, Timothy (2008). *Discourse on Civility and Barbarity*. Oxford: Oxford University Press.

Ford, Aníbal (1999). *La marca de la bestia: identificación, desigualdades e infoentretenimiento en la sociedad contemporánea*. Buenos Aires: Norma.

Fowler, C. (2007). *Chasing Tales: Travel Writing, Journalism and the History of British Ideas about Afghanistan*. Amsterdam and New York: Rodopi.

Francis, Mark (2007). *Herbert Spencer and the Invention of Modern Life*. Durham: Acumen Publishing Ltd.

Franklin, Bob (ed.) (1999). *Social Policy, the Media and Misrepresentation*. London: Routledge.

——, Hamer, Martin, Hanna, Mark, Kinsey, Marie and Richardson, John E. (2005). *Key Concepts in Journalism*. London: Sage.

Franks, Suzanne (2013). *Reporting Disasters: Famine, Aid, Politics and the Media*. London: C. Hurst & Co Publishers Ltd.

—— (2006). 'The CARMA report on Western media coverage of humanitarian disasters', *Political Quarterly*, 77(2): 281–4.

Franquet dos Santos, Miguel (2013). 'Gaza Burial, World Press Photo 2013: Between ethics and forensics', *Journal of Applied Journalism & Media Studies*, 2(2): 347–54.

Freedman, Russell and Hine, Lewis Wickes (1998). *Kids at Work: Lewis Hine and the Crusade against Child Labor*. Boston, MA: Houghton Mifflin.

Friedman, Milton and Rose (1980). *Freedom to Choose*. London: Pelican.

Friel, Howard and Falk, Richard A. (2007). *The Record of the Paper: How the "New York Times" Misreports US Foreign Policy*. London: Verso Books.

Frost, Chris (2002). *Reporting for Journalists*. London: Routledge.

Fuller, Jack (1996). *News Values*. Chicago, IL: University of Chicago Press.

Fukuyama, Francis (1992). *The End of History and the Last Man*. New York: Free Press.

Fürsich, Elfriede (April 2002). 'How can global journalists represent the "other"? A critical assessment of the cultural studies concept for media practice', *Journalism*, 3(1): 57–84.

Furtado, Celso (1967). *Development and Underdevelopment*. Berkeley, CA: University of California Press.

Galeano, Eduardo (1971 [2010]). *Las Venas Abiertas de América Latina*. Buenos Aires: Siglo XXI.

Galtung, Johan and Ruge, Mari Holmboe (1965). 'The structure of foreign news: The presentation of the Congo, Cuba and Cyprus crises in four foreign newspapers', *Journal of International Peace Research*, 2: 64–91.

Gans, Herbert J. (2007). Everyday news, newsworkers, and professional journalism', *Political Communication*, 24: 161–6.

—— (2004). *Deciding What's News: A Study of CBS Evening News, NBC Nightly News, Newsweek and Time*. Evanston, IL: Northwestern University Press.

—— (1979). *Deciding What's News*. New York: Pantheon Books.

Garnham, Nicholas (1994). 'The broadcasting market and the future of the BBC', *Political Quarterly*, 65(1): 11–19.

Gates, H.L. and Jarrett, G.A. (2007). *The New Negro: Readings on Race, Representation, and African American Culture, 1892–1938*. Princeton, NJ: Princeton University Press.

Gellhorn, M. (2012). *The Trouble I've Seen*. London: Eland.

George, Susan (1986). 'More food, more hunger: development', *Seeds of Change*, 1(2): 53–63.

Gerson, M. (2009). 'Dambisa Moyo's wrongheaded "Dead Aid"', *Washington Post*, 3 April http://www.washingtonpost.com/wp-dyn/content/article/2009/04/02/AR2009040203285.html (accessed 27 October 2011).

Gilens, Martin (1996). 'Race and poverty in America', *Public Opinion Quarterly*, 60(4): 515–41.

Gill, Peter (2010). *Famine & Foreigners. Ethiopia since Live Aid.* New York: Oxford University Press.

—— (1986). *A Year in the Death of Africa. Politics, Bureaucracy and the Famine.* London: Paladin.

Gilroy, P. (1987). *There Ain't No Black In The Union Jack.* London: Century Hutchinson.

GlobalNews (2007). *El Poder de los Argumentos.* Bueno Aires: Konrad Adenauer Stiftung.

Golding, Peter (1977). 'Media professionalism in the Third World: The transfer of an ideology', in James Curran (ed.), *Mass Communication and Society*. London: Sage Publications.

—— and Elliot, P. (1979). *Making the News*. London: Longman.

—— and Middleton, Sue (1982). *Images of Welfare. Press and Public Attitude to Poverty*. Oxford: Martin Robertson.

Goodman, Peter S. (2007). 'Ending battle, Wolfowitz resigns From World Bank', *Washington Post*, 18 May http://www.washingtonpost.com/wp-dyn/content/article/2007/05/17/AR2007051700216.html (accessed 12 January 2014).

Goodmana, Michael K. and Barnesa, Christine (2011). 'Star/poverty space: the making of the "development celebrity"', *Celebrity Studies*, 2(1): 68–85.

Gráda, C.Ó. (2009). *Famine: A Short History*. Princeton, NJ: Princeton University Press.

Graf, Heike (ed.) (2011). *Diversity in Theory and Practise. News Journalists in Sweden and Germany*. Göteburg, Sweden: Nordicom.

Graham, Harrison (2010). 'The Africanization of poverty: A retrospective on "Make Poverty History"', *African Affairs*, 109(436): 391–408.

Grattan, M. (1998). 'Editorial Independence: An outdated concept?', Part 1. Australia, Department of Journalism, University of Queensland. Australian Journalism Monographs.

Greenberg, Josh (2002). 'Framing and temporality in political cartoons: a critical analysis of visual news discourse', *Canadian Review of Sociology/Revue canadienne de sociologie*, 39(2): 181–98.

Grigoriadis, V. (2011). 'The womanizer's wife', *New York Magazine*, 8 August http://nymag.com/news/features/dominique-strauss-kahn-2011-8/index5.html (accessed 9 October 2011).

Grunig, James E. (1992). *Excellence in Public Relations and Communication Management*. Hillsdale, NJ: Lawrence Erlbaum Associates.

Guardian. Global Development website: http://www.guardian.co.uk/global-development (accessed 14 October 2011).

Guardian (2011). 'A fresh chapter is opening in Africa's history', editorial, 19 February http://www.theguardian.com/commentisfree/2011/feb/19/observer-editorial-africa-regeneration (accessed 21 August 2014).

Gudykunst, W.B. and Kim, Y.Y. (1992). *Communicating with Strangers: An Approach to Intercultural Communication*. New York: McGraw Hill.

Gumede, William (2010). 'Africa remains shrouded in myth', *Guardian*, 16 January http://www.theguardian.com/commentisfree/2010/jan/16/africa-western-view (accessed 21 August 2014).

Gunther, Richard and Mughan, Anthony (2000). *Democracy and the Media*. London: Cambridge University Press.

Hachten, William A. and Scotton, James F. (2006). *The World News Prism: Global Information in a Satellite Age*. London: Wiley-Blackwell.

Hackett, R.A. (2005). *Democratizing Global Media: One World, Many Struggles*. Lanham, MD: Rowman & Littlefield Publishers, Inc.

Hackett, Robert A. and Zhao, Yuezhi (1998). *Sustaining Democracy? Journalism and the Politics of Objectivity*. London: Garamond Press.

Hafez, Kai (2011). 'Global journalism for global governance? Theoretical visions, practical constraints', *Journalism*, 12(4): 483–96.

—— (2009). 'Let's improve global journalism!', *Journalism*, 10(3): 329–31.

—— (2008). *The Myth of Media Globalization*. Cambridge: Polity Press.

Haggard, H.R. (1885 [1993]). *King Solomon's Mines*. London: Wordsworth.

Hall, Stuart (1997). *Representation: Cultural Representation & Signifying Practices*. London: Sage.

—— (1981). 'The determination of photographs', in S. Cohen and J. Young (eds), *The Manufacture of News* (revised edn). London: Constable, pp. 226–46.

——, Critcher, C., Jefferson, T., Clarke, J., and Roberts, B. (1978). *Policing the Crisis: Mugging, the State, and Law and Order*. London: Macmillan.

Halliday, Josh (8 August 2011) 'London riots: how BlackBerry Messenger played a Key Role', *Guardian*, 8 August http://www.theguardian.com/media/2011/aug/08/london-riots-facebook-twitter-blackberry (accessed 25 August 2014).

—— (21 October 2011). 'BBC foreign correspondents warn cuts compromise impartiality', *Guardian* http://www.guardian.co.uk/media/2011/oct/21/bbc-foreign-correspondents-cuts (accessed 12 January 2012).

Hammett, Daniel (2001). British media representations of South Africa and the 2010 FIFA World Cup. *South African Geographical Journal*. Volume: 93 Issue: 1 Pages: 63-74.

Hanitzsch, Thomas; Hanusch, Folker; Mellado, Claudia; Anikina, Maria; Berganza, Rosa; Cangoz, Incilay; Coman, Mihai; Hamada, Basyouni; Hernandez, Maria Elena; Karadjov, Christopher D.; Moreira, Sonia Virginia; Mwesige, Peter G.; Plaisance, Patrick Lee; Reich, Zvi; Seethaler, Josef; Skewes, Elizabeth A.; Vardiansyah Noor, Dani and Yuen, Edgar Kee Wang (2011). 'Mapping journalism cultures across nations. A comparative study of 18 countries', *Journalism Studies*, 12(3): 273–93.

Hanrahan, John, (2009). 'World poverty: so important but so little coverage', *Nieman Watchdog* http://www.niemanwatchdog.org/index.cfm?fuseaction=background.view&backgroundid=419 (accessed 14 October 2011).

Harcup, Tony (2004). *Journalism: Principles and Practice*. London: Sage.

—— and O'Neill, Deirdre (2001). 'What is news? Galtung and Ruge revisited', *Journalism Studies*, 2(2): 261–80.

Harding, Phil (2009). *The Great Global Switch-Off International Coverage in UK Public Service Broadcasting*. Polis/OXFAM/International Broadcasting Trust. http://www.oxfam.org.uk/resources/papers/downloads/great_global_switch_off.pdf (accessed 20 October 2011).

Harding, R. (2011). 'Bernanke tells US to heed emerging economies, *Financial Times* 29 September http://www.ft.com/cms/s/0/318294a6-ea12-11e0-b997-00144feab49a. html#axzz1bzqJrOkj (accessed 27 October 2011).

Hariman, R. and Lucaites, J.L. (2007). *No Caption Needed: Iconic Photographs, Public Culture, and Liberal Democracy*. Chicago, IL: University of Chicago Press.

Harmon, Mark D. and Lee, Shu-Yueh (Autumn 2010). 'A longitudinal study of U.S. network TV newscast and strikes: Political economy on the picket line', *Journalism and Mass Communication Quarterly*, 87(3/4): 501–15.

Harris, P. (1985). 'The West African wire service of Reuters', in F.O. Ugboajah (ed.), *Mass Communication, Culture and Society in West Africa*. Oxford: Hans Zell Publishers, pp. 260–76.

Harrison, Jacquie (2006). *News*. London: Routledge.

Harrison, P. and Palmer, R. (1986). *News Out Of Africa: Biafra to Band Aid*. London: Hilary Shipman.

Hartley, John (April 2000). 'Communicative democracy in a redactional society: The future of Journalism Studies', *Journalism: Theory, Practice & Criticism*, 1(1): 39–48.

—— (1992). *The Politics of Pictures: The Creation of the Public in the Age of Popular Media*. London and New York: Routledge.

Harvey, D. (2005). *A Brief History of Neoliberalism*. New York, Oxford University Press.

Hastings, Max (2001). *Going to the Wars*. London: Macmillan.

Heikkilä, Heikki, and Kunelius, Risto (2008). 'Ambivalent ambassadors and realistic reporters. The calling of cosmopolitanism and the seduction of the secular in EU journalism', *Journalism*, 9(4): 377–97.

Heller, Steven (2002). 'What about cartoons makes people mad? An interview with Signe Wilkinson', *AiGA Voic*. http://blog.lib.umn.edu/mccu0154/mugwump/ madspread.pdf (accessed 21 January 2011).

Herbert, John (2001). *Practising Global Journalism: Exploring Reporting Issues Worldwide*. London: Focal Press.

—— (2000). *Journalism in the Digital Age*. London: Focal Press.

Herman, Edward S. and Chomsky, Noam (1988 [1994]). *Manufacturing Consent: The Political Economy of the Mass Media*. London: Vintage.

Herman, Edward S. and McChesney, Robert W. (1997). *Global Media: The New Missionaries of Corporate Capitalism*. New York: Continuum International Publishing Group Ltd.

Herrnstein, R.J. and Murray, C.A. (1994). *The Bell Curve: Intelligence and Class Structure in American Life*. New York: London, Simon & Schuster.

Himmelfarb, Gertrude (1992). *Poverty and Compassion: The Moral Imagination of the Late Victorians*. New York: Vintage Books.

Hobson, John A. (1891 [2004]). *Problems of Poverty. An Inquiry the Industrial Condition of The Poor*, 6th edn. Project Gutenberg.

Hodal, Kate, Kelly, Chris and Lawrence, Felicity (2014). 'Revealed: Asian slave labour producing prawns for supermarkets in US, UK', *Guardian Online*, 10 June http://www.theguardian.com/global-development/2014/jun/10/supermarket-prawns-thailand-produced-slave-labour (accessed 11 June 2014).

Hoge, J.F.J. (1994). 'Media pervasiveness', *Foreign Affairs*, 73: 136–44.

Höijer, Birgitta (2004). 'The discourse of global compassion: the audience and media reporting of human suffering', *Media, Culture & Society*, 26(4): 513–31.

Hollis, Patricia (1930 [1970]). *The Pauper Press. A Study in Working-Class Radicalism of the 1830s*. London: Oxford University Press.

Holt, Gerry (2011). 'As it happened: Liam Fox resigns', *BBC Online*, 11 October http://www.bbc.co.uk/news/uk-politics-15313986 (accessed 13 January 2014).

Holt, Hamilton (1909). *Commercialism and Journalism*. Cambridge, MA: The Riverside Press.

Howard, P., (2010). *The Digital Origins of Dictatorship and Democracy: Information Technology and Political Islam*. New York: Oxford University Press.

Hubbard, G. and Duggan, W. (2010). *The Aid Trap: Hard Truths About Ending Poverty*. New York: Columbia Business School Publishing.

Hulsen, Isabell (2011). 'Journalistic success, economic failure. Can free Web content save the *Guardian*?', *Spiegel Online International*, 30 September. http://www.spiegel.de/international/business/0,1518,789108-2,00.html (accessed 18 October 2011).

Hunter-Gault, C. (2002). *New News out of Africa*. London: Oxford.

Iyengar, Shanto (1990). 'Framing responsibility for the political issue: The case of poverty', *Political Behaviour*, 12(1): 19–40.

Jakubowicz, Karol (2007). 'Public service broadcasting in the 21st century. What chance for a new beginning?', *From Public Service Broadcasting to Public Service Media. RIPE@2007* http://www.nordicom.gu.se/en/publikationer/public-service-broadcasting-public-service-media (accessed 1 September 2014).

Jencks, C. (1985). 'How poor are the poor?', *New York Review of Books*, 9 May http://www.nybooks.com/articles/archives/1985/may/09/how-poor-are-the-poor/?pagination=false (accessed 19 February 2013).

Jimada, Usman (March 1992). 'Eurocentric media training in Nigeria. What alternative?', *Journal of Black Studies*, 22(3): 366–79.

Joffé, G. (2011). 'The Arab spring in North Africa: origins and prospects', *Journal of North African Studies*, 16(4): 507–32.

Jones, Gareth (2004). *An End to Poverty? A Historical Debate*. London: Profile Books.

Kahn, Joseph (2001). 'World Bank presses inquiry on economist who dissents', *New York Times* 7 September http://www.nytimes.com/2001/09/07/business/world-bank-presses-inquiry-on-economist-who-dissents.html?scp=1&sq=william+easterly+&st=nyt (accessed 27 October 2011).

—— (2000). 'Ideas & trends: a fork in the road to riches; redrawing the map', *New York Times* 25 June http://www.nytimes.com/2000/06/25/weekinreview/ideas-trends-a-fork-in-the-road-to-riches-redrawing-the-map.html (accessed 27 October 2011).

Kapur, Akash, 2009. 'Smart step to help rural India's poor', *New York Times* 27 August http://www.nytimes.com/2009/08/28/world/asia/28iht-letter. html?scp=1&sq=rural%20job%20scheme&st=cse (accessed 27 October 2011).

Kapuściński, Ryszard (2002 [2012]). *Los cínicos no sirven para este oficio. Sobre el buen periodismo.* Barcelona: Anagrama.

Katz, Michael B. (1989). *The Undeserving Poor.* New York: Pantheon Books.

Kendall, Diana (2005). *Framing Class: Media Representations of Wealth and Poverty in America.* Lanham, MD: Rowman & Littlefield.

Keeble, Richard (2001). *Ethics for Journalists.* London: Routledge.

—— and Wheeler, Sharon (2007). *The Journalistic Imagination: Literary Journalists from Defoe to Capote and Carter.* London: Routledge.

Kendall, D. (2005). *Framing Class: Media Representations of Wealth and Poverty in America.* Lanham, MD: Rowman & Littlefield.

Kennan, George F. (1993). 'Somalia: through a glass darkly', *New York Times*, 30 September http://www.nytimes.com/1993/09/30/opinion/somalia-through-a-glass-darkly.html?src=pm (accessed 20 December 2010).

Kenny, Timothy and Gross, Peter (2008). 'Journalism in Central Asia: A victim of politics, economics, and widespread self-censorship', *International Journal of Press-Politics*, 13(4): 515–25.

Kenynes, John Maynard (1920 [2005]). *The Economic of Consequences of the Peace.* New York: Harcourt, Brace and Howe.

Khondker, Habibul Haque (2011). 'Role of the new media in the Arab Spring', *Globalizations*, 8(5): 675–9.

Kim, Sei-Hill; Carvalho, John P. and Davis, Andrew G. (2010). 'Talking about poverty: News framing of who is responsible for causing and fixing the problem', *Journalism and Mass Communication Quarterly*, 87(3/4): 563–82.

Kiousis, S., Kim, S.Y., McDevitt, M., and Ostrowski, A. (2009). 'Competing for attention: Information subsidy influence in agenda building during election campaigns', *Journalism & Mass Communication Quarterly*, 86(3): 545–62.

Kipling, R. (1929). *The White Man's Burden: The United States & The Philippine Islands, 1899.* Rudyard Kipling's Verse: Definitive Edition, Garden City, NY: Doubleday.

Kitzberger, Philip and Pérez, Germán Javier (2009). *Los pobres en papel. Las narrativas de la pobreza en la prensa latinoamericana.* Buenos Aires: Fundación http://www. kas.de/wf/doc/kas_12547-1522-4-30.pdf?110209141915 (accessed 1 September 2014).

Kivikuru, Ullamaija (2001). *Contesting the Frontiers: Media & Dimensions of Identity.* Gothenburg, Sweden: Nordiskt Informationscenter.

Knightley, Phillip (2000). *The First Casualty: The War Correspondent as Hero and Myth-Maker.* London: Prion.

Kothari, Ammina (2010). 'The framing of the Darfur conflict in the *New York Times*: 2003–2006', *Journalism Studies*, 11(2): 209–24.

Kovach, Bill and Rosenstiel, Tom (2003). *The Elements of Journalism*. London: Atlantic Books for Guardian Newspapers.

Kovacs, Rachel (2006). 'Interdisciplinary bar for the public interest: What CSR and NGO frameworks contribute to the public relations of British and European activists', *Public Relations Review*, 32: 429–31.

Kristof, Nicholas (2011a). 'The birth control solution', *New York Times*, 2 November 2011 www.nytimes.com/2011/11/03/.../kristof-the-birth-control-solution.html (accessed 1 September 2014).

—— (2011b). 'Question a President (and me too) about Sudan', *New York Times*, 7 January 2011 http://kristof.blogs.nytimes.com/2011/01/07/question-a-president-and-me-too-about-sudan/?scp=6&sq=nicholas%20kristoff%20guinea%20worm&st=cse (accessed 18 October 2011).

—— (2010). 'Winning the worm war', *New York Times* 29 April 2010 http://www.nytimes.com/2010/04/29/opinion/29kristof.html?ref=guineawormdisease (accessed 18 October 2011).

—— (2007). 'Let's start a war, one we can win, *New York Times*, 20 February 2007 http://www.nytimes.com/2007/02/20/opinion/20kristof.html?ref= guineaworm-disease (accessed 18 October 2011).

Kumar, K. (1975). 'Holding the middle ground: the BBC, the public and the professional broadcaster', *Sociology*, 9(1): 67–88.

Küng-Shankleman, Lucy (2000). *Inside the BBC and CNN. Managing media Organisations*. London: Routledge.

Kyodo News (2013). 'Japan cuts foreign aid again', *Bangkok Post*, 24 December http://www.bangkokpost.com/most-recent/386440/japan-to-cut-foreign-aid (accessed 12 June 2014).

Lakoff, George (2004). *Don't Think of an Elephant. Know Your Values and Frame the Debate*. White River Junction, VT: Chelsea Green Publishing.

Lansley, Stewart (2012). *The Cost of Inequality*. London: Gibson Sqare.

Lazarsfeld, Pauk and Merton, Robert K. (1948). 'Mass media, popular taste and organized social action', in L. Bryson (ed.), *The Communication of Ideas*. New York: Harper Brothers.

Leiberman, T. (2001). 'Lifting the veil', *Columbia Journalism Review*, 29(5): 57–9.

Leigh, David and Evans, Rob (2007). 'How Blair put pressure on Goldsmith to end BAE investigation', *Guardian Online*, 21 December http://www.theguardian.com/world/2007/dec/21/bae.tonyblair (accessed 12 January 2014).

Lerner, James, Taylor, Anna Marie and Lerner, Richard Neil (eds) (2012). *Course of Action: A Journalist's Account from Inside the American League against War and Fascism and the United Electrical Workers Union (UE) 1933–1978*. New York: RNL Publishing.

L'Etang, Jacquie (2008). *Public Relations: Concepts, Practice and Critique*. London: Sage.

—— (2004). *Public Relations in Britain: a History of Professional Practice in the Twentieth Century*. Mahwah, New Jersey: Lawrence Erlbaum.

—— and Pieczka, Magda (1996). *Critical Perspectives in Public Relations*. London: International Thomson Business Press.

Lewis, Justin, Williams, Andrew and Franklin, Bob (2008a). 'A compromised fourth estate? UK news journalism, public relations and news sources', *Journalism Studies*, 9(1): 1–20.

—— (2008b). 'Four rumours and an explanation: A political economic account of journalists' changing newsgathering and reporting practices', *Journalism Practice*, 2(1): 27–45.

——, Thomas, James and Mosdell, Nick (2008c). *The Quality and Independence of British Journalism / Tracking the changes over 20 years*. Cardiff: Cardiff School of Journalism, Media and Cultural Studies. Journalism & Public Trust Project.

Lichtenberg, J. (1993). 'In sefence of objectivity', in J. Curran and M. Gurevitch (eds), *Democracy and the Mass Media*. Cambridge: Cambridge University Press, pp. 216–31.

Liddle, Dallas (2009). *The Dynamics of Genre: Journalism and the Practice of Literature in Mid-Victorian Britain*. Charlottesville, VA: The University of Virginia Press.

Liebovich, Louis W. (1994). *Bylines in Despair. Herbert Hoover, the Great Depression and the U.S. News Media*. Westport, CT: Greenwood Publishing Group, Inc.

Lightman, B. (1997). *Victorian Science in Context*. Chicago, IL and London: University of Chicago Press.

Lippman, Walter (1997). *Public Opinion*. London: Transaction Publishers.

Lister, Ruth (2008). 'Povertyism and "othering": why they matter', A talk by Prof Ruth Lister at the conference on 'Challenging Povertyism', *TUC* http://www.tuc. org.uk/social/tuc-15539-f0.pdf (accessed 12 March 2013).

—— (2004). *Poverty*. Cambridge: Polity Press.

Lloyd, J. (1999). 'The Russian devolution', *New York Times Sunday Magazine*, 15 August http://www.nytimes.com/1999/08/15/magazine/the-russiandevolution. html?pagewanted=all&src=pm (accessed 27 October 2011).

Lugard, F. (1926). *The Dual Mandate in British Tropical Africa*. London: Blackwood.

Lugo, J. (2007). 'A tale of donkeys, swans and racism: London tabloids, Scottish independence and refugees', *Communication and Social Change*, 1(1): 23–38.

Lugo-Ocando, Jairo (2011). 'Seeking refuge under the kilt: "Media campaigns" and asylum seekers in Scotland', in M. Alleyne (ed.), *Antiracism & Multiculturalism. Studies in International Communication*. Edison, NJ: Transaction Publishers (Rutgers University).

—— (2009). *ICTs, Democracy and Development*. Saarbrücken, Germany: VDM Verlag.

—— (2008). *The Media in Latin America*. Berkshire: Open University Press.

—— (1998). *Información de Estado: Como el gobierno se comunica con sus ciudadanos*. Maracaibo: Ediciones Corpozulia.

—— and Romero, Juan (2003). 'From friends to foes: Venezuela's media goes from consensual space to confrontational actor', *Sincronía*, 4(2) http://sincronia.cucsh. udg.mx/lugoromeroinv02.htm (accessed 1 September 2014).

——, Cañizález, Andres and Lohmeier, Christina (2010). 'When PSB is delivered by the "hand of God": The case of Roman Catholic broadcast networks in Venezuela', *International Journal of Media and Cultural Politics*, 6(2): 149–67.

——, Kent, Gregory and Narváez, Ancízar (2013). 'Need a hand? No thanks! Media Representations and Peace Building Indicators: The case of UK Foreign Aid Programs in Colombia', *Journal of Intervention and Statebuilding*, 7(4): 514–29.

Luhmann, Niklas (1993). *Communication and Social Order: Risk: A Sociological Theory*. Edison, NJ: Transaction Publishers.

MacBride, Sean (1980). *Many Voices, One World: Towards a New, More Just, and More Efficient World Information and Communication Order* (Critical Media Studies). UNESCO.

MacGregor, Brent (1997). *Live, Direct and Biased? Making Television News in the Satellite Age*. London: Arnold.

Malaolu, P.O. (2014). 'Sources and the news from Africa: Why are there no skyscrapers in Nigeria?', *Ecquid Novi: African Journalism Studies*, 35(1): 25–42.

—— (2010). 'Why there are no skyscrapers in Nigeria', unpublished thesis, University of Stirling.

Manheim, Jarol B. (2011). *Strategy in Information and Influence Campaigns*. London: Routledge.

Manning, P. (2001). *News and News Sources: A Critical Introduction*. London: Sage.

Maras, Steven (2013). *Objectivity in Journalism*. Cambridge: Polity Press.

Marriott, Stephanie (2007). *Live Television: Time, Space and the Broadcast Event*. London: Sage Publications.

Martin, Iain (2014). 'MPs' expenses: A scandal that will not die', *Telegraph*, 13 April http://www.telegraph.co.uk/news/newstopics/mps-expenses/10761548/MPs-expenses-A-scandal-that-will-not-die.html (accessed 13 January 2014).

Martín-Barbero, J. (1993). *Communication, Culture and Hegemony: From the Media to Mediations*. London: Sage.

Marx, K. (1963), cited in Blain, M. (2009).*The Sociology of Terrorism: Studies in Power, Subjection, and Victimage Ritual*. Boca Raton, FL: Universal-Publishers.

—— and Engels, F. (1841 [1987]). *Sobre Prensa, Periodismo y Comunicacion*. Madrid: Taurus Comunicacion.

Mattelart, Armand (1994). *Mapping World Communication: War, Progress and Culture*. Minneapolis: University of Minnesota Press.

McBriar, A.M. (1966). *Fabian Socialism and English Politics, 1884–1918*. Cambridge: Cambridge University Press.

McCarthy, Thomas (2009). *Race, Empire and the Idea of Human Development*. Cambridge: Cambridge University Press.

McChesney, R. (2010). 'The media system goes global', in D.K. Thussu (ed.), *International Communication – A Reader*. London: Routledge.

McCombs, M. and Reynolds, A. (2002). 'News influence on our Pictures of the world', in J. Bryant and D. Zillmann (eds), *Media Effects: Advances in Theory and Research*, 2nd edn. Mahwah, NJ and London: Lawrence Erlbaum Associates.

McCurry, Steve (2007). *In the Shadow of Mountains*. London: Phaidon.

McDonnell, L. (2001). 'Neither publishers nor reader clamor for stories about the poor', *Nieman Reports*, 55(1): 23–6 http://www.nieman.harvard.edu/reports/article/101726/Neither-Publishers-nor-Readers-Clamor-for-Stories-About-the-Poor.aspx (accessed 17 October 2011).

McGregor, J. (2002). 'Restating News Values: Contemporary Criteria for Selecting the News', in M.R. Power (ed.), *Communication Reconstructed for the 21st Century: Proceedings of the ANZCA 2002 Conference*. Coolangatta, Australia: Bond University.

McKendrick, J.H, Sinclair, S., Irwin, A., O'Donnell, H., Scott, G. And Dobbie, L. (2008). 'The media, poverty and public opinion in the UK', Joseph Rowntree Foundation http://www.jrf.org.uk/sites/files/jrf/2224-poverty-media-opinion.pdf. (accessed 12 January 2011).

McNair, Brian (2006). *Cultural Chaos*. London: Routledge.

—— (2003). *An Introduction to Political Communication*. (3rd Edition ed.) London: Routledge.

—— (2002a). *Journalism and Democracy*. London: Routledge.

—— (May 2000b). 'Journalism and democracy: A millennial audit', *Journalism Studies*, 1(2): 197–211.

—— (1998). *The Sociology of Journalism*. London: Arnold.

—— (1995). *An Introduction to Political Communication*. London: Routledge.

—— (1994). *News and Journalism in the UK*. London: Routledge.

Meadows, Michael (2001). *Voices in the Wilderness: Images of Aboriginal People in the Australian Media*. Westport, CT: Greenwood Press.

Media Standards Trust Report (2010). 'Shrinking World: The Decline of International Reporting in the British Press', 1 November 2010 http://mediastandardstrust.org/publications/shrinking-world-the-decline-of-international-reporting-in-the-british-press/ (accessed 12 October 2011).

Mehan, H. and Wood, H. (1975). *The Reality of Ethnomethodology*. New York: John Wiley and Sons.

Meinhof, U. and Richardson, K. (eds) (1994). *Text, Discourse and Context. Representations of Poverty in Britain*. Harlow: Longmans.

Mellor, Noha (2011). *Arab Journalists in Transnational Media*. New York: Hampton Press.

—— (2005). *The Making of Arab News*. Lanham, MD: Rowman & Littlefield.

Merill, J.C. (1964). 'The Image of the US in Ten Mexican Dailies', *Journalism Quarterly*, 39: 203–9.

Michnik, Adam (1998). 'An anatomy of dictatorship', *Index on Censorship*, 27(1): 17–24.

Mihelj, Sabina (2011) *Media Nations, Communication Belonging and Exclusion in the Modern World*. Basingstoke: Palgrave.

Miles, Hugh (2006). *Al-Jazeera: How Arab TV News Challenged the World*. London: Abacus.

Millet, D. and Toussaint, E. (2004). *Who Owes Who? Fifty Questions About World Debt*. London: Zed Books.

Miller, David and Dinan, William (2007). *A Century of Spin: How Public Relations Became the Cutting Edge of Corporate Power*. London: Pluto Press.

Miliner, Helen V. (1997). *Interests, Institutions and Information*. Princeton, NJ: Princeton University Press.

Mirowski, P. and Plehwe, D. (2009). *The Road From Mont Pelerin: The Making of the Neoliberal Thought Collective*. Cambridge, MA: Harvard University Press.

Mitchell, T. (1988). *Colonising Egypt*. Cambridge: Cambridge University Press.

Moeller, C. (1999). *Compassion Fatigue. How the Media Sells Disease, Famine, War and Death*. New York: Routledge.

Moore, Malcolm (2010). 'Inside Foxconn's suicide factory', *The Telegraph*, 27 May http://www.telegraph.co.uk/finance/china-business/7773011/ A-look-inside-the-Foxconn-suicide-factory.html (accessed 23 January 2011).

Moore, Martin (2010). 'Shrinking world: The decline of international reporting in the British press', *Media Standards Trust*, November http://mediastandardstrust.org/publications/shrinking-world-the-decline-of-international-reporting-in-the-british-press (accessed 4 March 2011).

—— (2007). 'Public interest, media neglect', *British Journalism Review*, 18(2): 33–40.

Morris, Nancy and Silvio Waisbord (2001). *Media and Globalization: Why the State Matters*. Lanham, MD: Rowman & Littlefield Publishers.

Morse, M. (1998). *Virtualities*. Bloomington: Indiana University Press.

Mosley, Paul (2013). 'Two Africas? Why Africa's "Growth Miracle" is barely reducing poverty, *BWPI Working Paper 191*. Manchester: Brooks World Poverty Institute, University of Manchester.

Moyo, Dambisa (2009). *Dead Aid. Why Aid is Not Working and How There is Another Way for Africa*. London: Allen Lane.

Mudimbe, Valentin Yves (1988). *The Invention of Africa*. Bloomington: Indiana Press University.

Munk, Nina (2007). 'Jeffrey Sachs's $200 Billion Dream'. *Vanity Fair*, July http://www.vanityfair.com/politics/features/2007/07/sachs200707 (accessed 21 February 2011).

Murdock, Graham and Golding, Peter (1989). 'Information poverty and political inequality: citizenship in the age of privatized communications', *Journal of Communication*, 39(3): 180–95.

Muro Benayas, Ignacio (2006). *Globalización de la información y agencias de noticias*. Barcelona: Paidos.

Murray, Charles (2001). *Underclass +10: Charles Murray and the British Underclass 1990–2000*. London: Institute for the Study of Civil Society.

—— (1984). *Losing Ground. American Social Policy 1950–1980*. New York: Basic Books.

Nash, Kate (2008). 'Global citizenship as showbusiness: the cultural politics of Make Poverty History', *Media, Culture and Society*, 30: 167–81.

Naude, Annelie M.E., Froneman, Johannes D. and Atwood, Roy A. (2004). 'The use of the internet by ten South African non-governmental organizations – a public relations perspective', *Public Relations Review*, 30(1): 87–94.

Negrine, Ralph (1996). *The Communication of Politics*. London: Sage Publications.

—— and D. Lilleker (2002). 'The professionalisation of political communication: continuities and change in media practices', *European Journal of Communication*, 17(3): 305–24.

Nelson, T.E., Clawson, A. and Oxley, Z.M. (1997). 'Media framing of civil liberties and its effect on tolerance', *American Political Science Review*, 91(3): 566–83.

Nerone, John (1987). 'The mythology of the penny press', *Critical Studies in Mass Communication*, 4: 376–404.

New York Times (2006). 'Still flying high', *New York Times*, 25 December http://www.nytimes.com/2006/12/25/opinion/25mon3.html (accessed 27 October 2011).

Newton, J. (2000). *The Burden of Visual Truth: The Role of Photojournalism in Mediating Reality*. London: Routledge.

Niblock, Sara (1995). *Inside Journalism*. London: Routledge.

Norris, Pippa (1995). 'The restless searchlight: Network news framing of the post-Cold War world', *Political Communication*, 12(4): 357–70.

Nyamnjoh, Francis B. (2005). *Africa's Media, Democracy and the Politics of Belonging*. London: Zed Books.

Ocwich, Denis (2010). 'Public journalism in Africa: trends, opportunities and rationale', *Journal of African Media Studies*, 2(2): 241–54.

Ogan, Christine L. (1982). 'Journalism/communication: The status of the concept', *International Communication Gazette*, 29(1–2): 3–13.

Ogbondah, Chris W. (1997). 'Communication and democratization in Africa. Constitutional changes, prospects and persistent problems for the media', *International Communication Gazette*, 59(4): 271–94.

Ojer Goñi, Teresa (2009). *La BBC, un modelo de gestión audiovisual en tiempos de crisis*. Ames, Spain: EuroEdiciones Ltd.

Okazaki, Shoko (1986). 'The Great Persian famine', *Bulletin of the School of Oriental and African Studies*, 49(1,): 183–92.

Okunna, C.S. (2005). 'Women: as "invisible" as ever in Nigeria's news media', *International Journal of Media & Cultural Politics*, 1: 127–30.

Olujobi, Gbemisola (2006). 'The Africa you need to know', *Truth Dig* http://www.truthdig.com/report/item/20061128_the_africa_you_need_to_know (accessed 21 July 2011).

Olsen, G.R., Carstensen, N. and Høgen, K. (2002). 'Humanitarian crises: What determines the level of emergency assistance?', *Disasters*, 27(2): 109–26.

Oreskes, N. and Conway, E. (2010). *Merchants of Doubt: How a Handful of Scientists Obscured the Truth on Issues from Tobacco Smoke to Global Warming*. New York: Bloomsbury Press.

O'S, J. (2013). 'Development in Africa. Growth and other good things', *Economist: Baobab Africa*, 1 May http://www.economist.com/blogs/baobab/2013/05/development-africa (accessed 10 March 2014).

Oso, Lai (1991). 'The commercialization of the Nigerian press: development and implications'. *Africa Media Review*, 5(3): 41–51.

——(1990). 'The Role of the mass media in rural development: A critical appraisal', in L. Oso and L. Adebayo (eds), *Communication and Rural Development in Nigeria*. Abeokuta, Nigeria: Millennium Publishers.

Pace, Patricia (2002). 'Staging childhood: Lewis Hine's photographs of child labor', *The Lion and the Unicorn*, 26(3): 324–52.

Pakenham, Thomas (1990 [1991]). *The Scramble for Africa*. London: Weidenfeld & Nicolson.

Pallister, David (2007). 'How the US sent $12bn in cash to Iraq. And watched it vanish', *Guardian Online*, 8 February http://www.theguardian.com/world/2007/feb/08/usa.iraq1 (accessed 12 January 2014).

Patterson, T.E. (2013). *Informing the News*. London: Random House LLC.

Paulson, Tom (2001). 'A breakdown of our primary health care system', *Seattle Post-Intelligencer*, 21 March http://www.seattlepi.com/news/article/A-breakdown-of-our-primary-health-care-system-1050911.php (accessed 21 August 2014).

Payne, R.K. (2005). *A Framework for Understanding Poverty*. Highlands, TX: Aha Process, Inc.

Pedelty, M. (1995). *War Stories: The Culture of Foreign Correspondents*. London: Routledge.

Pérez, E. (1999). *The Decolonial Imaginary: Writing Chicanas into History*. Bloomington: Indiana University Press.

Peters, L. (2013). *Dickens and Race*. Manchester: Manchester University Press.

Petros, G., Collins, O., Airhihenbuwa, L., Simbayi, S.R. and Brown, B. (2006). 'HIV/AIDS and "othering" in South Africa: The blame goes on', *Culture, Health & Sexuality*, 8(1): 67–77.

Pflanz, Mike (2011). 'Horn of Africa famine spreads', *Telegraph*, 29 July http://www.telegraph.co.uk/news/worldnews/africaandindianocean/somalia/8670779/Horn-of-Africa-famine-spreads.html (accessed 21 August 2014).

——(2008). 'How the mobile phone in your pocket is helping to pay for the civil war in Congo', *Telegraph*, 8 November http://www.telegraph.co.uk/news/worldnews/africaandindianocean/congo/3407217/How-the-mobile-phone-in-your-pocket-is-helping-to-pay-for-the-civil-war-in-Congo.html (accessed 21 August 2014).

Philo, Greg (1993). 'From Buerk to Band Aid. The media and the 1984 Ethiopian famine', in Eldridge, John (ed.). *Getting the Message. News, Truth and Power*. Abingdon: Routledge and Glasgow Media Group.

——, Beharrell, Peter and Hewitt, John (1995). 'Reasonable men and responsible citizens: economic news', in Philo, Greg (ed.), *The Glasgow Media Group Reader*,

Vol. II: *Industry, Economy, War and Politics: Glasgow University Media Reader*. London: Routledge.

Pilger, John (2011). 'Welcome to the violent world of Mr Hopey Changey', *News Statesman*, 30 May: 18.

Pirie, M. (2012). *Think Tank: The Story of the Adam Smith Institute*. London: Biteback.

Polgreen, Lydia (2009). 'Rural India gets chance at piece of jobs boom', *New York Times*, 12 November 2009 http://www.nytimes.com/2009/11/13/world/asia/13india. html (accessed 27 October 2011).

—— (2006). 'Nigerian states mired in corruption', *New York Times*, 24 November http://www.nytimes.com/2006/11/24/world/africa/24iht-nigeria.3660236. html?pagewanted=all&_r=0 (accessed 14 August 2014).

Polman, Linda (2010). *War Games. The Story of Aid and War in Modern Times*. London: Penguin/Viking.

Press Association (2006). 'Nigerian money scams cost Britain million, says report', *Guardian*, 20 November http://www.theguardian.com/business/2006/nov/20/ money.scamsandfraud (accessed 30 August 2014).

Preston SF Group (June 20, 1995). 'Steve Bell interviewed'. Internet Archive, *WayBack Machine* http://web.archive.org/web/20000608225535/http://freespace.virgin. net/g.hurry/s_bell.htm (accessed 14 June 2011).

Project for Excellence in Journalism (2011). 'Return of foreign news', 7 July http:// www.journalism.org/numbers_report/return_foreign_news (accessed 28 October 2011).

—— (2008a). 'The changing newsroom, changing content', 21 July http://www. journalism.org/node/11963 (accessed 28 October 2011).

—— (2008b). *The Changing Newsroom: What is Being Gained and What is Being Lost in America's Daily Newspapers, Summary Report 2008*, 21 July 2008 http://www. journalism.org/files/PEJ-The%20Changing%20Newspaper%20Newsroom%20 FINAL%20DRAFT-NOEMBARGO-PDF.pdf (accessed 28 October 2011).

—— (2005). *The State of the News Media 2005: An Annual Report on American Journalism* www.fpjq.org/fileadmin/FPJQ/pdf/06-02_state-of-media.pdf (accessed 3 October 2011).

Qasim, Maryan (2011). 'Why can't we end famine in Somalia?', *Comment is Free. The Guardian*, 28 July http://www.guardian.co.uk/commentisfree/2011/jul/28/ somalia-famine-crisis (accessed 28 July 2011).

Raghavan, Chakravarthi (1993). 'The New World Order: A view from the South', in Kaarle Nordenstreng and Herbert I. Schiller (eds), *Beyond National Sovereignty: International Communications in the 1990s*. New York: Ablex Publishing Corporation.

Ramirez, M. (2013). 'Editorial cartoons. Michael Ramirez', *Creators.com* http://www. creators.com/editorialcartoons/ramirez-caricatures-about.html (accessed 4 May 2014).

Randall, D. (2000). *The Universal Journalist*. London: Pluto Press.

Rangel, Eleazar (1967). *Pueblos Sub-Informados*. Caracas: Monte Avila Editores.

Rapport, M. (2009). *1848, Year of Revolution*. New York: Basic Books.

Ravallion, Martin, Chen, Shaohua and Sangraula, Prem (2008). *Dollar a Day Revisited*. World Bank, May http://econ.worldbank.org/external/default/main?pagePK=6 4165259&piPK=64165421&theSitePK=469372&menuPK=64216926&entit yID=000158349_20080902095754 (accessed 12 October 2010).

Rawls, John (1971). *A Theory of Justice*. Cambridge, MA: Belknap Press of Harvard University Press.

Razaq, Rashid (2010). 'Maid "drank acid to kill herself after being treated like a slave"', *London Evening Standard*, 21 April http://www.thisislondon.co.uk/standard/article-23826551-maid-drank-acid-to-kill-herself-after-being-treated-like-a-slave. do (accessed 12 July 2011).

Reich, Zvi (2011). 'Source credibility as a journalistic work tool', in Bob Franklin and Matt Carlson (eds), *Journalists, Sources, and Credibility*. London: Routledge.

Reinert, E.S. (2008). *How Rich Countries Got Rich and Why Poor Countries Stay Poor*. London: Constable & Robinson Ltd.

Reinikka, R. and Svensson, J. (2005). 'Fighting corruption to improve schooling: Evidence from a newspaper campaign in Uganda', *Journal of the European Economic Association*, 3: 259–67.

Reiss, Matthias (2006). 'The image of the poor and the unemployed: The example of Punch, 1841–1939', in Andreas Gestrich, Steven King and Lutz Raphael (eds), *Being Poor in Modern Europe. Historical Perspectives 1800–1940*. Bern, Switzerland: Peter Lang AG.

Reuters (2011). 'Clinton warns against "new colonialism" in Africa', 11 June http://www.reuters.com/article/2011/06/11/us-clinton-africa-idUSTRE75A0RI20110611 (accessed 12 May 2014).

Rice, Xan (2011). 'Somali rebels deny lifting ban on foreign aid groups', *Guardian*, 22 July http://www.theguardian.com/world/2011/jul/22/somali-rebels-deny-lifting-ban (accessed 25 August 2014).

Rich, S. (2007). 'Africa's village of dreams', *Wilson Quarterly*, Spring http://www.wilsonquarterly.com/article.cfm?aid=969 (accessed 27 October 2011).

Richey, Lisa Ann and Ponte, Stefano (2008). 'Better (Red)™ than Dead? Celebrities, consumption and international aid', *Third World Quarterly*, 29(4): 711–29.

Ricoeur, Paul (1994). *Oneself as Another*. Chicago, IL: Chicago University Press.

Rideout, Lisa (2011). 'Representations of the "Third World" in NGO advertising: Practicalities, colonial discourse and western understandings of development', *Journal of African Media Studies*, 3(1): 25–41.

Riggins, Stephen Harold (1997). 'The rhetoric of othering', in Stephen Harold Riggins (ed.), *The Language and Politics of Exclusion*. London: Sage Publications.

Rist, Gilbert (1997 [2002]). *The History of Development, From Western Origins to Global Faith*. New York: Zed Books.

Robinson, G.J. and Sparkes, V.M. (1976). 'International news in the Canadian and American press: A comparative news flow study', *International Communication Gazette*, 22: 203–18.

Robinson, P. (2002). *The CNN Effect: The Myth of News, Foreign Policy and Intervention.* London: Routledge.

Rocha, Glauber (1965). 'An aesthetics of hunger', in Randal Johnson and Robert Stam (eds). *Brazilian Cinema.* Rutherford, NJ: Fairleigh Dickenson University Press.

Rodino, V. (2005). 'African debt, war and imperialism are linked: Why Bono and Geldof got it wrong', *Global Research* http://www.globalresearch.ca/index.php?context=va&aid=787 (accessed 12 March 2013).

Rogovin, Milton (1985). The *Forgotten Ones.* Washington, DC: University of Washington Press.

Roig-Franzia, Manuel, Sheridan, Mary Beth and Ruane, Michael E. (2010). 'Security fears mount in lawless post-earthquake Haiti', *Washington Post*, 18 January.

Roper, Juliet (2002). 'Government, corporate or social power? The internet as a tool in the struggle for dominance in public policy', *Journal of Public Affairs*, 2(3): 113–24.

Rosanvallon, Pierre (2011 [2012]). *La Sociedad de los Iguales.* Barcelona: RBA Libros.

Ross, Eric (1998). *The Malthus Factor. Poverty, Politics and Population in Capitalist Development.* London: Zed Books.

Rudin, Richard and Ibbotson, T. (2002). *An Introduction to Journalism.* London: Focal Press.

Sachs, Jeffrey (2006). *The End of Poverty: Economic Possibilities.* New York: Penguin.

Sage, Alexandria and Labb, Chine (2013). 'Former IMF chief Dominique Strauss-Kahn to be tried for pimping', *NBC News Online/Reuters*, 26 July http://www.nbcnews.com/news/other/former-imf-chief-dominique-strauss-kahn-be-tried-pimping-f6C10759860 (accessed 13 January 2014).

Sainath, P. (1996). *Everybody Loves a Good Drought.* New Delhi: Penguin India.

Sallot, Lynne M., Steinfatt, Thomas M. and Salwen, Michael B. (1998). 'Journalists' and public relations practitioners' news values: Perceptions and cross-perceptions', *Journalism & Mass Communication Quarterly*, 75(2): 366–77.

Sambrook, Richard (2010). *Are Foreign Correspondents Redundant? The Changing Face of International News.* Oxford: Institute for the Study of Journalism of the University of Oxford.

Sartor, T. and Page, D. (2008). 'Foreign coverage shrinking, not gone', 23 July http://www.journalism.org/node/12042 (accessed 28 October 2011).

Scannell, P., and Cardiff, D. (1982). 'Serving the nation: public service broadcasting before the war', in B. Waites, T. Bennett and G. Martin (eds), *Popular Culture: Past and Present.* London: Croom Helm, pp. 161–88.

Schlesinger, Phillip (1990). 'Rethinking the sociology of journalism', in M. Ferguson (ed.), *Public Communication.* London: Sage, pp. 61–83.

—— (1978). *Putting 'Reality' Together.* London: Constable and Company Ltd.

Schlesinger, V. (2007). 'Rebranding African poverty', *Harper's Magazine*, April http://www.harpers.org/archive/2007/05/0081512 (accessed 12 October 2011).

Schiffrin, Anya (2010). *Bad News: How America's Business Press Missed the Story of the Century*. New York: The New Press.

Schneider, Barbara (2013). 'Reporting homelessness. Practice, product, profession', *Journalism Practice*, 7(1): 47–61.

—— (2011). 'Sourcing homelessness: How journalists use sources to frame homelessness', *Journalism*, 13(1): 71–86.

Schraeder, Peter J., and Endless, Brian (1998). 'The media and Africa: The portrayal of Africa in the *New York Times* (1955–1995)', *A Journal of Opinion*, 26(2): 29–35.

Schudson, Michael (2001). 'The objectivity norm in American journalism', *Journalism*, 2(2): 149–70.

Schutz, A., Walsh, G. and Lehnert, F. (1967). *The Phenomenology of the Social World*. Evanston, IL: Northwestern University Press.

Scott, Martin (July 2009). 'Marginalized, negative or trivial? Coverage of Africa in the UK press', *Media, Culture & Society*, 31(4): 533–57.

Scott, J. (1994). *Poverty & Wealth: Citizenship, Deprivation and Privilege*. New York: Longman.

Seaton, Jane (2005). *Carnage and the Media. The Making and Breaking of News About Violance*. London: Penguin.

Seib, P. (2008). *The Al Jazeera Effect: How the New Global Media Are Reshaping World Politics*. Herndon, VA: Potomac Books Inc.

—— and Fitzpatrick, K. (1994). *Public Relations Ethics*. Orlando, FL: Harcourt Brace.

Sen, Amartya Kumar (1999). *Development as Freedom*. Oxford: Oxford Press University.

—— (1981). *Poverty and Famines: An Essay on Entitlements and Deprivation*. Oxford: Clarendon Press.

Serle, John R. (1995). *The Construction of Social Reality*. London: Penguin Books.

Seymour, David (2009). *Reporting Poverty in the UK*. York: Joseph Rowntree Foundation.

Seymour-Ure, Colin (2008). 'Cartoons', in Bob Franklin, (ed.), *Pulling Newspapers Apart. Analysing Print Journalism*. New York: Routledge.

Shah, Hemant, (2011). 'Race, mass communication, and intellectual networks and the flow of ideas'. in Mark Alleyne (ed.), *Anti-Racism & Multiculturalism*. New Brunswick, CT: Transaction Publishers.

Shaw, Ibrahim Seaga (2011). *Human Rights Journalism: Advances in Reporting Distant Humanitarian Interventions*. Basingstoke: Palgrave Macmillan.

Shaw, Martin (1996). *Civil Society and Media in Global Crises – Representing Distant Violence*. London: Pinter/Cassell.

Shieldsa, Todd G. (2001). 'Network news construction of homelessness: 1980–1993', *The Communication Review*, 4(2): 193–218.

Shoemaker, P.J. and Reese, S.D. (1996). *Mediating the Message: Theories of Influences on Mass Media Content*. New York: Longman.

Shohat, E. and Stam, R. (1994). *Unthinking Eurocentrism: Multiculturalism and the Media*. London: Routledge.

Shraeder, P.J. and Endless, B. (1998). 'The Media and Africa: The Portrayal of Africa in the *New York Times*', *Journal of Opinion*, 26(2): 29–35.

Shumate, Michelle and O'Connor, Amy (2010). 'The symbiotic sustainability model: Conceptualizing NGO-corporate alliance', *Communication. Journal of Communication*, 60(3): 577–609.

Sigal, L.V. (1973). *Reporters and Officials: The Organization and Politics of Newsmaking*. Lexington, MA: Heath.

Signitzer, Benno H. and Coombs, Timothy (1992). 'Public relations and public diplomacy: Conceptual convergences', *Public Relations Review*, 18(2): 137–47.

Silverstone, Roger (2002). 'Complicity and collusion in the mediation of everyday life', *New Literary History*, 33: 761–80.

Sinclair, Upton (1919 [2003]). *The Brass Check. A Study of American Journalism*. Urbana and Chicago: University of Illinois Press.

Sisco, H., Collins, E. and Zoch, L. (2010). 'Through the looking glass: A decade of Red Cross crisis response and situational crisis communication theory', *Public Relations Review*, 36(1): 21–7.

Skjerdal, Terje S. (2009). 'Between journalism "universals" and cultural particulars: challenges facing the development of a journalism programme in an East African context', *Journal of African Media Studies*, 1(1): 23–34.

Smith, Adam (1776 [1982]). *An Inquiry into the Nature and Causes of the Wealth of Nations*. Book 1, Chapter 8 'Of the wages of labour'. London: Penguin Classics.

Smith, David (2010). 'China says booming trade with Africa is transforming continent', *Guardian*, 23 December http://www.theguardian.com/world/2010/dec/23/china-africa-trade-record-transform (accessed 2 September 2014).

Smith, Joe, Edge, Lucy and Morris, Vanessa (2006). *Reflecting the Real World?: How British TV Portrayed developing Countries in 2005*. London: International Broadcasting Trust.

Smith-Spark, Laura (2005). 'New Orleans violence "overstated"', *BBC News*, 29 September http://news.bbc.co.uk/1/hi/world/americas/4292114.stm (accessed 24 May 2011).

Soley, Lawrence C. (1992). *The News Shapers. The Sources Who Explain the News*. New York: Praeger Publishers.

Somerville, K. (2011). 'Violence, hate speech and inflammatory broadcasting in Kenya: The problems of definition and identification', *Ecquid Novi: African Journalism Studies*, 32(1): 82–101.

Sontag, Susan (2003). *Regarding the Pain of Others*. London: Penguin.

—— (1971 [1977]). *On Photography*. London: Penguin Books.

Sonwalkar, Prasun and Allan, Stuart (2007). 'Citizen journalism and human rights in northeast India', *Media Development*, 54(3): 31–5.

Sparks, Colin (2007).*Globalization, Development and the Mass Media*. London: Sage.

Spelman, E.V. (1999). '"Race" and the labor of identity', in S. Campbell and S.Babbit (eds), *Racism and Philosophy*. Ithaca, NY: Cornell University Press, pp. 202–15.

Spivak, Gayatri C. (1988). 'Can the subaltern speak?', in C. Nelson and L. Grossberg (eds), *Marxism and the Interpretation of Culture*. Urbana: University of Illinois Press.

Spurr, David (1993). *The Rhetoric of Empire. Colonial Discourse in Journalism, Travel Writing and Imperial Administration*. Durham, NC: Duke University Press.

Stannard, David E. (1992 [1994]). *American Holocaust: The Conquest of the New World*. New York: Oxford University Press.

Starkey, Guy (2007). *Balance and Bias in Journalism*. London: Palgrave.

Starkman, Dean (2014). *The Watchdog That Didn't Bark: The Financial Crisis and the Disappearance of Investigative Journalism*. New York: Columbia University Press.

Steel, John (2013). *Journalism and Free Speech*. London: Routledge.

Steinbach, S. (2012). *Understanding the Victorians: Politics, Culture, and Society in Nineteenth-century Britain*. London and New York: Routledge.

Stevenson, Nick (1999). *The Transformation of the Media: Globalisation, Morality and Ethics*. Harlow: Pearson Education Limited.

Stiglitz, Joseph (2012). *The Price of Inequality*. London: Penguin.

—— (2006 [2007]). *Making Globalization Work*. New York: Norton & Company, Inc.

—— (2004). 'The Post-Washington Consensus', *The Initiative for Policy Dialogue* http://policydialogue.org/files/events/Stiglitz_Post_Washington_Consensus_Paper. pdf (accessed 2 June 2011).

Stiglitz, Joseph, Sen, Amartya and Fitoussi, Jean-Paul (2010). *Mis-Measuring Our Lives. Why GDP Doesn't Add Up*. New York: The New Press.

Straughan, Dulcie M. (1989). 'An experiment on the relation between news values and reader interest', *International Communication Gazette*, 43: 93–107.

Street, John (2001). *Mass Media, Politics and Democracy*. Basingstoke: Palgrave.

Streicher, L.H. (1967). 'On a theory of political caricature', *Comparative Studies in Society and History*, 9(4): 427–45.

Stott, W. (1973). *Documentary Expression and Thirties America*. London: Oxford University Press.

Suttles, Gerald D. and Jacobs, Mark D. (2011). *Front Page Economics*. Chicago, IL: University of Chicago Press.

Sutton Trust (2006). 'The educational backgrounds of leading journalists' http:// www.suttontrust.com/research/the-educational-backgrounds-of-leading-journalists/ (accessed 21 March 2011).

Swanger, W. and Rodger, S. (2013) 'Revisiting fundraising encroachment of public relations in light of the theory of donors' relations', *Public Relations Review*, 39(5): 566–8.

Taiwo, O. (1999). 'Reading the colonizer's mind: Lord Lugard and the philosophical foundations of British colonialism', in S. Babbitt and S. Campbell (eds), *Racism and Philosophy*. Ithaca, NY: Cornell University Press, pp. 157–88).

Tatarian, Roger (1978). 'News flows in the Third World: An overview', in Philip C. Horton (ed.), *The Third World and Press Freedom*. New York: Praeger Publishers.

Taylor, Philip M. (1997). *Global Communications, International Affairs and the Media since 1945.* New York: Routledge.

Terkel, Studs (1997). *The Studs Terkel Reader. My American Century.* New York: The New Press.

Tettey, W.J. (2001). 'The media and democratization in Africa: Contributions, constraints and concerns of the private press', *Media, Culture & Society*, 23(1): 5–31.

Thompson, E.P. and Yeo, Eileen (1973). *The Unknown Mayhew.* London: Pelican Classics.

Thoreau, Henry David (1849). 'Civil Disobedience', Parts I–III, *Thoreau Reader* http://thoreau.eserver.org/civil1.html (accessed 21 May 2014).

Thussu, Daya Kishan (2000). *International Communication. Continuity and Change.* London: Arnold.

Tiffen, R. (1989). *News and Power.* Sydney: Allen & Unwin.

Tomaselli, Keyan G. (2009). 'Repositioning African media studies: thoughts and provocations', *Journal of African Media Studies*, 1(1): 9–21.

Tomlinson, J. (1999). *Globalization and Culture.* Cambridge: Polity Press.

Townsend, Frances Fragos (2006). *The Federal Response to Hurricane Katrina. Lessons Learned.* Washington, DC: Department of Homeland Security http://library. stmarytx.edu/acadlib/edocs/katrinawh.pdf (accessed 12 June 2014).

Townsend, Peter (1993). *The International Analysis of Poverty.* London: Harvester/ Wheatsheaf.

Tuchman, G. (1978). *Making News: A Study in the Construction of Reality.* Glencoe, IL: Free Press.

Tuchman, Gaye (1972). 'Objectivity as a Strategic Ritual', *American Journal of Sociology*, 77: 660–79.

Tunstall, Jeremy (1971). *Journalists at Work.* London: Constable.

Uche, Luke Uka (1991). 'Ideology, Theory and Professionalism in the African Mass Media', *Africa Media Review*, 5(1): 1–16.

United Nations (2009). *Rethinking Poverty. Report on the World Social Situation 2010.* New York: Department of Economic and Social Affairs, United Nations.

UNDP (2010a). Press Coverage of the 2010 *Human Development Report* http://hdr. undp.org/en/reports/global/hdr2010/news/ (accessed 12 October 2011).

UNDP (2010b). 'The Real Wealth of Nations: Pathways to Human Development' http://hdr.undp.org/en/reports/global/hdr2010/ (accessed 12 October 2011).

Usherwood, S. (1972). 'The BBC and the General Strike'. *History Today*, 22: 858–65.

Van Belle, Douglas A. (2004). *Media, Bureaucracies, and Foreign Aid: A Comparative Analysis of the United States, the United Kingdom, Canada, France and Japan.* Basingstoke: Palgrave Macmillan.

Van den Bulcka, Hilde and Panisa, Koen (2010). 'Michael as he is not remembered: Jackson's "forgotten" celebrity activism', *Celebrity Studies*, 1(2): 242–4.

van Dijk, T.A. (1998). *Ideology: A Multidisciplinary Approach.* London: Sage.

van Ginneken, J. (1998). *Understanding Global News – A Critical Introduction*. London: Sage.

Van Leeuwen, M. (2007). *Global Media Discourse: A Critical Introduction*. London: Routledge.

van Leuven, Sarah, Deprez, Annelore and Raeymaeckers, Karin (2013). 'Increased news access for international NGOs? How *Médecins Sans Frontières*' press releases built the agenda of Flemish newspapers (1995–2010)', *Journalism Practice*, 7(6): 1–16.

Van Tright, Anke M., De Jong-Van Den Breg, Lolkje T., Voogt, Linda M., Willems, Jaap, Trompt, T. (Drirk) F.J. and Haaijer-Ruskamp, Flora M. (1995). 'Setting the agenda: Does the medical literature set the agenda for articles about medicine in the newspapers?', *Social Science & Medicine*, 41(6): 893–9.

von Hayek, Friedrich (1944 [2001]). *The Road to Serfdom*. London: Routledge.

Verma, Gita (2003). *Slumming India: A Chronicle of Slums and their Survivors*. London: Penguin Books.

Vernon, James (2007). *Hunger: A Modern History*. Cambridge, MA: Harvard University Press.

Wahl-Jorgensen, K. and Hanitzsch, T. (2009). *The Handbook of Journalism Studies*. New York: Routledge.

Waisbord, Silvio (2013). *Reinventing Professionalism. Journalism and News in Global Perspective*. Cambridge: Polity Press.

—— (2010 [2012]). 'Rethinking development journalism', in Stuart Allan (ed.), *The Routledge Companion to News and Journalism*. London: Routledge.

—— (2001). 'Introduction: Journalism and new technologies', *Journalism*, 2: 171–3.

Wall, Melissa A. (2003). 'Press conferences or puppets. NGOs vs. street groups' communication in the Battle of Seattle', *Javnost – The Public*, 10(1): 33–48.

Ward, David (2006). *Can the Market Provide? Public Service Media, Market Failure and Public Goods. Making a Difference: Public Service Broadcasting in the European Media Landscape*. Eastleigh: John Libbey Publishing.

Ward, Stephen J.A. (2010). 'A theory of patriotism for journalism', in Stephen J.A. Ward and Herman Wasserman (eds), *Media Ethics Beyond Borders: A Global Perspective*. New York: Routledge.

—— (2005). 'Philosophical foundations for global journalism ethics', *Journal of Mass Media Ethics: Exploring Questions of Media Morality*, 20(1): 3–21.

Warsemah, Abdurrahman (2011). 'Armed militia grab the famine business', Inter-Press Service, 7 September http://www.africafiles.org/article.asp?ID=25698 (accessed 25 August 2014).

Wasburn, Philo C. (2002). *The Social Construction of International News*. Westport, CT: Praeger.

Way, Lyndon (2013a). 'Discourses of Somali piracy. Intervention and legitimacy', *Journalism Practice*, 7(6): 2–16.

—— (2013b). 'Orientalism in online news: BBC stories of Somali piracy', *Journal of African Media Studies*, 5(1): 19–33.

Weaver, David H. (2005). 'Who are the journalists?', in Hugo Burgh, *Making Journalists*. London: Routledge.

Webber, J. (2007). 'The re-invention of journalism', *The Times*, 1 October http://technology.timesonline.co.uk/tol/news/tech_and_web/the_web/article2569470 (accessed 21 July 2011).

Wells, H.G. (1895/2012). *The Time Machine*. London: Penguin.

Westley, Robert (1998). 'Many billions gone: Is it time to reconsider the case for black reparations', *BC Third World LJ*, 19: 429.

Whynne-Hammond, C. (1979). *Elements of Human Geography*. London: Allen & Unwin.

Wilkinson, Richard and Pickett, Kate (2009 [2010]). *The Spirit Level. Why Equality is Better for Everyone*. London: Penguin Books.

Williamson, John (1990). *Latin American Adjustment: How Much Has Happened?* Washington, DC: Institute for International Economics.

Wilby, David (2006). 'The General Strike 1926', *History of the BBC* http://www.bbc.co.uk/historyofthebbc/resources/bbcandgov/pdf/generalstrike.pdf (accessed 2 May 2014).

Wilson, John (1996). *Understanding Journalism*. London: Routledge.

Winfield, Betty Houchin (1990). *FDR and the News Media*. Champaign, IL: University of Illinois Press.

Wodak, R. (2004). 'Critical discourse analysis', in C. Seale, G. Gobo, J. Gubrium and D. Silverman (eds), *Qualitative Research Practice*. London: Sage.

Wojcieszak, Magdalena (2007). 'Al Jazeera. A challenge to the traditional framing research', *International Communication Gazette*, 69(2): 115–28.

World Bank (2011). 'World Bank Program Budget' https://finances.worldbank.org/Budget/World-Bank-Program-Budget/gprm-cvxz (accessed 12 October 2011).

—— (2010). *World Development Report* http://econ.worldbank.org/WBSITE/EXTERNAL/EXTDEC/EXTRESEARCH/EXTWDRS/0,,contentMDK:20227703~pagePK:478093~piPK:477627~theSitePK:477624,00.html (accessed 11 October 2011).

Wright, D.R. (1983 [1986]). 'Racism in school textbooks', in D. Punter (ed.), *Introduction to Contemporary Cultural Studies*. London: Longman.

Zayani, Mohamed (ed.) (2005). *The Al Jazeera Phenomenon: Critical Perspectives on New Arab Media*. London: Pluto Press.

Zelizer, B. (2007). 'Introduction: On finding new ways of thinking about journalism', *Political Communication*, 24: 111–14.

—— (2001). *About to Die: How News Images Move the Public*. New York: Oxford University Press.

—— (1990). 'Achieving journalistic authority through narrative', *Critical Studies in Mass Communication*, 7(4): 366–76.

—— and Stuart Allan (eds) (2002 [2011]). *Journalism After September 11*. London: Routledge.

Zhang, Juyan and Swartz, Brecken Chinn (2009). 'Towards a model of NGO media diplomacy in the Internet age: Case study of Washington Profile', *Public Relations Review*, 35: 47–55.

Zuberi, Tukufu (2001). *Thicker than Blood: How Racial Statistics Lie*. Minneapolis: University of Minnesota Press.

Index

Printed in Great Britain
by Amazon.co.uk, Ltd.,
Marston Gate.